Yellow Jack

How Yellow Fever Ravaged America and Walter Reed Discovered Its Deadly Secrets

John R. Pierce

Jim Writer

WILEY

John Wiley & Sons, Inc.

Copyright © 2005 by John R. Pierce and James V. Writer. All rights reserved

Published by John Wiley & Sons, Inc., Hoboken, New Jersey
Published simultaneously in Canada

Photo credits: pages 123, 124, 125, 126 (top), 134 (top), courtesy of the National Library of
Medicine; pages 126 (bottom), 127, 128, 129, 130, 131, 134 (bottom, left and right), courtesy of the
Philip S. Hench Walter Reed Yellow Fever Collection, the Claude Moore Health Sciences Library,
University of Virginia; page 132, United States Veterans Administration VA File Number C
2,486,530; page 133, Record Group 112, National Archives and Records Administration

For general information about our other products and services, please contact our Customer Care
Department within the United States at (800) 762-2974, outside the United States at
(317) 572-3993 or fax (317) 572-4002.

Wiley also publishes its books in a variety of electronic formats. Some content that appears in print
may not be available in electronic books. For more information about Wiley products, visit our web
site at www.wiley.com.

Library of Congress Cataloging-in-Publication Data:
Pierce, John R., date.
Yellow jack : how yellow fever ravaged America and Walter Reed discovered
its deadly secrets / John R. Pierce and James V. Writer.
p. cm.
Includes bibliographical references and index.
ISBN 0-471-47261-1 (cloth)
1. Yellow fever—History.   2. Reed, Walter, 1851–1902.
I. Writer, James V., date.   II. Title.
RA644.Y4R447   2005
614.5′41′0973—dc22
2004013845

Printed in the United States of America
10 9 8 7 6 5 4 3 2 1

*To our children, Rachel, Ann, and John Pierce
and Kathleen, Helen, and James Writer Jr.,
and especially to our wives,
Kathe Pierce and Susan Writer,
all of whom have been living with a
chronic case of yellow fever for many years*

Contents

Illustrations begin on page 123

Preface

THIS BOOK COULD NOT HAVE BEEN WRITTEN WITHOUT THE assistance of Dr. Philip S. Hench, someone whom neither of us has met. In fact, Dr. Hench died more than thirty-five years before we began writing this fascinating tale of death and triumph. Death was delivered by one of God's smallest and seemingly most insignificant creatures. Triumph was due to the combined efforts of many of God's most complex creatures.

In the beginning, the simple, noncomplex, nonreasoning, nonthinking carried away many of the more complex to their graves. But over the course of many years, the complex finally won out. Surely it must always be that way; the intelligent, sophisticated, reasoned would dominate the unthinking, uncomplicated, reflexive, and primitive. But at the cost of how many lives? Thousands, tens of thousands, hundreds of thousands, and even more. Today we are fortunate to have never seen and even rarely heard of this disease, yellow fever. But the story of this dreadful malady will fascinate and captivate you just as it did Philip Hench six decades ago. And it is to Dr. Hench we owe a tremendous debt of gratitude for his interest and his remarkable actions driven by that interest.

Born in Pennsylvania in 1896, Hench received his bachelor's degree from Lafayette College and his medical degree from the University of Pittsburgh. After his early medical training, he joined the Mayo Clinic in 1923, and other than a couple of years studying abroad, he remained at Mayo the rest of his career. His academic interest was in the field of rheumatology; his observations of his patients led him to believe that an internally produced steroid helped relieve the pain of arthritis. Dr. E. C. Kendall had isolated several steroids from the human adrenal gland, and in collaboration with Dr. Hench, he gave these to arthritic patients. The substance was initially called Compound E, and later cortisone. Hench, Kendall, and Tadeus Reichstein received the Nobel Prize in Physiology or Medicine in 1950 for their work.

While impressed with and thankful to Dr. Hench for his contributions to medical knowledge and better health, we are selfishly grateful to him for one of his hobbies. In 1937, he was asked by a friend to make some comments at the dedication of a new chemistry building at Washington and Jefferson College to be named for an alumnus, Jesse W. Lazear. Lazear had died almost forty years before from yellow fever while serving in the army in Cuba. At the time of his death, Lazear was a member of the U.S. Army Yellow Fever Board with Walter Reed and two other army physicians. Looking for information, Hench wrote one of the surviving yellow fever volunteers, John J. Moran. This launched Hench into a more than twenty-year odyssey to learn and discern the truth of the extraordinary world-changing events that had taken place in the search for the cause of this dread disease.

Hench's dogged pursuit of this story led him all around the United States and to Cuba several times. He met, interviewed, and befriended all of the living participants and many of the families of the deceased who played in this drama. Through force of personality, persistence, character, integrity, honesty, and hard work, he convinced almost every one of these folks to give him their letters, documents, pictures, artifacts, and anything else they might have about their or their loved ones' participation in this splendid little war against this splendidly awful disease. He pursued the history of yellow fever with a passion most of us will never know. How much of his own time and money was spent on travel, hotel rooms, taxis, copies of documents, photographs, and stenographers to transcribe hundreds of his letters is unknown. He planned on writing the definitive book, but died before he realized this dream. After his death, his remarkable collection was given to the University of Virginia. Dr. William Bean relied heavily on it for his biography of Walter Reed published in 1983. When we spoke to Dr. Hench's son, he said, "Bill Bean wrote my father's book."

In 1999, the Institute for Museum and Library Services awarded the University of Virginia a grant to select, transcribe, and digitize a large complement of original materials from the Philip S. Hench Walter Reed Yellow Fever Collection.

Since then, other manuscripts from other collections have been added. These include items from the Henry Rose Carter Papers, the William Bennett Bean Papers, and the Wade Hampton Frost Papers, as well as the Jefferson Randolph Kean Papers, and a number of Walter Reed's letters. In addition, the collection holds many reproductions and photostats from originals in the National Archives and Records Administration in Washington, D.C. In January 2004, the collection allowed online access to an extraordinary 7,400 documents at www.yellowfever.lib.virginia.edu/reed/ collection. During our research, we relied heavily on the material in the Hench Collection for critical information about yellow fever and the work of the U.S. Army Yellow Fever Board.

The story of yellow fever presented in this book covers many years before and after the work of the Army Board, the main interest and subject of the Hench Collection. Therefore we have relied on the writings and publications of many others to fill in that part of this story. To those scientists, historians, and writers we are grateful. But to Philip Hench we are indebted, as will be any future student of this truly wonderful and inspiring story.

As is always the case when trying to write a historically correct account of dramatic events, there are differences in dates and times in the various documents one encounters. For the sake of uniformity, we relied on the published work of the U.S. Army Yellow Fever Board and other scientists involved in yellow fever research for names of individuals, dates, and times of events concerning their research.

Introduction:
The Forgotten Scourge

THE HOUSTON OIL AND GAS EXECUTIVE TOM MCCULLOUGH PRE-
sented at a Corpus Christi, Texas, emergency room on March 10, 2002, complaining of abdominal pain, severe headache, and a high fever. He was diagnosed with a rickettsial infection, given antibiotics, and released. Two days later, he returned in obvious distress; the fever and headache had worsened, and he was battling what a U.S. Centers for Disease Control and Prevention (CDC) report called "intractable vomiting."[1] While the doctors continued ordering tests to identify the cause of his distress, he was treated for malaria. On March 15, he developed shock, seizures, and bleeding from his needle puncture sites. The forty-seven-year-old McCullough died the next day, his disease still undiagnosed.

The CDC conducted a series of diagnostic tests and investigations using blood and tissue collected from McCullough before and after his death. Serum taken during his hospitalization and a liver sample taken at autopsy tested positive for yellow fever RNA, the genetic component of the virus.

Thus, Tom McCullough became the third person to die of yellow fever in the United States since 1996, the first deaths from yellow fever in seven decades. Like the others, one in 1996 and another in 1997, he picked up the infection while on a trip to South America. He had recently returned from a six-day fishing trip with colleagues on the Rio Negro in the Brazilian state of Amazonas. He didn't recall being bitten by mosquitoes, and he had taken appropriate steps to avoid their sting. While on the river, he slept in an air-conditioned fishing boat, and while fishing, he wore clothes impregnated with DEET—an insect repellent. According to a story in the Corpus Christi *Caller-Times*, he repeatedly asked his wife, "What is happening to me?"[2]

1

One hundred or more years ago, he likely would have known what was happening, and strangely enough, his doctors, unlike those in Corpus Christi, would have known long before the patient died that this was a case of yellow fever.

In many areas of the United States during the eighteenth and nineteenth centuries, yellow fever was a dreaded visitor familiar to medical professionals and laypersons. American port cities from Galveston, Texas, to Portsmouth, New Hampshire, were struck with epidemics. Until the early 1800s, the disease was an occasional unwelcome summertime guest as far north as New York and Boston. During the summer and fall of 1793, the disease terrorized Philadelphia and carried away nearly five thousand souls, one-tenth of the city's population. After 1822, epidemics were limited to southern cities, with the northernmost reach of yellow fever being Norfolk, Virginia.

If McCullough had lived in the late 1800s in a southern port town, there was a very good chance that his doctor would have quickly recognized a severe case of yellow fever in his patient. And the presence of yellow jack, as it was sometimes called in honor of the yellow quarantine flag that infected ships flew, would have altered life in that town for months. There is not a single disease today that can terrorize a community the way yellow fever did. Not AIDS, SARS, or West Nile virus. The closest one could get to the dread that gripped a community visited by yellow fever is bioterrorism. Only the intentional introduction of smallpox or anthrax into a city could mimic the horrors of a nineteenth-century yellow fever epidemic. Dysentery, typhoid, smallpox, and many unnamed or unrecognized diseases killed many more people more frequently and in more places than yellow fever. Yet, people learned to live with them. Perhaps it was the relative rarity of yellow fever, the randomness of its attacks, and the inability to discern a pattern in how it chose its victims that gave it a certain horrifying cachet.

With the first report of the disease, those who could fled in every direction to places historically free of yellow jack. Tar and pitch fires burned in the streets, and sanitary campaigns were mounted to rid the infected city of the filth that many thought harbored the poisons of yellow fever. Almost all normal public intercourse—commerce, churchgoing, the theater, and any socializing with friends and family—stopped. Businesses failed and governments collapsed. People shunned their friends and relations. One witness to an outbreak noted that handshaking disappeared as a greeting and people crossed over to the opposite side of a street to avoid acknowledging acquaintances. Families disintegrated as parents abandoned sick children and children left their parents. People died alone in their beds with no one to care for them, and many were buried without ceremony in potter's fields out of fear that their corpse could spread the yellow jack. Until 1905, the fear of yellow fever, if not the disease itself, arrived each summer as sure as heat and humidity and those pesky mosquitoes. Only the coming of the first frost allowed the citizens of a yellow fever city to let out a sigh of relief.

When the army major and physician Walter Reed and his three associates gathered together outside Havana, Cuba, in June 1900, yellow fever was nearly as much an enigma as when the first cases had been reported in the Yucatan in 1648. The four physicians constituted the board of medical officers that Surgeon General of the Army George Sternberg had created to investigate the diseases attacking Americans and others on the newly liberated island nation. In post–Spanish-American War Cuba, disease was striking down U.S. soldiers and civilians at an alarming rate. Reed was named chairman of the investigating board. He sailed to Cuba from New York aboard the *Sedgwick* with the army contract surgeon James Carroll. These two doctors joined contract surgeons Jesse Lazear and Aristides Agramonte, who were already investigating diseases on the island. The board's orders didn't specifically mention yellow fever, but the four knew their main mission was to unravel its mysteries.

The Spanish-American War made the United States a worldwide power. Cuba was one of its prizes, as were the Philippines, Guam, and Puerto Rico. For the first time, the United States had possession of and responsibility for overseas colonies and all the problems that come with colonies. Cuba, though mandated by an act of Congress to be returned to the Cuban people, was in 1900 the crown jewel of America's small new empire.

Even under Spanish rule, Cuba had a close relationship with the United States. With the defeat of the Spanish, abundant financial and political rewards awaited anyone willing to accept the challenges of rebuilding the country. American soldiers, government officials, businessmen, adventurers, as well as many Spanish immigrants, poured into Cuba. Most of these new arrivals had never before been exposed to yellow fever. Instead of riches, some found only their graves awaiting them. In an effort to cleanse the island of yellow jack and other diseases, military sanitarians tried washing decades' worth of filth from Cuban cities, the legacy of many years of Spanish neglect and civil war. The military doctors had limited success; dysentery and typhoid fevers declined, but as the cities and towns got cleaner, yellow fever carried more victims away.

Present in the Caribbean for 350 years and first reported in the British-American colonies in 1693, yellow fever long plagued American seaports. Cuba, many thought, was the fount of yellow fever, spewing infection to faraway cities and towns in the north. Ships, along with their sailors and cargoes, were all suspect in the continuing struggle against the contagion. The U.S. victory in Cuba gave the United States an opportunity to attack one of the most feared diseases of the day in its home port.

The four army doctors understood the importance of conquering yellow fever. Hundreds of thousands of souls and many millions of dollars had been lost to it in just the past hundred years. The doctors also understood the depth of the mystery surrounding the disease. At the end of the nineteenth century, as medicine transformed itself from art to science, the healing profession was still torn by disagreement and controversy on nearly every aspect of yellow fever. Three hundred and fifty years of medical discourse by the best and worst medical minds, and all the minds in between, had produced little more than confusing and contradictory theories of its origin, spread, treatment, and control. But while little progress was made in understanding yellow fever, real scientifically based advancements in medical science were accelerating.

Reed's success was built on the science that came before. In Europe, Louis Pasteur and Robert Koch demonstrated the role of specific bacteria in the causation of specific diseases, thus becoming the fathers of modern microbiology. In the Americas, Louis Daniel Beauperthuy and Carlos Juan Finlay, among others, proposed the mosquito as a carrier of yellow fever and other diseases. Finlay, working in Cuba in the 1880s and 1890s, correctly identified the species of *Culex* mosquito—later called *Stegomyia* and now *Aedes*—most often associated with transmission of the illness, but alas, he could never prove the connection. In 1897, Ronald Ross, an English doctor assigned to India, conclusively demonstrated the life cycle of the malaria parasite in another mosquito species, the *Anopheles*, thereby confirming the transmission of the disease by the insect. Last, Henry Rose Carter, a doctor with the United States Marine Hospital Service, the forerunner of the Public Health Service, noted a two-week interval between the first case of yellow fever in a community and subsequent cases. He called this the period of "extrinsic incubation"—a period needed for some change to occur in the yellow fever germ before it could be passed on.

When the U.S. Army Yellow Fever Board assembled in Cuba, they stood atop the accumulated scientific knowledge. Also in Havana were two leading but yet unrecognized leaders in the study of yellow fever. Now in the nineteenth year of his failed attempts to convincingly prove that the mosquito carried the disease, Carlos Juan Finlay was still busily breeding mosquitoes. In Havana harbor, the quarantine officer was none other than Henry Rose Carter. The Army Board was at the eye of the perfect scientific storm, and they were about to ride it to glory.

Using what was known and making their own best guesses about the unknowns, they devised simple but elegant experiments to pursue the cause of the disease as far as 1900 science would allow. During their short stay in Cuba, they overturned the leading theories of the day on its cause, spread, and control while presenting scientifically sound and defensible new theories.

On New Year's Eve 1900, Walter Reed sat alone in his quarters and wrote to his wife of his triumph, then known only to him and a few others:

> Only 10 minutes of the old Century remain, lovie [sic], dear. Here I have been sitting reading that most wonderful book—La Roche on Yellow fever—written in 1853. Forty-seven years later it has been permitted to me & my assistants to lift the impenetrable veil that has surrounded the causation of this [most] dreadful pest of humanity and to put it on a rational & scientific basis. I thank God that this has been accomplished during the latter days of the old century—May its cure be wrought out in the early days of the new century! The prayer that has been mine for twenty or more years, that I might be permitted in some way or sometime to do something to alleviate human suffering, has been answered! *12 midnight!* A thousand happy new years to my precious, thrice precious wifie and daughter![3]

At that moment, Walter Reed was Christopher Columbus approaching landfall on Hispaniola, Lewis and Clark at the Pacific Ocean, or Sir Edmund Hillary pulling himself up onto Mount Everest's summit.

As the twentieth century began, yellow fever was in retreat, soon forced out from many of its Caribbean and South American strongholds. The army sanitarian William Gorgas, who had once recommended that troops burn the little Cuban town of Siboney to the ground in a misguided effort to eradicate yellow fever, now applied less draconian but more effective measures to chase it out of Havana. Within weeks of the Army Board's key experiments, Gorgas was on a search and destroy mission in the streets of Havana, looking for mosquito breeding areas and other harborages. By the end of 1901, Havana was free of yellow fever for the first time in over one hundred years. A few small outbreaks occurred until the last case faded away in 1905—the same year yellow fever was banished from the United States.

The victory, as many victories do, had its costs and its glory. Within six months of their first welcoming handshakes in Havana, one of the four doctors was dead—killed in action by yellow fever. Another was severely wounded by the disease he was battling. One began to fade into history, an almost unknown supporting player in one of medicine's greatest triumphs. And one became an icon of the can-do American military, a medical man prominent and revered in the early twentieth century.

This is the story of yellow fever's two-and-a-half-century killing spree across the United States. It is also the story of how Americans lived and died with it and how it was finally defeated.

Chapter 1

Yellow Fever Comes to America

Y ELLOW FEVER IS AN ACUTE VIRAL HEMORRHAGIC DISEASE caused by the yellow fever virus. The virus belongs to the flavivirus group, which includes the West Nile and dengue fever viruses. Infection results in a wide spectrum of disease, from mild symptoms to severe illness and death, making the disease difficult to diagnose. Doctors may confuse it with malaria, typhoid, rickettsial diseases, other arthropod-borne viral fevers, viral hepatitis, and even some poisonings.

While some infections will have no symptoms, most people with yellow fever will experience an acute illness normally characterized by fever, muscle pain, backache, headache, shivers, loss of appetite, nausea, and vomiting. Their eyes may be bloodshot and their tongue fuzzy. While in many febrile illnesses a high fever is accompanied by a rapid pulse, in yellow fever, the pulse is often slowed down, a phenomenon called Faget's sign. During the acute phase, which lasts about three days, there is virus circulating in the patient's blood and that person can be a source of infection. In most patients, the illness will not progress beyond these symptoms, and most victims will improve and recover. However, about 15 percent will enter a "period of intoxication"[1] within two to twenty-four hours after the acute phase appears to be resolving. In these patients, fever reappears and jaundice develops along with severe abdominal pain and vomiting. Bleeding can occur from the mouth, nose, eyes, and stomach. Digested blood may appear in the feces or vomit. The Spanish were struck by this feature and named the disease *el vomito negro*. It often heralds death. Kidney function may be affected, ranging from abnormal protein levels in the urine, called albuminuria, to complete kidney failure with no urine production, called anuria. Half of the patients in the toxic phase die within ten to fourteen days after becoming ill.

Yellow fever is an arboviral disease, meaning that it is transmitted to humans by an arthropod vector. Arthropods include insects and ticks. Adult female mosquitoes pick up the virus from infected individuals while

7

feeding. Males do not feed and cannot carry the disease. Humans and monkeys are generally the only animals that can be infected.

After the mosquito ingests infected blood, the virus is carried to the mosquito's midgut. There it reproduces or replicates in the cells lining the midgut wall. The virus is then released into the mosquito's hemolymph, or blood, and travels to her salivary glands. The virus is now ready for release into the mosquito's next victim. The time needed for the virus to complete this part of its life cycle is about seven to seventeen days and is called "extrinsic incubation." The mosquito cannot transmit the virus until after this time.

The female mosquito can also pass the virus via infected eggs to its offspring. These eggs can lie dormant through dry conditions, hatching when conditions are right. Therefore, the female mosquito and its eggs are the true reservoir of the virus, ensuring transmission from one year to the next.

Today scientists recognize three different transmission cycles for yellow fever: sylvatic or jungle, intermediate, and urban. All three cycles exist in Africa, but in South America, only sylvatic and urban yellow fever occur. Until the 1930s, only the urban cycle was known. Each cycle has its own specific ecology and may involve several different species of *Aedes* and *Haemagogus* mosquitoes.

In jungle yellow fever, monkeys in tropical rain forests are infected by wild mosquitoes that may bite humans entering the forest, resulting in sporadic cases of yellow fever. Intermediate yellow fever occurs in the humid or semihumid savannas of Africa, where small-scale epidemics occur. In this cycle, semidomestic mosquitoes infect both monkey and human hosts in areas where their habitats intersect. Urban yellow fever has historically been the type most associated with the large-scale deadly outbreaks in the United States, the Caribbean, and Central and South America. In this setting, the tiny black-bodied silver-striped domestic mosquito, *Aedes aegypti*, which prefers to breed in man-made containers, carries the virus from person to person. It also stays close to home, having a flight range of only about a thousand feet.

There is no specific treatment for yellow fever, but several strategies are used to prevent the disease or control an outbreak. The most important and effective is vaccination. Also important, especially in urban settings, but perhaps less effective over the long term, is mosquito control.

Some four hundred years after the first cases of the disease were described in Mexico and the Caribbean, the mystery surrounding the origin of yellow fever remains unsolved. Among the many theories of its origin is one that claims the yellow fever virus existed in the rain forests of the New World but needed the African *Aedes aegypti* mosquito to carry it to humans. The consensus among virologists and disease ecologists, however, is that both the disease and the *Aedes aegypti* mosquito arrived in the Western Hemisphere from Africa as a consequence of the early slave trade. Molecular biology may end the debate. The case for an African origin of the disease is supported by recent work in the evolutionary genetics of the yellow fever virus. There is more genetic variation in the African strains than in the South American strains, pointing to a longer evolutionary history for the virus in Africa. Therefore, Africa is most likely yellow fever's ancestral home.

There is little or no question that the mosquito has its roots in Africa. On that continent, there are many mosquito species closely related to *A. aegypti*. As with the virus, this suggests a common evolutionary path. In the Western Hemisphere, this particular mosquito has no close relatives, making it likely that it was recently introduced. In Africa, *Aedes* was primarily a forest-dwelling pest that bred in water-filled tree holes. Over time, it adapted itself to life in close proximity to human habitats and became domesticated. By the middle of the twentieth century, it was found in many of the world's tropical and subtropical regions and even made its way into the more temperate zones of North America, North Africa, and the Middle East. Since that time, aggressive mosquito control efforts, especially in the Western Hemisphere, have greatly reduced its range.

Whether it was the vector and disease or the vector alone that was brought from Africa, there is no debate on how they came to meet in the Americas—trade. In much the same way that the global economy of the twenty-first century facilitates the movement of diseases like SARS or West Nile around the world, the opening of trade routes in an earlier time resulted in the movement of disease. Yellow fever was not the only disease on the move. Spanish conquistadors brought measles and smallpox to the Inca and Mayan societies and the Carib Indians. In turn, the Spanish probably took home syphilis. Most likely it was the trafficking in human cargo that delivered yellow fever to the Americas.

Infectious diseases love social upheaval. War, mass migrations of people, changes in climate, and other events that alter human ecology often create incubators for illness. The American Revolution and a continent-wide smallpox epidemic were joined in time and place. The 1918 influenza pandemic that took 20 million lives worldwide began at the tail end of World War I. HIV/AIDS took advantage of changing sexual mores. Yellow fever was born of the mating of slavery and sugar.

At the midpoint of the 1600s, significant changes came to Caribbean agriculture and the labor pool that supported it. Until this time, indentured servants from Europe mainly worked the small farms that dominated colonial West Indian agriculture. These laborers exchanged three to five years of their lives for passage to the Americas; some voluntarily, some at the point of a sword. But the indentured labor pool was shrinking, and many of these workers, it was discovered, were not up to the backbreaking work and hardships of tropical farming. A new source of cheap labor was needed.

The Spanish-Portuguese monopoly on the African slave trade that had been in place since the early 1500s was also coming to an end. Dutch, British, and French slavers were increasingly taking over the trade—sometimes by force. The Dutch were among the most aggressive and seized Spanish-controlled slave ports on the west coast of Africa. With more players in the trade, the number of slaves transported to the Americas dramatically increased.

The typical slave ship of the time may have been similar to a Dutch flute: a small three-masted wooden ship with two decks, top and below. The crew of about twenty would sail from Europe to slave-trading outposts such as Benin and Old Calabar on Africa's west coast. There, ship and crew plied coastal Africa for many months, cutting their best deals for slaves who were hunted down and sold by other Africans and Islamic traders. Before departing, the ships loaded up on provisions. Sweet potatoes and other native African fare were put up for the journey across the Atlantic. These foods were for the slaves. Many captains had learned that a European diet, especially one of dried meats and hardtack, could not sustain their human cargo. Too much of their high-priced inventory was lost to dysentery and other digestive disorders during a crossing without native foods.

Water was also essential for the trip. Casks of water were loaded in Africa for the three-month journey. It can be assumed that a few days out of port, wigglers, or mosquito larvae, danced just below the surface of the water. Several days later, the mature mosquitoes would have emerged. Slaves and crews provided the blood meals female mosquitoes needed to produce eggs. The sated females returned to the water casks and cisterns to lay their eggs. During the voyage across the Middle Passage, as the Africa to America journey was called, the mosquitoes could pass through several generations.

Between the time they left Africa and the time they docked in Pernambuco, Guadeloupe, or Barbados, a ship's crew was likely reduced by 20 percent, almost entirely by sickness. The extent to which yellow fever contributed to this mortality rate will never be known; such things were kept "conveniently dark."[2] The death rate among the ship's human cargo, due to disease, suicide, and murder, was about the same in this period. It is very likely that only the mosquito population had increased on the crossing.

Slaves and mosquitoes disembarked into the New World. Slave labor was desperately needed to work the new large plantations that were displacing the smaller family farms. In Barbados in the mid-1600s, the ten-acre plot worked by a family and a few indentured servants was disappearing, replaced by large plantations averaging three hundred acres; some stretched over a thousand acres. As the plantations grew, the number of property holders fell from over 11,000 to under 800. The demand for a huge slave labor force also grew, and the slavers were ready to comply. Barbados had 5,600 black slaves in 1645, up from near zero a few years earlier. By 1667, there were more than 82,000 Africans working the island's plantations.

Many of the shifts in land use and the labor force were the result of a major change in West Indian agriculture. Europe and the European colonies to the north had developed a sweet tooth. Where cotton and tobacco were once grown, the green spiky leaves of sugar cane now waved in the Caribbean trade winds. Whether it was packed into cones of sugar, turned into molasses, or fermented into rum, demand was high, prices were higher, and the incentive to forsake other crops in favor of cane was even higher.

While the slaves went to work in the fields and plantation homes of the Caribbean, *Aedes aegypti* mosquitoes, now freed from their water casks, went in search of blood meals. And while blood was essential for laying eggs, it was not required for sustenance. Sugar water, now abundant on the islands, could sustain them quite well until they happened on a warm-blooded mammalian feast.

Sporadic cases of yellow fever probably occurred for many years before the virus and the vector were sufficiently established to cause a devastating epidemic. Historians have reported several disease outbreaks before 1648 as yellow fever. Among those were an epidemic that ravaged Christopher Columbus's troops and the Carib Indians they engaged at the 1495 battle of Vega Real in Hispaniola. Much later, in 1643, an illness dubbed the *Coup de Barre* struck Guadeloupe. Four years later, a mysterious illness visited Bridgetown, Barbados. Both this outbreak and *Coup de Barre* have been called the first reports of yellow fever. It is uncertain whether any of these were yellow fever.

The Vega Real outbreak is too poorly documented for us to know its cause. The *Coup de Barre*, described by the French priest Pere Duptertre and named for the extreme muscle pains that accompanied it, was unlikely to be yellow fever. It was similar to a previously known disease and had too low a death rate for yellow fever. While conditions may have been right for yellow fever on Barbados in 1647, not enough is known about the outbreak to name it. Whatever it was, it was devastating. Writing to Governor Winthrop of New England, a correspondent described "an absolute plague, very infectious and destroying."[3] In the writer's parish, twenty people were buried in one week, and in many weeks during the epidemic there were fifteen or sixteen burials.

The first relatively certain occurrence of yellow fever was in the Spanish stronghold on the Yucatan in 1648. Writing in his *Historia de Yucathan*, Lopez de Cogolludo noted that conditions that year were ripe for a great calamity. In March, one of the signs of impending disaster was the arrival of a fog so dense that for several days the sun appeared eclipsed. For the old Mayan Indians the fog was "a sign of great mortality of people in this land, and for our sins." The first cases of the mystery illness appeared in Campeche in June. Cogolludo said the city was "totally laid waste." The *peste*, as he called it, continued throughout the summer. The Spanish established roadblocks around Campeche in an effort to confine the contagion. But the disease spread. There was little confidence in the authorities' ability to halt the sickness. After all, many reasoned, what good were human barriers if their Lord God did not protect the city? Moving from Campeche, its apparent place of origin, to Merida, the *peste* appeared to jump over the villages between as if carried directly from one city to the other. A resident of Merida, where the epidemic hit in August, wrote in a letter,

"With such quickness it came on great and little, rich and poor, that in less than eight days almost the whole city was sick at one time and many of the citizens of highest name and authority died."[4]

Accounts describing the spread and symptoms of the disease leave little doubt that it was yellow fever. Indians fell ill a few days after arriving in the city of Merida. Initially, only friars who left their cloisters to care for the sick became ill. But soon cases of the *peste* appeared in the cloisters seventeen to twenty days after the first friars fell ill. This timing is in keeping with the now known time needed for the virus to reproduce in the infected mosquito, the extrinsic incubation, and for symptoms to develop in people. Henry Rose Carter, who discovered and described the extrinsic incubation period, wrote in his exhaustive 1931 *History of the Origin of Yellow Fever,* published after his death, that the known epidemiology of yellow fever dovetails so perfectly with that reported from the Yucatan "as to almost compel of the diagnosis of it or some other host-borne disease."[5]

Cogolludo's recounting of the malady's symptoms almost certainly confirms it as yellow fever. Victims of the *peste* were "taken with a very severe and intense pain in the head and of all the bones of the body, so violent that it appeared to dislocate them or to squeeze them as a press."[6] Many but not all of the sick progressed to a "vehement fever" often accompanied by delirium. The truly unfortunate began vomiting "putrefied blood and of these very few remained alive."[7] Those who worsened often died on the fifth day. Except for dying two or more days earlier than most yellow fever patients today, the descriptions of the *peste* symptoms offered by Cogolludo mirror what is now known of the disease.

Who or what brought the disease to the Yucatan is not known. Contemporary writers have noted that there was a lot of pirate activity in the Caribbean that year. Perhaps increased shipping traffic and encounters between ships for pillaging helped transport the virus or the vector to Campeche. The Mayan Indians had their own theories, as reported by Cogolludo: "The malady was a judgment of God, since they were sick only in the [Spanish] cities and towns."[8] But the disease raged in the Yucatan for two years, and eventually even the Indian pueblos couldn't escape the scourge. Attributing the disease to the wrath of God, however, remained a consistent feature of yellow fever epidemics for the next two hundred and fifty years.

The French colonies of St. Kitts and Guadeloupe also suffered a *peste* in the summer of 1648. One-third of St. Kitts's population perished within eighteen months. A mysterious disease visiting Guadeloupe that summer was unlike 1635's *Coup de Barre* but epidemiologically and clinically similar to yellow fever. Residents claimed the French ship *La Boeuf* brought it to the island in late July. The ship's crew was sick and dying when it arrived at the capital of Basse Terre. Soon after it docked, Father R. P. Aramand de la Paix boarded the ship to hear the crew's confessions and to administer the Church's sacraments to the afflicted. He took ill while aboard the *La Boeuf* and died on August 4.

The disease soon struck Cuba. From 1511, when Velasquez brought three hundred settlers to Cuba from Santo Domingo and permanently established a Spanish presence on the island, until about 1620, there was no record of any significant disease outbreaks in the colony. Starting in 1620, residents of the island and ship crews calling at its ports began experiencing malignant fevers. Dr. Carlos Finlay, Cuba's pioneering yellow fever researcher in the late nineteenth century, believed these were outbreaks of yellow fever, but too little is known about them to draw that conclusion.

A virulent and horrible disease that struck Cuba in 1649, though the year has also been given as 1648, was almost certainly yellow fever. In Havana, a third of the city's residents died between May and October. If the 1649 date is correct, it is likely that the disease was introduced from the Spanish colony at the Yucatan. Yellow fever was present on the island until 1655. It then either disappeared completely or remained at such a low level as to be almost unnoticeable until infected prisoners from Vera Cruz who arrived to build Cabañas reintroduced it in 1751. It remained endemic on Cuba until 1901.

Throughout most of the Caribbean during much of the late 1600s and early 1700s, yellow fever was a sporadic visitor. Still, it may have been the best defender of the Caribbean against European colonists. During this time, it devoured British and French military expeditions. In 1665, a British squadron, noted to be in good health, seized St. Lucia. A garrison of fifteen hundred troops placed on the island was quickly reduced to eighty-nine by a virulent epidemic of yellow fever. Similar stories of ill-fated military missions were common.

Along with immigrants to the Caribbean, newly arrived soldiers and sailors were among those who suffered the most. Yellow fever became known as a "fever of acclimation." If newcomers survived three years without dying of it, chances were that something else would have to kill them.

Not known at the time was that once infected, a person is immune for life. A constant influx of emigrants from Europe or North America was needed to keep yellow fever alive in the Caribbean. These newcomers were immunologically naive; never having been exposed to yellow fever, they lacked the antibodies needed to protect against infection.

How much of the mortality attributed to yellow fever during its early history really was the result of infection with the yellow fever virus is unknown. Standardized medical nomenclature simply didn't exist, and a variety of names were applied to it. In English-speaking colonies, the name "yellow fever" didn't become routinely associated with the sickness until the mid-1700s. The descriptive *el vomito negro* used by the Spaniards had been in use much longer. The disease had other names. *Mal de Siam* was applied to the disease during a 1690 epidemic in Martinique, where a French man-of-war, the *Oriflamme*, docked after traveling from Siam, known today as Thailand. The ship was believed to have carried the fever. Since yellow fever has never been known to occur in Asia, the sickness more likely came aboard during a port call the ship made in Brazil a few weeks earlier.

Complicating matters, while the symptoms of severe yellow fever are nearly unique to the disease, those in less virulent cases can be shared by other diseases. Milder cases that did not progress much beyond flulike symptoms would have been impossible to diagnose as yellow fever with any certainty. Even today, blood tests and urinalysis for biochemical changes and immunological markers of infection are needed to make a definitive diagnosis.

After the 1690 *Mal de Siam* epidemic, as yellow fever settled into the Caribbean, cases of the disease were being exported along with rum and sugar. In 1693, Boston was the first British North American colony struck by an epidemic. Admiral Joseph Wheeler's fleet, recently arrived from the West Indies, was blamed for the introduction. Charleston and Philadelphia also came under attack. A year later, the admiral lost almost his entire squadron to the scourge while preparing to mount an assault on Martinique.

Over the next hundred years, yellow fever epidemics occasionally struck port cities up and down the East Coast. In 1699, Philadelphia and Charleston were again visited. Both cities lost about 7 percent of their residents: 220 people in Philadelphia and 178 in Charleston. New York City lost 10 percent of its population to yellow fever in 1702. During the century after the first Boston epidemic, major outbreaks were reported in only fifteen of those years. There were two notable periods, however, when the disease made back-to-back annual visits. Starting in 1737, eastern seaports suffered through seven consecutive yellow fever summers and then were yellow fever–free until 1762. Between 1762 and 1765, yellow fever returned each year to North American cities. It then disappeared for nearly three decades.

During this time, outbreaks in the Caribbean were also sporadically occurring. While a continuous influx of immigrants provided fresh victims throughout the early and mid-1700s, few outbreaks were reported for the twenty years after 1770. Dr. William Wright, a British physician practicing in Jamaica from 1764 to 1777 and 1783 to 1786, claims to have never seen a case. This was also a time of peace in the region, but that was about to change.

In the wake of the 1789 French Revolution, the French colony on the island of St. Domingue (now Hispaniola) was torn by civil war. Whites, powerful landowners, and the lower class *petits blancs* battled one another over independence from France. Meanwhile, the Free Coloreds, a mix of free blacks and mulattos, were fighting for full rights as citizens. Initially, the black slaves watched as these warring factions fought one another.

Taking advantage of the turmoil, thousands of slaves rose up against the island's white society on the night of August 21, 1791. The Haitian revolution on St. Domingue was under way. In the northern provinces of St. Domingue, the slaves butchered their white owners and other whites, torched hundreds of plantations, and forced refugees to flee into Cap François, now Cap Haitien, and a few other heavily defended strongholds.

A Revolutionary Commission, led by Léger Sonthonax and backed by seven thousand troops, was dispatched from Paris to take control of the island. As malaria and yellow fever decimated his French troops, the Republican leader aligned himself with the Colored militia and imposed a reign of terror on the island's whites, most of whom he believed were monarchists. St. Domingue's whites turned on Sonthonax. In June 1793, to strengthen his position, he offered freedom to all blacks who joined his revolutionary cause. Accepting his offer, a band of black fighters set upon Cap François on June 20. They killed ten thousand mostly white residents. The survivors fled the island. Among the ships heading away from Haiti that summer was the *Mary*. Loaded with refugees, it sailed north for Philadelphia.

The turmoil its passengers left behind continued for another eleven years. St. Domingue was a battleground for French, British, and Spanish troops all maneuvering for control of the once productive and prosperous colony. In addition to the black warriors, the Europeans were confronted by yellow fever. British forces lost one hundred thousand soldiers and sailors—half of them killed; half disabled—to disease in Haiti, with most, it is believed, succumbing to yellow fever.

Francois Dominique Toussaint-Louverture, the George Washington of Haiti, who led his forces against the French general Victor-Emmanuel LeClerc and his twenty-thousand-man-strong army, was greatly aided in his struggle by yellow fever. One-third of the French troops who landed at Cap François in January 1802 were lost to the malady. Despite his loses, LeClerc forced the surrender of Louverture in May. Yellow fever fought on, and LeClerc knew he could not hold on without reinforcements from Europe.

On May 8, 1802, he wrote to the French minister of marine, "I have at this moment 3,600 men in hospital. I have been losing from 30 to 50 men a day in the colony. . . . To be master of San Domingo, I need 25,000 Europeans under arms."[9] Many of his generals and their staff were sick, dying, or dead. He ordered a report on the sickness: "According to this report, it seems that this sickness is that sickness which is called Yellow fever or Siamese disease."[10] On October 22, 1802, LeClerc himself succumbed to yellow fever. His replacement, General Rochambeau, arrived to face the disease and the Haitian insurgents. He surrendered what remained of his French army in November 1803. On January 1, 1804, rebel leader General Jean-Jacques Dessalines declared Haitian independence.

The refugees, who had sailed north out of Cap François in 1793 aboard the *Mary* and other ships, left behind the horrors of Haiti's decade-long war of independence. Among the cargoes they carried with them to Philadelphia and other cities was Haiti's great defender, yellow fever.

The devastating Philadelphia epidemic of 1793 ushered in the longest and deadliest string of yellow fever years yet known in North America. While other U.S. cities were stricken, Philadelphia suffered the greatest losses during the tumultuous thirteen-year span of annual yellow fever epidemics that followed. In 1793, 5,000 people, one-tenth of Philadelphia's population, died. After several milder outbreaks in the mid-1790s, the disease again swept away staggering numbers of Philadelphians. In 1797, 1,500 perished, another 3,500 died in 1798, and 1,000 more died in 1799.

The repeatedly high mortality rates were probably the result of a continuous stream of emigrants from elsewhere in the United States and foreign immigrants into the city. The newcomers, both those carrying yellow fever as they fled the ongoing turmoil in the Caribbean and those never exposed to yellow fever, helped ignite and fuel the illness as it burned through Philadelphia and other U.S. cities.

Some blamed the recurring yellow fever epidemics for hindering Philadelphia's growth. Between 1790 and 1800, the city's population increased about 44 percent, from 28,522 to 41,220, but from 1800 to 1810 it grew only by 30 percent, to 53,722. Despite the high mortality rates from disease, European cities seemed to thrive, but the threat of yellow fever was seen as a deterrent to the emergence of the U.S.'s new and emerging metropolises. Thomas Jefferson, no fan of the urban environment, recognized the yearly epidemics as "evil" but saw slowed growth as a bit of good news among the bad. In an 1800 letter to Philadelphia's leading physician, Benjamin Rush, he wrote, "The yellow fever will discourage the growth of great cities in our nation & I view great cities as pestilential to the morals, the health and the liberties of man."[11] The Jeffersonian ideal clashed with the view of many that growth and prosperity went hand in hand. City fathers felt they had to control yellow fever and the other diseases then prevalent in their young metropolises if they were to successfully compete for trade and business. The fear of this disease could not be allowed to endanger economic health.

Yet each spring, Americans living in seaport cities came to dread the approaching summer. This seasonal anxiety lasted for over a hundred years, though after the 1820s it was almost entirely confined to southern cities and towns. Throughout the entire nineteenth century, as yellow fever destroyed lives and ruined businesses, residents of these threatened cities struggled with the most basic questions about yellow fever: where did it come from, how could it be prevented, why were some cities stricken and others missed, and why did certain people fall ill and others remain well? Many theories came and went as doctors, especially those in the South, became intimately acquainted with the scourge. No matter what the "theory of the decade" was, city leaders—and before the American Civil War, public health was almost exclusively a local responsibility—relied on two methods in an often fruitless attempt to prevent or control yellow fever.

These were the ancient practice of quarantine and the newer emerging science of sanitation.

Northern cities acted quickly to contain the suffering caused by their worst yellow fever epidemics. Philadelphia, Baltimore, and New York convened boards of health to manage the repeated invasions. Controversial, but supported by the contagionists, quarantine was one of the most used and perhaps most potent tools available to the boards. Previously it had been applied to halt smallpox and plague, among other diseases, but its use against yellow fever was relatively recent. Ships arriving from yellow fever–infested areas—their crews, cargoes, and passengers—were held on islands or other secluded areas for forty days or more. Infected ships were ordered to fly a yellow flag, giving the disease its common nickname, yellow jack. Overland travelers from suspect cities were also subject to quarantine, as were those living in a city who took ill or had contact with the sick. They were directed to pest houses or camps outside of town.

Pestilence and quarantine have been linked throughout history; both can be traced to early human history. The Bible's Old Testament book of Leviticus laid out the methods for halting the spread of leprosy. In the fourteenth chapter, forty-sixth verse, the Lord tells Moses and Aaron how to manage a leprous person: "He shall live alone, and his dwelling shall be outside the camp."[12] The modern concept of quarantine began to emerge during the great plague of Europe in the fourteenth century. Venice, southern Europe's leading maritime port, established a code of quarantine in 1448. All ships arriving from places where disease was known to exist or was suspected of being prevalent had to anchor outside the harbor for forty days. No cargo or persons could go ashore. A few years later, the seaport created the first lazarettos for the care and treatment of plague victims on a small nearby island. The sick and their families were deported to the pest house and were not allowed to return to their homes until forty days after the disease abated.

The word "quarantine" comes from the Latin *quaranta*, meaning forty. The reason for selecting forty days as the period of confinement is not known. Historians have suggested several theories. Forty days is a recurring number in major biblical events such as the nights and days of rain that Noah and his menagerie endured aboard their ark. It was the time period assigned to Moses's stay on Mt. Sinai, and in Mosaic law it was the period appointed for cleansing unclean lepers. In the New Testament, Jesus's trial in the wilderness lasted forty days, and it is the number of days of spiritual cleansing in the Christian Lent. The number appeared in Greek medicine, which declared forty critical days for the development of a contagious disease. While forty may be an unnecessarily long confinement for most diseases, including yellow fever, fear and uncertainty demanded a greater rather than lesser period of isolation.

Before the 1793 yellow fever epidemic, Philadelphia used quarantines to prevent the spread of smallpox. A ten-pound fine was levied on anyone harboring a sick person who had been banished to the pest house. In 1774, when a smallpox epidemic swept through the city, a provision was added to the law subjecting any person escaping quarantine to a fifty-pound fine. If unable to pay, the escapee got twenty lashes, well laid-on, upon the bare back. As a nineteenth-century wag noted, this was "a soothing application to the desquamating skin of a small pox convalescent!"[13]

Merchants and businessmen saw quarantine as a costly failure. After all, between 1794 and 1820, the practice failed to prevent eight major East Coast epidemics. Because normal trade was halted, goods were blocked from entering and leaving town, and many believed quarantine was more injurious to a port's commercial interests than were the diseases it was guarding against. As the nineteenth century progressed, even health officials made the decision to establish a quarantine based more on economic rather than on health concerns.

The shipping industry despised quarantine at U.S. ports, and some traders took a cynical view of the reasons behind the practice. In the late 1850s, twenty-two ship captains whose vessels were sitting at quarantine vented their frustrations in the New York *Commercial Advertiser*. They complained that the decisions for sending a ship to quarantine were based on flimsy evidence and were driven less by a need to "preserve the health of New York, but for the benefit of whom it may concern."[14] They then listed those concerned who benefited. The port health officer got $6.50 a ship. The port warden's fee was $5.00, and a fumigator got $6.00 for tossing about a bit of chloride of lime. Others collected fees for services both needed and unneeded. Finally, all dunnage had to be burned at a cost of $6.00.

Despite the questionable efficacy of quarantine and the high costs associated with it, the practice survived into the twentieth century. Taken together, quarantine and sanitary improvements may have been the reason yellow fever fled the northern cities and took refuge in the South. Several public health historians credit both these interventions as key elements in the demise of yellow fever above the Mason-Dixon line after 1822. Anti-contagionists and health reformers in afflicted communities championed sanitary reforms. In response to these demands, local governments began to examine their roles and responsibilities in protecting health and ensuring the welfare of their citizens.

Community responsibility for public and personal health was a newly emerging concept. Following the 1800 Baltimore outbreak, which claimed nearly twelve hundred lives, an anonymous writer noted, "We have fire companies, we have insurance companies, and we have banking companies; but no company could equal the extensive or essential benefits desirable from a health company."[15] Baltimore established a "health company" of sorts in 1801. For a five-dollar subscription, members could refer up to two patients to the newly established city dispensary in the Fells Point section of town. The system quickly drew criticism since many of the people it was created to help, the city's poor, could not afford the five dollars and sponsors were scarce.

Public health reforms enacted to improve the health of the entire population were more common and successful. In response to repeated invasions of yellow fever, which clearly caused great economic disruption and soiled a city's reputation, boards of health were established in such cities as New York, Boston, Baltimore, and Philadelphia. These agencies began to look inward as well as outward for the source of the yellow fever poison.

In the time before germs were linked to disease, the boards of health focused on filth as a reservoir of the unknown agents of yellow fever, cholera, and smallpox. Public works projects spurred on by the need to control these diseases included trash removal, draining swamps, and building municipal water and sewage systems. The boards' edicts, issued in ignorance of any of these diseases' true causes, were based on common sense and good intentions. Sanitary improvements also resulted in tangible evidence of a board's worth. There was clear evidence of progress for politicians to point to. Citizens could see and smell the changes in their surroundings. And public works projects created jobs.

More important, the improvements did reduce sickness and mortality. In the case of yellow fever, eliminating standing water could significantly reduce the threat of an outbreak. The still-to-be-discovered carrier of yellow fever, the *Aedes aegypti* mosquito, thrived in standing water and the urban environment. To become an efficient yellow fever vector, the mosquito needed to rapidly increase its population. Close proximity to both blood meals and breeding grounds was essential for her survival. The mosquitoes' life cycle was fatally disrupted by working street drains, closed water supply systems, and underground sewage lines.

Beginning with the great Philadelphia epidemic of 1793, some combination of sanitation and quarantine was the standard response to the arrival of yellow fever. In some places and in some time periods, one or the other dominated public health practice. That battle for supremacy also began in 1793, as the city's physicians split into contagionist and anticontagionist camps.

Chapter 2

The Capital Under Siege

IN 1793, PHILADELPHIA WAS PROSPEROUS AND CONFIDENT, SECURE IN ITS place as America's premier city. Perhaps not quite on equal footing with London or Paris, it was the center of learning, religion, commerce, trade, and government for the newly founded United States. It was a city where "learning, manufactures, and human improvement of every kind thrive and flourish."[1] Some of America's greatest thinkers argued science, law, philosophy, and literature and the arts in the College of Philadelphia and the American Philosophical Society. But it was also a city of artisans and craftsmen, merchants and traders, lawyers and bankers. The mix of religions, races—including a free black society—and nationalities undoubtedly made it the most cosmopolitan town in the New World.

In part, the temporary presence of the federal government contributed to Philadelphia's prosperity. In 1790, the growing bureaucracy established itself in the Quaker City—a brief stop as it made its journey from New York City to the nascent city of Washington, D.C. Those wanting to be close to the central government flocked into town. Between 1790 and 1800, the population in the city proper increased from 28,522 to 41,220, an incredible 45 percent gain. In nearly every street, new homes were being built "in a very neat, elegant style."[2] Demand must have outpaced supply as house rents became extravagant.

In the city's cafes, business doubled and even tripled as ordinary citizens and the leaders of a new nation—George Washington, John Adams, Alexander Hamilton, and Thomas Jefferson—met to drink and eat while arguing the future of their creation.

Not everyone was happy with the transformations taking place in Philadelphia. Prosperity came with costs. Luxury and wealth were not universally accepted virtues. Mathew Carey was among those increasingly concerned by what he saw as an encroaching decadence. Carey, a Roman Catholic, was born in Ireland and had emigrated to Philadelphia in 1784 after publishing a paper attacking the British government that landed him in an English jail. By 1793, he was one of Philadelphia's most prominent publishers and booksellers. At the end of 1793, he rushed into print his account of that year's tragic yellow fever epidemic. As the year began, Carey worried that the temperance and sober manners needed for the "liberty and happiness of a nation"[3] were less and less practiced. He saw a steady erosion of the city's wholesome habits. Others observed this moral decay, at least in retrospect. Dr. Benjamin Rush described a "bitter and unchristian spirit"[4] taking hold in 1793.

Rapid growth brought other problems. Sanitation was less than ideal. The new redbrick homes and crowded cafes lined streets that ran with sewage and other unpleasant and odorous wastes. The Philadelphia physician William Currie found his town to be quite agreeable, though plagued with "a few nuisances . . . such as slaughter-houses, tan-yards, and grave-yards."[5] The summer heat intensified the stench emanating from some of these nuisances. In many neighborhoods, the air was barely breathable.

The spring of 1793 had been wet and warm. Fruit trees blossomed in the first week of April. Migratory birds returned two weeks early. The early summer was hot and dry, giving way to a "temperate and pleasant"[6] August. The various dysenteries and remitting fevers were common. Yet, Dr. Rush recalled that "[t]here was something in the heat and drought of the summer months which was uncommon in their influence upon the human body."[7] Philadelphians, however, didn't let this influence keep them from enjoying a "merry and sinful" summer.[8]

The fifth of August began warm and clear. Dr. Benjamin Rush was called on to attend the daughter of his colleague Dr. Hugh Hodge. The Hodge family lived at the eastern edge of the city along Water Street, two blocks down and six blocks north of Dr. Rush's home. The young girl was struck with a bilious fever in the last week of July. When Rush arrived, she was vomiting blood and the yellow tint of jaundice infused her skin. The girl was too far gone for even such a prominent and successful physician as Dr. Rush to save. She died later in the day.

If Dr. Rush walked up Water Street from Chestnut, he passed the bustling crowded wharves where longshoremen unloaded the goods needed to support the city of Philadelphia and its surrounding communities. He may have seen the *Mary*, recently arrived from St. Domingue loaded with refugees. Also recently in from the Caribbean and points south were other vessels like the *Amelia*, *Flora*, *Sans Culottes*, and *Il Constant*. As he walked through town past these recent arrivals, Philadelphia's leading physician may have slapped away the mosquitoes that seemed more prevalent than in most years.

Almost as common as the mosquitoes were refugees from St. Domingue. The island's civil war, begun in 1791, continued unabated. Those who could flee, fled, many arriving in Philadelphia. French was becoming almost as common as English in the streets and shops, as more than one thousand refugees arrived in July, followed by another thousand in August.

Over the next two weeks, Dr. Rush was called to the sickbeds of ten more patients with similar symptoms, and rumors of other cases flew around the city. On August 19, Benjamin Rush was summoned to the home of Peter La Maigre on Water Street, between Race and Arch. His wife, Catherine, was the twelfth victim Rush treated who had signs and symptoms of the malignant bilious fever then prevalent in the city. Her home was near Ball's wharf, where a pile of coffee lay putrefying in the summer heat.

The stench of the coffee was so "excessively offensive that the people in the neighborhood could hardly bear to remain in the back part of their homes."[9] Captain John Foulke, the health officer for the Port of Philadelphia, felt that the coffee, along with other decaying vegetable and animal matter, was the source of the fevers that Dr. Rush and others were treating. Rush agreed, and following his visit to Mrs. La Maigre, he declared the presence of bilious yellow fever caused by the poisons escaping from that foul pile of coffee.

Catherine La Maigre died on August 20. Late on the night of August 21, an admittedly fatigued Dr. Rush sat down and wrote a letter to his wife. She, as was her habit, was spending the summer in Trenton, New Jersey, with her family. He told her of the malignant fever loose in the Water Street neighborhood and noted the possible connection between the sickness and the coffee. In addition to Mrs. La Maigre and Dr. Hodge's daughter, one other of his patients had died and seven or eight were recovering.

The fever distressed him a bit. While few were ill, it was a violent disease. A 1780 influenza epidemic had brought him more patients, he told his wife, but "most of the cases I [now] attend are acute and alarming and require an uncommon degree of vigilance and attention."[10]

What Dr. Rush probably didn't realize was that the fever was breaking out all along Water Street and possibly beyond the wharf area. Several sailors and refugees from St. Domingue had taken ill in and near Richard Denney's Water Street boardinghouse. Other similar cases and deaths were reported from towns north and south of Philadelphia.

In a city with more than its share of prominent and learned physicians, Benjamin Rush stood near the top of the pyramid, if not perched precariously on the point. He was born on January 4, 1746, some thirteen miles north of Philadelphia. His father, a farmer and gunsmith, died when young Benjamin was five years old. His mother ran a grocery store to support the family.

An uncle took in the boy and provided for his education, which included Princeton College in New Jersey and apprenticeships in the medical arts across the Delaware River with some of the Colonies' leading doctors. He attended lectures at the newly established College of Philadelphia. In 1762, the young medical apprentice was confronted with a yellow fever epidemic that swept through Philadelphia. American medicine was young, and to receive a proper education, a fledgling doctor with ambition needed to journey to Europe. Rush left for the University of Edinburgh in 1766. He received his medical degree in 1768 and continued his training at St. Thomas Hospital in London, where in the heart of the British Empire he met and befriended one of Philadelphia's most prominent citizens, Benjamin Franklin.

Rush returned home in 1769 and began his medical practice. Over the next several years, as the rift between Great Britain and its American colonies grew, he exchanged revolutionary thoughts with such people as Thomas Jefferson, John Adams, and Thomas Paine. These thoughts became actions, and in 1776, Rush served as a delegate to the Constitutional Congress. His new father-in-law, Richard Stockton of Princeton, also attended; Rush had married his seventeen-year-old daughter, Julia, the year before. Both Rush and Stockton signed the Declaration of Independence.

Rush went on to serve as surgeon general in the Middle Department of the Continental Army. He found the conditions of army hospitals and army medicine abysmal. Not willing to accept these circumstances, he took his concerns to his superiors and then to the Continental Congress. An unsigned letter describing the unhealthful conditions made its way to General George Washington, who believed Rush to be the author. Having lost the confidence of Washington, Rush resigned his post and returned to the private practice of medicine.

In 1787, he made a brief return to elected political office, serving on the Pennsylvania ratifying convention for the new federal constitution.

The same year, he was a founding member of the Philadelphia College of Physicians.

In late August 1793, he realized he was again coming face-to-face with that great scourge, yellow fever. He and his colleagues were worried by the increasing number of cases. By the end of August, over three hundred citizens would die, more than twice that expected in any given month. Of course, not every case was seen by a physician, and not every death was properly diagnosed and recorded, so the true extent of the insidious infection was unknown. Yellow fever had announced its presence but not its intentions. Rush, who had observed the 1762 epidemic as an apprentice, and other experienced physicians knew that the disease came on in late summer and did not depart until the first frost.

Rush sounded the alarm on August 21. He called on Mayor Matthew Clarkson and told him of his fears: a great epidemic was stirring in the city. This was a homegrown disease, the mayor was told, the result of the frightful effluvia carried in the air from the waste products of a great and teeming city. In Philadelphia, as in most major cities at the time, open sewers ran through streets littered with waste.

The city, aware that sanitation and good health worked in tandem, had a law on its books requiring the proper disposal of wastes, but in the summer of 1793, it was all but ignored. At Rush's urging, the mayor ordered that the ordinance be republished and enforced along with weekly trash removal. He also called for a meeting of the College of Physicians. Their collective knowledge and experience was needed to halt the sickness. The meeting was set for Sunday, August 25. It was the first time since the founding of the college that the city government called on it for guidance.

On August 22, Rush wrote his last letter until November that did not dwell on the devastating disease now spreading through Philadelphia. Instead, he described a celebration he had attended. About a mile outside town, the freed black community had held a roof raising on their new "African Church."[11] Calling it one of his most pleasant days, the staunch abolitionist recounted a plentiful dinner, accompanied by fine liquors and a simple dessert of melons. When he returned to the city after a two-hour absence, he had enough new business to keep busy till after ten o'clock.

On the night of August 24, Rush lost two patients to the fever. He knew of five other fever deaths in the neighborhood and four more elsewhere. Having decimated the waterfront, the disease was being reported from neighborhoods away from Water Street.

Most frightening to the doctors trained to fight disease, even as crudely as was done in the eighteenth century, this fever was mocking the power of their medicine. Despairingly, Rush told his wife, "I even strive to subdue my sympathy for my patients; otherwise, I would sink under the accumu-lated loads of misery."[12]

Such was Rush's state of mind as the College of Physicians convened. Its members were the premier doctors in town, as recognized by one another. There was Rush's mentor, John Redman, William Currie, Phillip Physick, and Hugh Hutchinson, whose daughter was one of the first known victims of yellow fever, among others. Not counted in the mem-bership were the less well regarded doctors, barber-surgeons, bleeders, and assorted healers, many of whom were seeing a different side of the emerg-ing epidemic than the top-drawer doctors.

Sixteen of twenty-six college fellows set to work on Sunday afternoon. A committee was formed to draft directions for checking the spread of the disease. The committee imposed on Rush to produce the document. By the time he sat down that night to write his wife, the directives were written. They were published on Tuesday, August 27.

Among the steps to be taken to halt the illness's onslaught were: avoid every infected person, as much as possible; avoid fatigue of the body and mind; dress according to the weather; avoid intemperance; mark every house with sickness in it; place patients in the center of well-ventilated rooms, change their clothes often, and remove all offensive matter; stop tolling bells at once; transport the dead in closed carriages and bury them as quickly as possible; clean the streets and keep them clean; stop building fires in homes, instead burn gunpowder and use vinegar and camphor lib-erally; and, called most important by the committee, provide a large and airy hospital near the city to receive the poor people infected with the dis-ease who have no one else to care for them.

Perhaps stopping the tolls of the bells was initially the most welcome recommendation. In part marking deaths, the city's church bells had been pealing nearly constantly. Mathew Carey wrote that they terrified the healthy and drove the sick to their graves: "Dismay and affright were visi-ble in almost every person's countenance."[13]

The bells notwithstanding, fear was dominating the town. Philadelphia averaged three to four deaths a day in the 1790s. The day after the College of Physicians published its treatise, twenty-two burials were recorded.

From the Delaware River ports inland, yellow fever was moving through the city's neighborhoods. Thousands left town; others locked themselves behind their doors and shuttered windows, afraid to walk the streets.

Two of Rush's sons had stayed in Philadelphia for the summer. On August 26, he told their mother that the boys had "so much apprehension" of getting yellow fever from their father's clothes that he had concluded they would be better off in Trenton.[14] Both suffering headaches, the boys set out on August 27 with the admonishments to "go to bed as soon as they reach Trenton, and by no means expose themselves to cold, heat or fatigue."[15]

On August 27, the Pennsylvania legislature met at the State House, now Independence Hall. Eleven of eighteen senators and about half of the seventy-six representatives attended. They remained in session for three days, over which they were described as becoming increasingly "uneasy."[16] The House doorkeeper, Joseph Fry, was found dead in the west wing of the State House on the twenty-ninth. Yellow fever was uncomfortably close.

Addressing the lawmakers, Governor Thomas Mifflin blamed the disease on the foreigners flooding the city from the West Indies. He pointed out "the necessity of more strongly guarding the public health, by legislative actions."[17] His pronouncement was in direct conflict with the College of Physicians' and Dr. Rush's assertion that the disease was of local origin, but Mifflin was supported by other prominent doctors.

The governor went on to call for the city's health officer and physician of the port, assisted by the police and college faculty, to use "every rational measure to allay the public inquietude, and effectively remove its cause."[18] It was the governor's belief that the vigorous enforcement application of quarantine and inspection was needed. He ordered ships coming up the Delaware to stop at Mud Island, where they were to be boarded by a doctor and inspected for signs of disease. He gave the health officer of the port funds to buy a boat for this purpose and to hire assistants.

In an open letter to Mayor Clarkson, Mifflin found fault with the city's response to the emergency. He demanded that the mayor institute all of the recommendations from the college. And he promised state money to pay for any measures the city council and mayor could not or would not pay for.

At the governor's request, the mayor dispatched a troop of militia from Ft. Mifflin to drag a cannon through the streets. They fired it every few yards to chase away the contagion. In the already stressed town, the noise was unwanted and the action generally recognized as useless.

The mayor attempted to answer the governor's criticism while demonstrating to his political allies and the people of Philadelphia that he was taking action. Clarkson described the definitive steps the city was taking to stem the epidemic. The mayor's call for improved sanitation was being enacted. City officials were receiving clear orders to visit the wharves and market streets and to clean them of any offensive materials. Those scavengers available to work were directed to continuously remove wastes and not limit their collections to once a week.

While the leading politicians postured and defended their actions, the civil and social structure of America's premier city was collapsing. As people packed up and left, took ill or died, many shops and businesses closed their doors. Night watchmen, the town criers, called the hours wrong, as the clocks were not maintained. At the dock, stranded ships stayed tied up because there were not enough healthy sailors to man them. Despite the mayor's call to clean the city, garbage and other wastes piled up in the streets. Bodies went unburied. The scavengers and gravediggers were in short supply. People from all walks of life, all social classes, fled in all directions.

Those who ventured into the streets took what they believed were appropriate precautions. Some wore scarves or other cloths soaked in vinegar or camphor as recommended by Rush. They kept off the footpaths and walked down the middle of the street to avoid homes known to house yellow fever victims. "Acquaintances and friends avoided each other in the streets, and only signified their regard by a cold nod," wrote Mathew Carey. "The old custom of shaking hands fell into such general disuse, that many were affronted at even the offer of a hand."[19]

Within families, fear of yellow fever broke the bonds of marriage and blood. Rush's descriptions of life under siege were particularly poignant and chilling: "[P]arents desert their children as soon as they are infected, and in every room you enter you see no person but a solitary Black man or woman near the sick."[20] In many families, the first sign of a headache, a common harbinger of the disease, was enough to thrust a family member into the street.

In some homes, infants were found suckling the breasts of their dead mothers. In one home, a woman went into labor, her dead husband still beside her. Neighborhood women would not enter the sick house, and she lay in anguish until finally she reached a window and cried out for help. Two passing men went to her aid, but she was beyond help and died in their arms.

Scenes like this were being reported from across all quarters of Philadelphia.

At the midpoint of the epidemic, Dr. Rush, greatly disturbed by the coldhearted acts occurring in every quarter of town, wrote an open letter to the citizens of Philadelphia. It was published in the September 12 *Federal Gazette*. Rush explained that the risk of contracting yellow fever by being in the same room with a patient or even caring for the sick was not greater than that from walking the streets. While he most likely was correct, there seemed to be little science or experience to back up his assertion.

In these dark days, the burden of caring for the poor and sick fell to the "Overseers and Guardians of the Poor." A semiofficial social welfare organization, the Guardians was weakened by sickness and deserters in its ranks. Yet the demands upon it grew. Almshouses and other sanctuaries for the city's destitute would not take in the ill. Still, they had to be cared for somewhere.

In keeping with the College of Physicians' call for a large and airy hospital near the city to take in the poor, the Guardians seized John Ricketts's circus. The troupe had taken their show to New York.

Seven yellow fever victims were quickly moved in; two died that night. Residents in the neighborhood surrounding the circus at Twelfth and High streets were terrified at the prospect of hosting a haven for the stricken in their backyards. They threatened to burn the building to the ground.

In a hastily called meeting on August 29 attended by half the available Guardians, a handful of aldermen, and the mayor, the need for an infectious disease hospital, or lazaretto, was deemed too important to let such niceties as the law impede its establishment. In the absence of citizens volunteering their homes, the group decided to seize any available and appropriate property.

Two miles northwest of the city center, across the Delaware and Schuylkill Canal, stood Bush Hill. Built in 1740 by Andrew Hamilton, the architect of Independence Hall, the estate was currently owned by his grandnephew William. For a short time in 1791 and 1792, Vice President John Adams and his wife, Abigail, had rented the house. She described the house as spacious. A contemporary engraving shows a three-story Federal-style home with two large chimneys and several outbuildings. While the Adamses had a "fine view of the whole city" from their bedroom window, Abigail found the surrounding countryside wearing and not stimulating to the imagination. She complained that "the country round has too much of the level to be in my style."[21] She felt like a prisoner of the estate, especially in winter when impassable roads made the two-mile trip to town all but impossible, and the Adamses soon departed Bush Hill for Philadelphia itself.

At the end of August 1793, its owner in England, the house stood empty. Initially, the Guardians tried to appropriate several of the outbuildings for their patients, but the caretaker and his family occupied the buildings, so the main house was taken. On August 31, four surviving patients of the original seven housed in Ricketts's circus were moved to Bush Hill. They were the first of hundreds.

In town, the disease "raged with great virulence." It was greater in "violence and mortality" than any other disease seen by the medical men of Philadelphia.[22] Dr. Rush, his letters consumed with tallies of the dead and dying, described the symptoms he encountered. Although different in different people, they were clearly those of classic yellow fever.

He told Julia it sometimes comes on with "a chilly fit and high fever but more frequently it steals on with headache, languor, and sick stomach." These are followed by "[s]tupor, delirium, vomiting, a dry skin, cool or cold hands, [and] a feeble slow pulse, sometimes below in frequency the pulse of health." By the third or fourth day of the disease, the eyes are bloodshot, and soon become yellow, and sometimes the skin takes on a yellow cast. "Few survive the 5th day, but more die on the 2nd and 3rd."[23]

Impending death was often heralded by "[l]ivid spots on the body, a bleeding at the nose, from the gums, and from the bowels, and a vomiting of black matter."[24] Some patients retained their dignity to the end. Dr. Rush wrote of a patient who stood and shaved the morning he died.

As August came to a close, Dr. Rush counted 325 dead of the malignant fever. Mayor Clarkson put the number at 140. It is unlikely that either number was correct, but Rush's was probably closer to the truth. He reported that thirty-eight persons, from eleven families, had died on Water Street during the last nine days of August. Christ Church and St. Peter's Episcopal Church were burying twelve people a day—this in addition to the other churchyards and the city's potter's field.

On September 1, Rush opened his letter to Julia by quoting from a prayer: "I am enabled yet to thank God 'that I am alive, while others are dead.'"[25]

It was clear to Rush and the many other physicians in town that yellow fever could not be treated by the traditional methods. Peruvian bark (a source of quinine, effective against malaria), wine, blisters, vinegar, cold baths, and warm blankets had all failed.

On Sunday, September 8, Thomas Jefferson, writing to James Madison from his summer cottage in Gray's Ferry, noted that the physicians were stymied and "no two agree in any one part of their process of cure."[26] On that day, forty-two persons were buried, the highest daily total yet.

People continued to pour out of town, the governor among them.

Chapter 3

Nothing but a Yellow Fever

Y ELLOW FEVER STUBBORNLY REFUSED TO SURRENDER TO THE
Philadelphia physicians. But instead of uniting against the invader,
the doctors split apart, each falling back on his own theories and experiences to explain and treat the disease.

There were two major schools of thought on yellow fever's origin. On one side were Dr. Benjamin Rush and his allies. They were the anticontagionists, who believed the yellow fever was produced and spread by environmental conditions. They were certain it was a homegrown sickness rising out of the unhealthy miasma and foul effluvia of the city. To them, the rotting coffee on Ball's Wharf was the likely source of the epidemic because of its proximity to the first cases where yellow fever appeared.

Opposing the anticontagionists were, of course, the contagionists. They were certain yellow fever had been imported into the Quaker City, most likely by passengers and cargo arriving aboard ships traveling up from the Caribbean. The Cap François refugees were their prime suspects. Dr. William Currie and his allies stood behind this theory. They supported the quarantine of ships, cargo, and passengers as the only way to end the devastating assault.

There was also little agreement on treatment. Rush was a proponent of what was called "heroic" medicine. He taught his medical students that the doctor must reject "undue reliance on Nature" and "wrest the cure of all violent and febrile disease out of her hands."[1] When necessary, physicians defeated diseases by engaging them in a fierce battle for their patient's body. Aggressive bleeding and purging were needed to restore the body to its healthful balance.

On the flip side were those healers who believed the physician's job was to aid nature in its efforts to reclaim a victim's health. Milder treatments such as cinchona bark (effective in malaria but useless in yellow fever), teas, and cold baths, along with good nursing care, were essential components of these physicians' prescriptions. This approach was sometimes referred to as the West Indian method because French-trained doctors who'd practiced in the Caribbean often espoused it.

In the late eighteenth century, the classical theories of the ancient Greeks, which had dominated medical practice for nearly two thousand years, were being replaced by new theories. These were largely based on emerging knowledge of human anatomy and physiology. The old theory of medicine ascribed disease to an imbalance of the four humors—blood, phlegm, black bile, and yellow bile. It was the doctor's role to restore the patient's fluid balance through bleeding, purging, sweating, and medicines that mimicked the properties of each humor.

Benjamin Rush, while at the University of Edinburgh, had learned a new approach to the patient based on managing the nervous system. In short, the nervous system could be overstimulated or understimulated. Each condition would result in tension in the nerves, muscles, or vasculature and lead to disease.

Rush went a step further and saw an interaction of both over- and understimulation as leading to disease. Therefore, he proposed treating both at the same time. He also felt that all fevers shared a common mechanism. The emerging science of nosology, or the naming and classifying diseases based on a patient's specific signs and symptoms, offended Rush. To him nosology was "as repugnant to truth in Medicine as polytheism is to truth in religion."[2]

On September 3, Rush, with unwarranted optimism, wrote the Trenton, New Jersey, doctor Nicholas Belleville that "the fever which has ravaged our city for some weeks past is at last arrested in its fatality."[3] He attributed this great success to calomel, a chloride of mercury and a powerful purgative. In Rush's cure, the calomel was given with an equal dose of a purgative derived from the ground-up tuberous roots of a Mexican vine called jalap. Rush recommended about ten to twenty grains of each, to move the mercury through the bowels faster. On the same day he wrote this letter, he announced his cure to Philadelphia's College of Physicians. So confident was he in his treatment that he began telling patients they had "nothing but a yellow fever," even as scores died daily around him.[4]

As the epidemic progressed, Rush combined his mercuric purges with bleeding. In mid-September, drawing off ten to twelve ounces of blood seemed to work for Rush, but by early October, he was advocating blood losses of sixty to eighty ounces, or nearly one-half of the patient's entire blood supply.

One colleague called the treatments a "prescription for a horse."[5] Layman William Cobbett snidely noted that Rush had made "one of those great discoveries which have contributed to the depopulation of the earth."[6] But Rush saw things differently, noting that the only people dying in Philadelphia were the poor, who lacked medical and nursing care, and those in the upper classes getting their care from "quacks or enemies of mercury."[7]

Dr. Currie strongly opposed Dr. Rush's heroic medicine. On Rush's advice to further physically stress an already sick patient he commented that "nothing is more pernicious, or even more fatal, than that any part or function should be forced to make exertions incompatible with its strengths, and there is the more danger of ill-timed remedies in the present fever."[8] Currie published a handbook describing the milder treatments he advocated.

Currie's attacks became personal. He went so far as to challenge not only Rush's science but his morality as well. Rush's motive for continuing to prescribe what Currie clearly believed were mortal treatments came into question. Currie compared Rush to the fictional Dr. Sangardo in the satirical novel *Gil Blas*. Doctor Sangardo revealed to the title character Gil Blas that his prescription for the treatment of dropsy was wrong, yet he noted that it was better that all in town die "than for me to change my opinion."[9]

It is unlikely, however, that Rush thought his treatment was wrong. His training and experience convinced him otherwise. He saw his prescription as working in ninety-nine out of one hundred patients who tried it, claiming that he prescribed it more than fifty times a day. How many actually had yellow fever will never be known. And while his assessment of the effectiveness of treatments may have been clouded by his own encroaching fatigue and frustrations—at times he was seeing 150 patients a day on less than a few hours' sleep—those treatments grew out of his theories of human physiology. Although it would have been nearly impossible, Rush believed he suffered through two bouts of yellow fever during the 1793 epidemic and he twice applied the heroic treatment to himself. He also employed them with his beloved sister, who died of the disease in early October of that year. Until his own death, he continued to teach his philosophy of disease and heroic treatment methods. The mainstream medical establishment generally accepted his teaching until the 1820s.

Dr. Currie's accusations and the snide comments of others stung Dr. Rush. He wrote his wife on September 13 that in addition to having to battle yellow fever, he had to contend with the "prejudices, fears, and falsehoods of several of my brethren, all of which retard the progress of truth and daily cost our city many lives."[10] In another letter later in the same month, he complained that few doctors in the city had adopted his treatment regime, and he accused those who did not of "murder by rule." He believed his colleagues were conspiring to spread calumnies against him and that Currie was "the weak instrument of their malice and prejudices."[11]

Currie and Rush disagreed on another key element of the outbreak—how many diseases were afflicting the people of Philadelphia. Currie believed yellow fever accounted for a relatively small proportion of the cases and that other bilious fevers were responsible for the rest. Rush saw yellow fever everywhere he looked.

The lay citizens of Philadelphia also had opinions on things medical and what constituted good medical care. A leading resident reminded his town of Benjamin Franklin's observation that in Barbados the sick began to recover "only after the doctors had run out of medicine."[12]

Others were tiring of the feuding doctors. A writer to a local paper told his fellow Philadelphians to "be no more pestered with the disputes about a doctrine, which hath been a bone of contention for a couple of centuries." He noted, "At this moment [it] is as far from a decision as when it commenced."[13]

While the physicians bickered, Philadelphia plunged deeper into despair. Treasury Secretary Alexander Hamilton was stricken on September 5. He recovered, but his illness was a symbol of the capriciousness of yellow fever. On September 10, President George Washington rode away from his Walnut Street home. The annual return to Mount Vernon, his Potomac River plantation, was long-planned and even delayed until he could no longer justify the risk to his family, especially since there was little business for him to conduct in the capital. "The disorder has blockaded the Federal Government," Washington said.[14] Yet, his departure further demoralized the citizens left behind.

Sickness and desertion were taking their toll. Halfway through September, some six to seven weeks into the epidemic, Philadelphia was collapsing. Newspapers ceased publication; nearly all shops and taverns were shuttered. Half the population was gone. Farmers could not or would not bring food into the city, the port was shut down, and many surrounding communities blockaded the metropolitan area, refusing admittance to its desperately fleeing citizens.

The city needed help, and the white community turned to a largely untapped resource. The free blacks of Philadelphia operated in a parallel society to the whites. As the epidemic spread through town, it seemed that blacks were spared the horrors of yellow fever. This was not unexpected.

In the eighteenth and nineteen centuries, many doctors and laypersons, both black and white, believed blacks had special innate immunity to yellow fever. This may have arisen from the lifelong immunity conferred by a childhood infection. Blacks born in Africa or the Caribbean were more likely than whites to have been exposed to yellow fever when young. In children, the disease was more likely to cause a mild flulike illness rather than the fulminating, often fatal, disease seen in many infected adults. This acquired immunity could have been mistaken for natural immunity.

Believing along with many others in their God-given immunity, Richard Allen and William Grey, free blacks and members of Philadelphia's African Society, argued that they had a special obligation to help the beleaguered whites of Philadelphia. They called on Mayor Clarkson and offered their services. He immediately accepted their assistance. The city ran an appeal in the newspapers calling on the black community to step forward. The mayor even freed black prisoners from the Walnut Street jail to work in the lazaretto, or fever hospital, at Bush Hill.

The response was overwhelming. Soon blacks were filling many jobs unwanted or unfillable by whites, such as nurses, street sweepers, scavengers, undertakers, and gravediggers, among others. While one of the epidemic's chroniclers, Mathew Carey, accused the African Society of price gouging, thievery, and other crimes, their work and contributions were defended and accepted by the vast majority of citizens. In a January 1794 letter to Absalom Jones and Richard Allen, who were largely responsible for recruiting their fellow blacks to aid the city, Mayor Clarkson praised these citizens, noting, "Their diligence, attention and decency of deportment, afforded me, at the time, much satisfaction."[15]

By mid-September, the myth of divine immunity was crumbling as many blacks became ill. Even Rush, a believer in black immunity, admitted on September 22 that the disease occurred frequently among blacks, though the cases were milder than in whites.

Physical illness was not the only effect of the epidemic. As it wore on, the emotional toll mounted. Mathew Carey recorded his observations on the loss of compassion and emotional fatigue setting in. "Less concern was felt for the loss of a parent, a husband or an only child," he wrote, "than on other occasions would have been caused by the death of a servant, or even a favourite lap dog."[16]

The doctors felt the same fatigue. The number of potential patients overwhelmed them. Accosted in the street and implored to visit a sick wife, husband, parent, or child, Rush, with some reluctance, had to tear himself away from the petitioners. Adding to the burden, sickness and desertion among the city's doctors removed many from practice.

Rush's description of how families reacted to illness in their midst mirrored Carey's. He told his wife that "parents desert their children as soon as they are infected" and that "many people thrust their parents into the streets as soon as they complain of headaches." "These scenes," he reported, "now cease to move me."[17]

On the streets, orphaned children wandered among the sick, dying, and dead. Food supplies, even in a city whose population was reduced by half, grew short as farmers refused to enter the city and those who did faced possible exile for exposing themselves to the contagion. The shortages were most acute among the poor, who now faced the threat of starvation in addition to yellow fever.

On September 12, the same day a meteorite crashed down into Third Street, Mayor Clarkson addressed a group of his fellow citizens who gathered at city hall. He told them that the state of their city was not good and was slipping toward anarchy. The citizens rose to his challenge and voted two days later to create a volunteer committee to take on almost any job that needed doing. In effect, these citizens, drawn mainly from the city's middle classes—tradesmen, artisans, and the like—many of whom had not participated in the civic life of their town before, became the de facto government of the City of Philadelphia. Benjamin Rush's nemesis, Dr. William Currie, and Mathew Carey also signed on. Their mandate included procuring supplies, borrowing money to pay for those supplies as well as for labor, and recruiting doctors, nurses, and other caregivers.

Mayor Clarkson, the stalwart leader who was bravely guiding his city through the worst crisis of its young existence, was named committee chair. While others, including most city and state government employees, fled, he remained; the door to his vinegar-soaked offices was open to all comers.

As the committee began its work, the epidemic was clearly worsening. The daily mortality counts ranged from sixty-seven on September 16 to ninety-six on September 24. While there was some fluctuation in the day-to-day death tallies, the numbers clearly were creeping up.

The lazaretto at Bush Hill was in dire need of immediate attention and direction. Two committee members, Stephan Girard and Peter Helm, volunteered to administer the fever hospital. They divided the job into two domains. Peter Helm, a cooper and Moravian who dressed in the plain-cloth required by his faith, took on the outside. In addition to caring for the outbuilding, he coordinated moving in patients and supplies and moving out the dead or recovered. Stephan Girard, a merchant who had come to town from France fourteen years earlier, took on the inside operations—ensuring that the patients received care, food, and other essentials. Described as a decent but not extraordinary man, Girard devoted himself to transforming the hospital.

Helm and Girard would be there nearly every day throughout the epidemic, doing any job that needed doing. And as they began, everything needed attention. Bush Hill was filthy. Its staff was indifferent, at best, to the needs of their wards. There were too few beds, not enough supplies, and certainly too few skilled caregivers. A medical student working at Bush Hill recalled that "the sick, the dying and the dead were indiscriminately mixed together." He called it "a great slaughter house."[18]

Helm and Girard took an advertisement in the few publishing papers. "Generous wages will be given to persons capable and willing to perform the services of nurses at the hospital at Bush Hill," they wrote.[19] Girard also chose a physician to supervise care. He was Jean Derève, a French military surgeon and refugee from Cap François. The doctor's name was submitted to the citizens' committee for approval.

Derève would not have been the committee's first choice. He was a recently arrived Frenchman unknown to the city's medical establishment. He also was an anticontagionist and believed in the more gentle treatments espoused by the French teachings—though he occasionally bled patients—rather than the heroic methods of the English-Scottish school then prevalent in the city. His opinion of heroic medicine was certain: "Being in the habit of seeing the diseased, and to observe nature, can alone guide the practitioner," adding that those doctors who follow an arbitrary treatment plan and ignore nature are "a scourge more fatal to the human kind than the plague itself would be."[20]

Four doctors practicing part-time at Bush Hill rose up against the appointment. The committee, afraid to offend the College of Physicians, balked. Girard pushed back. He wanted Derève to oversee medical care at Bush Hill.

The battle over Derève raged for a week. In the end, Girard, the American doctors, and the committee came to a compromise. Derève was given medical control of Bush Hill—but only until the number of patients "considerably exceed those now in the Hospital."[21] The four doctors resigned their posts, and the Philadelphia physician Benjamin Duffield was appointed to assist.

Two miles to the southeast of Bush Hill, the rest of the committee began making progress against the demise of their town. Of the twenty-six members, thirteen were able to remain active throughout the crisis. They met every day from September 14 through the month of October. The members crisscrossed the city looking for situations to improve—they didn't have to look far or hard. The committee's courage, it has been noted, infected the city, a much-needed counter-note to the infection brought by the yellow fever.

The orphan problem was worsening and demanded their attention. The committee found housing, collected donated clothes, provided food, and tried to place the children in homes. During the last six weeks of the epidemic, the committee took charge of 194 "helpless innocents."[22] Homes were found for 94, 27 died, and 71 remained wards of the city. The fate of 2 was not reported.

The city was running out of burial space. The city's potter's field was full by the end of September. The committee seized land at the North West Public Square between Eighteenth and Twentieth streets and Vine and Race streets. Getting people to burial was another problem. Shoddy casket construction allowed the bodily fluids of the dead to leak and foul the streets of Philadelphia. The risk of disease and the stench forced the committee to demand well-constructed leakproof coffins.

It was the members of the committee and other unheralded citizens that Mathew Carey referred to when he wrote, "Amidst the general abandonment of the sick that prevailed there were to be found many illustrious instances of men and women . . . who, in the exercises of the duties of humanity exposed themselves to dangers, which terrified men, who have hundreds of times faced death without fear, in the middle of battle."[23]

As the battle raged in Philadelphia, surrounding cities and states took steps to protect themselves from yellow fever. Fueled by the awful truth of the epidemic and the often exaggerated reports in the press, cities and towns in New York, Maryland, and New Jersey set up roadblocks to keep Philadelphians out or designated quarantine houses to warehouse them. To ward off yellow fever, postmasters in distant towns dipped letters from Philadelphia in vinegar.

In Alexandria, Virginia, boats patrolled the harbor in an attempt to intercept ships traveling from the Quaker City. Outside Baltimore, militia blocked the Baltimore-Philadelphia Road; while in the city, it was resolved that none of its citizens should grant shelter to anyone traveling from Philadelphia. In New York City, vigilantes worked the ferry slips along the Hudson River looking for and turning back travelers suspected of fleeing north from the epidemic.

But as in Philadelphia itself, where coldhearted neglect and indifference mixed with scenes of heroism, the response of the infected city's near and distant neighbors was not entirely obstructive. The citizens of Springfield, New Jersey, met and chose to open their town as a sanctuary to people fleeing across the Delaware River. Elizabeth, New Jersey, to the north and Elkton, Maryland, to the south also welcomed the refugees.

While many cities turned away travelers and cargo, they also understood Philadelphia's plight. Whether through pure altruism, a sense of "there but for the grace of God go I," compassion, or something in between, these communities gave aid and support to the struggling, worn-down but still battling, yellow fever–infected town. J. H. Powell, who has produced one of the most comprehensive historical studies of the epidemic, wrote, "Carts laden with livestock, vegetables, supplies of all sorts came in over roads already thronging with refugees fleeing the city."[24] From New York City came $5,000. The influx of supplies and cash must have been a welcome show of support for people increasingly besieged and cut off from normal commerce and communication with their neighbors.

As September faded and October began, there was no sign that yellow fever was ready to release its stranglehold on Philadelphia. Yet, the burden was becoming easier to bear. "Courageous leadership," Powell noted, "brought people out of panic to resolution, and beyond resolution to hope."[25] As the daily death toll approached its zenith of one hundred or more, the city was actively fighting back.

The optimism was not blind to the realities of the time. Rush recalled meeting a man on October 1 who was busily stacking firewood for the coming winter. Such long-term planning surprised him, and he told his wife,

"I should as soon have thought of making provision for a dinner on the first day of the year 1800."[26]

One hundred and nineteen deaths were reported in Philadelphia on October 11, the single highest one-day loss of life recorded since the disease had first sailed into town two and half months earlier. On October 14, Rush reported that the disease raged in the city with "unabating mortality."[27] But three days after that, he wrote, "Satisfactory accounts still arrive from all quarters that the disease evidently declines."[28] For nearly the next two weeks, the number of new cases and deaths fell.

The day that the city's doctors and veterans of other yellow fever epidemics in the temperate zones had been waiting and hoping and often praying for arrived. On the morning of October 29 the 7 A.M. temperature was below freezing for the first time that fall. The same was true the next morning. The arrival of frost, they knew, always signaled the end of yellow fever.

Then on October 31, a white flag was unfurled at Bush Hill. It was not a flag of surrender but one proclaiming victory—the hospital wards were free of yellow fever patients. It came down the next day as yellow fever returned to the hospital, but no one who saw that flag could deny that the city's horrible visitor was about to depart.

Dr. Rush publicly expressed his disgust with many of his colleagues' refusal to accept, in his own opinion, his miraculous treatments. On November 7, in the waning days of the outbreak, he wrote a letter to Dr. John Redman, his mentor and College of Physicians president: "I beg you would convey, by means of this letter, my resignation of my fellowship" in the college. In the second sentence of the three-sentence letter, he asked that the members accept "a copy of Dr. Wallis' edition of the *Works* of Dr. Sydenham."[29] The book was his parting shot at the college. Thomas Sydenham was called the English Hippocrates. He believed one fever could displace another; as such, yellow fever became the only fever present in Philadelphia as the epidemic progressed. He also believed in the use of strong purges and bloodletting. Like Rush, he was persecuted for these beliefs.

While the resignation was an expression of Rush's desire to separate himself from the college, the presentation of Sydenham's book was a clear statement that the college had a lot to learn about the art of medical practice. In his autobiography, written twenty years after the 1793 epidemic, Rush explained his reasons for sending the book with his resignation. In part it was a defense of his practice, but it was also meant as "a rebuke of the ignorance of many of the members of the College, of the most common laws of Epidemicks."[30]

Rush was still reporting yellow fever deaths to his beloved Julia on November 11. Four had recently died and a few more deaths were expected. Still, the crisis was over. George Washington had ridden back into town the day before. A day later, Julia Rush was resting three miles out of town on her journey home.

The true number of yellow fever deaths in Philadelphia during 1793 will never be known. Mathew Carey counted 4,041 deaths in his history of the epidemic. Modern estimates put the death toll above five thousand. About one in ten residents of Philadelphia and its suburbs were carried away. The real death rate was even higher when one remembers that twenty thousand people fled the city and its environs that fall.

For Rush, the passage of time did not lessen the "the painful recollection of the events of that melancholy year."[31] Addressing the people of Philadelphia in his autobiography, Rush defended his actions, stating that he sought no profit, in money or reputation, through his obstinate allegiance to the heroic cure. "[C]itizens of Philadelphia," he wrote, "it was for your sakes only that I opposed [the other physicians'] errors and prejudices, and to this opposition many thousand people owned their lives."[32]

An analysis of Rush's case-fatality rates, or the proportion of people who died compared to those who survived, suggests the heroic treatments were not as effective as Rush perceived and claimed them to be—and, in fact, were possibly as dangerous as his critics claimed. Although the issue is complicated by poor record keeping and uncertainty over who had yellow fever and who did not, as well as a lack of comparison with the case-fatality rates of other Philadelphia physicians, it appears that about 46 percent of Rush's patients died. Historically, about 20 percent of yellow fever victims die of the disease.

In 1793, objective assessments of case-fatality rates and other epidemiological measures of a disease's severity or the success of a therapy were decades away. Even without these statistics, it is probably safe to assume that Rush's and his followers' patients did not fare well. It is very likely that the heroic purges and copious bloodletting hastened one's demise. Yet, proof that Rush caused harm and Currie affected cure simply did not and does not exist. At a time when medicine was very much an art, aspiring to be a science, the audience's visceral response counted more than reason. For most Philadelphians, Rush's art was more acceptable than the others' performances. Despite the verbal and published fisticuffs, Rush's relentless war against yellow fever, unyielding faith in his treatments, and obvious concern for his fellow citizens endeared him to the populace, and he emerged the hero of the crisis.

The medical debates that first simmered and boiled over during Philadelphia's 1793 yellow fever epidemic continued well into the next century. Many of Rush's beliefs soon fell out of favor. Rush's principles of heroic medicine were taught until the 1820s, and some three thousand medical students were schooled in it before the practice was abandoned by mainstream medicine.

The great quarrel between the contagionists and the anticontagionists continued well into the 1800s despite Stubbins Ffirth's definitive yet repellent experiments. Ffirth, a doctoral candidate working under the Philadelphia physician Caspar Wistar, took on the question of yellow fever and contagion. He, like many anticontagionists of the day, saw little to support the idea of person-to-person transmission of yellow fever. Unlike many of his contemporaries, he went beyond the philosophizing that often passed for medical research in the late eighteenth and early nineteenth centuries, and conducted actual experiments. His research subjects included birds, cats, dogs, and himself.

Starting in early 1802, he performed experiments similar to those carried out by Dr. Issac Cathrall in 1799. Ffirth fed and inoculated his animals with black vomit. The animals did not get sick. Unknown to Ffirth, they were not susceptible to the disease. He then began using himself as a guinea pig. He started by intentionally exposing himself to yellow fever patients. Despite sleeping alongside extremely ill patients and receiving "the breath of my patients in my face," as he described his practice, he remained well.[33]

In late 1802, he began a more aggressive series of experiments in an effort to infect himself. He made cuts in both of his arms, placed black vomit under the skin, and closed the wound. While his arms became red and swollen, Ffirth otherwise remained well. He tried similar experiments using blood, saliva, bile, sweat, and urine from yellow fever patients. He placed the vomit in his right eye and water in his left. He heated black vomit in dishes and inhaled the vapors. In several sets of experiments, he drank the reduced and thickened liquid remaining in the dish. In other attempts, Ffirth swallowed half an ounce of black vomit with a water chaser. When that failed to produce disease, he upped the dose of vomit to two ounces.

No matter what he did, Ffirth could not conjure up a case of yellow fever. He correctly concluded in his 1804 doctoral thesis, "The disease cannot be communicated by the secretions or excretions" of patients.[34]

Chapter 4

Yellow Fever Moves South

B ETWEEN THE LAST CASES OF YELLOW FEVER IN THE NORTH IN THE early 1820s and its eradication from the southern states in 1905, the disease, along with malaria and hookworm, had a profound effect on the North's view of the South as both backward and disease-ridden. The fear and fact of yellow fever were retarding the South's economic and social growth. This was quite an accomplishment for a sickness that rarely spread beyond urban port cities, appeared only sporadically in many places, and, compared to other diseases, sickened and killed relatively few people.

While quarantine was a common practice below the Mason-Dixon line, sanitary improvements lagged far behind those being implemented in the North. This unfortunate and deadly public health failure gave yellow fever a refuge from the increasingly hostile northern cities. Through the combination of unsanitary environment and insect-friendly climate, the seaport cities ringing the Gulf of Mexico such as New Orleans, Galveston, Mobile, and Pensacola came to provide a more welcoming habitat for the yellow fever mosquito than New York, Boston, and Philadelphia. The relatively harsh northern winters killed off the mosquito, and public health reforms prevented its return. But in the Deep South, *Aedes* mosquitoes could lie dormant through the mild winters and survive until spring, when conditions for their emergence were right.

Unlike in the North, where yellow fever could be established only by the arrival of both carrier mosquitoes and disease, in the South, mosquitoes might already be patrolling the wharf area waiting for an infected traveler. In some southeastern and most Gulf Coast cities, the mosquito populations could reach critical mass before disease-ridden ships docked. Locally bred mosquitoes simply waited for the arrival of yellow fever from the West Indies or South America and then propagated an explosive epidemic.

Before the American Civil War, southerners and southern doctors struggled to understand yellow fever. The study of the occurrence and distribution of disease is called epidemiology. Practitioners try to define the *who, what, when, where,* and *how* of disease in a population. In the 1820s, only the *when* was known: yellow fever came in the summer and left with the first frost. The *where* was becoming better defined; seaports and their environs and their trading partners seemed to be at highest risk. *Who* got sick was also largely a mystery, but certain people seemed to be at increased risk; these were the newcomers to yellow fever endemic areas. Blacks, on the other hand, seemed to be at lower risk. The questions of *what* and *how* were nearly completely unknown. And as the South grew more intimate with yellow fever, these two questions generated the most interest.

For over two hundred years, close observers of yellow fever had recognized the unusually high rate of disease among newcomers to infested islands and cities. Immigrants to the West Indies had to go through one or several summers to become seasoned. In the American South, a certain period of acclimation was necessary for recent arrivals before they could get through an epidemic alive. Many doctors and laymen accepted the fact that once exposed to the disease, a person was granted lifetime immunity. Others disputed this. Benjamin Rush, for one, claimed that he experienced two separate bouts of yellow fever in the 1793 epidemic.

Yellow fever became known as the "Stranger's Disease" because it seemed only newcomers got it. In New Orleans and across much of the South, the phenomenon of acclimatization or "creolization" was widely accepted. An 1802 traveler reported that Americans were particularly susceptible, followed by the French and then the Spanish. The Americans' origin in a cooler climate and their intemperance were the cause, he said; they "[revel] on succulent meats, and spices, and [have] often the bottle or glass to [their] mouth."[1] Following the Louisiana Purchase in 1803, New Orleans grew increasingly more American, in the sense that it attracted more and more immigrants. Many arrived from the cooler climates of the United States and Europe. In 1852 and 1853, over twenty thousand Irish and German immigrants arrived in New Orleans. The new arrivals were fresh fodder for the virus, and they paid dearly for their immunologic naivete. Of the eight thousand to eleven thousand yellow fever deaths during the city's worst epidemic in 1853, more than seven thousand were among these recent arrivals.

In 1853, as scores of strangers were carried away, being acclimated was a point of pride for many longtime city residents. The *Weekly Delta* newspaper reported that when many fled the onslaught, the creolized man "walk[ed] along the street with a tremendously bold swagger." Meanwhile, the unacclimated proceeded "timidly and nervously, recounting the mortality of the previous twenty-four hours."[2] Some residents of New Orleans saw the lack of seasoning among some segments of society as having great benefits to the city. The more successful citizenry regarded the too many poor, struggling immigrants as filthy, lazy, and immoral. Their living conditions and lifestyles were considered a threat to the rest of New Orleans. In addition, many saw the filth and squalor of the immigrants' ghettos as the breeding ground for the annual yellow fever attacks. The immigrants not only provided the tinder that fueled the epidemic, but they were often blamed as the source of the illness. An occasional reduction in their numbers was not universally mourned. Yet, not all of New Orleans agreed with the benefits of a good cleansing epidemic. An editorial in the *New Orleans Medical and Surgical Journal* castigated these "narrow-minded and selfish individuals for believing that frequent and severe epidemics were good for the city."[3]

Undesirables in the antebellum South were often poor whites, especially immigrants, rather than blacks. Blacks were a commodity, and an especially valuable one following the official end of the U.S. slave trade in the 1820s. As in post-Revolution Philadelphia, the issue of race and resistance to yellow fever in the pre–Civil War South remained a potent topic of discussion. The perception that blacks had a natural immunity to the disease was generally accepted. The reduced mortality among blacks when compared with whites had been recognized by the French and Spanish in the Caribbean and during several North American epidemics. In the 1853 epidemic, 7.4 percent of white New Orleans residents perished, compared to 0.2 percent of blacks. Since the slave trade had ended three decades earlier, immunity acquired in Africa or the Caribbean was an unlikely explanation for the difference. Eventually, it became clear that blacks were as likely to become ill as whites, but died at a much lower rate.

In the antebellum South, black immunity was as much a political as a scientific quandary. Slaves, if unaffected or only mildly affected by yellow fever, were essential to the southern economy. White laborers could not work though an epidemic; some even believed that a white person brought yellow fever on himself by doing the "Negroes' work." Some supporters of slavery attributed the blacks' resistance to yellow fever to their bondage. Slavery, it was said, was "a condition best suited to the [Negro] as it excepts him from a destructive disease, to which he would render himself liable by the exercise of freedom."[4]

Dr. Samuel Cartwright, who once identified a "running away" disease that afflicted slaves, was a defender of the theory that manual labor caused yellow fever in whites. "Nature scorns to see the aristocracy of the white skin . . . reduced to drudgery work under a Southern sun," he wrote. Whites—no matter their origin—"shall not be hewers of wood, or drawers of water or wallow in the sloughs of intemperance, under pain of three-fourths of their number being cutoff" by yellow fever. To the doctor, this was an "immutable law" of nature.[5]

Abolitionists had an opposing view. They saw yellow fever not as a blessing on blacks but as a plague on whites for the evils of slavery.

To slave masters, black immunity was a blessing and a curse. While whites were stricken during an epidemic and blacks presumably remained healthy and able to work, the risk of slave revolt rose. In an 1833 outbreak at Alexandria, Virginia, a doctor reported that the slaves who were left alone as whites fled planned an insurrection. The rebellion was discovered and defused.

While acclimatization and racial resistance were interesting academic problems for most southerners, the prevention and control of the disease were clearly the most important and immediate concerns. In warmer southern climates, annual outbreaks gave local physicians ample opportunity to observe and study the disease as no Yankee ever could. Yellow fever came more often, came earlier in the year, and stuck around longer, especially in the Deep South. With ample opportunity to observe the scourge, southern physicians began devising their own theories of origin and transmission.

The prevailing medical thought at this time was that yellow fever was a disease of local origin in the South—an extension of Benjamin Rush's anticontagionist theories. From the 1790s until the 1840s, the local origin theory ruled southern medical thought on yellow fever. Overcrowded cities, turned soil, dead animals in the streets, and generally filthy conditions were among the necessary ingredients for an outbreak. According to the proponents of spontaneously arising epidemics, it just took the right spark to ignite the mixture, and an explosion of yellow fever would tear through the community.

An 1819 epidemic at Natchez, Mississippi, illustrates the persistence of the anticontagionists' miasma model. Contemporary accounts of that outbreak show that residents believed the source of their distress was located in their town. Built on a bluff overlooking the river and named for the Natchez Indians, the city is the oldest settlement on the Mississippi. In 1819, it was a growing community, and improvements to its infrastructure were under way. The unpaved streets along the bluffs of the upper town were graded that summer, disturbing the dirt. Turning soil, many believed, released the noxious toxins of yellow fever and other diseases contained in decaying matter. But a more significant event added to the disaster believed set in motion by street grading. A flood swept through the lower town and into the surrounding countryside. Throughout and around the town, uprooted trees, decaying vegetable matter, and drowned animals lay where the receding waters left them. Townspeople and physicians accused the waste of harboring and releasing disease-causing effluvia.

As the summer went on, malignant remittent and intermittent fevers terrorized Natchez, most likely malaria and yellow fever, respectively. An exodus began. Those who couldn't or didn't want to leave stayed and took their chances; everyone else left. The authorities moved the sick poor out of town. Eventually, 250 died.

Yellow fever returned to Natchez in 1822, taking 312 more lives. John A. Quitman, a resident, described the rumors that swirled about town. The epidemic, it was said, brought on a breakdown of social mores. The city's potential victims adopted an "eat, drink and be merry attitude." "I hear curious details of the saturnalia, the debauchery and excesses that occurred here when the fear was at its worst—wine parties after funerals, card-playing on coffins, shrouded figures whirling in the waltz," he wrote.[6]

Local origin, however, did not provide a satisfactory explanation for all observed epidemics, and other southern physicians and their colleagues in the North spoke up in support of the possibility that yellow fever was imported from somewhere else. A particularly nasty 1826 epidemic in Washington, Mississippi, was blamed on infected materials brought in from Natchez. "It is very justly believed to have been carried in there by means of the fomites contained in the blankets and articles of merchandise, with which Washington was crowded . . . when the citizens of Natchez fled from the yellow fever," reported *The Mississippi and Louisiana Digest*.[7] Washington, a town of 250, suffered 52 deaths in 110 cases.

Increasingly, doctors believed that yellow fever, whatever its origin, was not contagious in the traditional sense. Certainly, anyone familiar with Stubbins Ffirth's research, in which he exposed himself to and consumed yellow fever–infected material, could believe this to be fact. Even if his research was unknown, there was enough experience with the disease for a keen observer to draw a similar conclusion. Repeatedly, epidemics demonstrated that those who had close contact with the sick often remained well. Compared to smallpox epidemics, in which person-to-person spread usually struck down susceptible caregivers, relatives, friends, and others exposed to its first victims, yellow fever carried off very few of these people; the ill did not appear to carry the disease. Yet, it seemed to move from place to place—Cuba could send it to New Orleans, from where it might travel to Mobile or Galveston, or up the Mississippi River valley. Fomites— clothes, bedding, and other items that were exposed to the sick—became the leading suspects in its spread, as did cargo carried on ships arriving from ports where yellow fever was prevalent.

If not contagious, the disease must be transportable, and a new theory took hold. Supporters of transportability pointed out that ships apparently free of disease could travel across hundreds of miles of ocean and still unleash yellow fever's poison upon arrival in a new city. By the 1840s, the theory of "transportability," discussed since the early part of the century, was maturing and replacing local origin as the primary explanation for yellow fever outbreaks.

Professor Wesley Carpenter of the Medical College of Louisiana was a leading proponent of transportability and its close relative, transmissibility. He wrote in 1844, "Under certain circumstances of temperature, population, [etc.], the introduction of cases of the disease from abroad; or of air of other cities, where the disease is prevailing, whether in boxes or in the holds of vessels, will tend to generate such a condition in the place, as to give rise to new cases and finally to an epidemic of the disease."[8] The exact mechanism of disease spread was unknown but not necessary to his conclusion: "The point which we desire to prove is, that the disease is transmissible, and consequently importable; and the question as to whether this transmission is by contagion or infection, does not enter into the general problem at all."

Over the next decade, debate over transportability and transmissibility continued. The spread and timing of yellow fever outbreaks seemed to support the new theory. But old convictions died hard. Two Mississippi doctors who reluctantly shed their local origin stance in favor of transportability noted, "These [new] convictions ... have been forced on us from observation and reflection, in opposition to early imbibed impression, and views of those in whose opinions we were thoroughly indoctrinated."[9]

Doctor Josiah C. Nott was a firm believer in the transportability of yellow fever. The prominent Mobile, Alabama, doctor, a careful observer of the disease, could not imagine any reasonable person doubting the veracity of this theory. He saw no other explanation for the way the sickness moved from house to house and neighborhood to neighborhood, sometimes skipping over houses and neighborhoods in its travels. "Yellow Fever, in 1842 and 1843," he wrote, "traveled from house to house for more than a month, as would the tax collector."[10] He also noted that within a vessel or a building, yellow fever may only affect a specific section. This kind of behavior did not follow the laws governing the movement of vapor, gases, or miasmas.

In 1848, Nott published a landmark paper in the *New Orleans Journal of Medicine and Surgery* explaining his theories on yellow fever. He based his theses on several scientific disciplines—recent research into the existence and role of microorganisms, observations of insect biology and behavior, and the prevailing theories on yellow fever epidemiology. He made two key points in the paper. First, he argued that yellow fever was a disease entity unto itself. Intermittent, remittent, and pernicious fevers were not yellow fever, he said. Yellow fever's uniqueness was an emerging but not yet universally accepted truth.

The second major argument of his lengthy, sometimes rambling article advocated his "Insect Theory" of yellow fever. This theory has often been misinterpreted and misrepresented by historians as the first to link yellow fever transmission and mosquitoes. It was far from that, but it was still an important evolutionary step in the ongoing attempts to explain the great enigma.

With the discovery of the microscopic world by Antony van Leeuwenhoek in the 1660s, scientists began trying to define the ecological niche occupied by bacteria, protozoa, and other new life-forms. By the early 1800s, Christian Gottfried Ehrenberg, a Prussian doctor, was describing the "animalcules"—as the creatures were often called—he saw through his microscope. Ehrenberg coined the term "bacteria" to describe the tiniest rod-shaped structures swimming under his lens, but he was convinced that they had no role in human disease. Nott felt otherwise. And while he prominently mentioned Ehrenberg's research in his article, he referred to the work of the French microscopist Alfred Donné to make the link between the animalcules and disease. Nott noted that Donné was "one of the best microscopic observers of the day . . . [and] asserts that the pus of Buboes contains animalcules, which account for the transmissibility of Syphilis."[11]

Nott claimed that the transportability of yellow fever and some other diseases could be explained by ascribing insect behaviors to animalcules. In his mind, the insect was not the carrier of the yellow fever germ. Instead, the yellow fever germ—some unknown animalcule—could fly on its own, move, or otherwise be transported from place to place in the same way as an insect. Further, it could lie dormant until climatic or other conditions were ripe for the germ to reproduce and strike. This explained the apparent spontaneous generation of an epidemic. According to Nott, victims of yellow fever did not get sick because an infected mosquito stung them— he never seemed to consider this. Instead, he claimed, the illness came from a specific yellow fever–causing animalcule landing on or being inhaled or swallowed by a susceptible person.

There is no indication that Nott's theory had a significant impact on his fellow medical practitioners. Nott's enduring fame stems more from a misreading of his paper rather than from its actual arguments. However, an event associated with the physician may have been Nott's greatest contribution to the defeat of yellow fever. On October 3, 1853, he attended the birth of Amelie and Jonah Gorgas's son, William Crawford, at a home outside Mobile, Alabama. Mrs. Gorgas had been moved there from her own Mobile home because of a yellow fever epidemic. Years later, William C. Gorgas would survive an attack of yellow fever and become a major figure in its conquest.

The 1853 epidemic that forced Mrs. Gorgas from Mobile was an extension of a disastrous epidemic that struck New Orleans that summer. Officially, 8,100 lives were lost among 146,000 residents. Unofficially, the death toll ranged as high as 11,000. Using either number, it was the worst loss of life, in total numbers though not the percentage of dying, from yellow jack ever reported in New Orleans. Day and night, tar and pitch fires burned in the streets. This centuries-old practice for warding off the miasma poured thick acrid smoke into the atmosphere. As in Philadelphia sixty years earlier, gunpowder explosions boomed out across the city in another misguided attempt to stop the epidemic. The firings were halted after only two days because of the stress they caused the population. But as in Philadelphia and many other U.S. and Caribbean cities, the smoke and explosions, vinegared face masks, and other preventatives failed to chase the scourge away. The city and its citizens were overwhelmed. Unburied coffins were left on the streets in the summer heat until the bloated remains of yellow fever victims burst them, spilling their noxious contents onto the ground.

New Orleans was the city most often and most viciously attacked by yellow jack, but despite the growing acceptance of the transportability of yellow fever, its physicians clung to local spontaneous origination as the source of the illness. The official Sanitary Commission Report on the 1853 epidemic pointed to the conditions of heat, humidity, and filth as the conjurers of disease. The possibility that yellow fever was imported was not seriously considered. However, the commission did permit one concession to the new notions about yellow fever's movements. While the disease's origin was local, once present it could be transported from place to place; this, the commission report said, "no one now disputes."[12] Although a lukewarm endorsement of transportability, it was another shovelful of dirt on local origin.

Foot dragging by health officials may have contributed to the high mortality of the 1853 epidemic, which also spread across the lower Mississippi valley. There had been no yellow fever in New Orleans since 1847, and complacency and denial may have played a role in the failure to recognize the insidious visitor. Or its presence may have been intentionally ignored.

Many southern boards of health were too slow to attack an emerging epidemic. Their mandate was based on two conflicting considerations. One was the preservation of health. But increasingly, the second was to protect commerce and lessen the economic blow to the town. It was not always clear which of these two objectives took precedence. In fairness, the *how* and *what* of yellow fever's epidemiology were still unanswered questions. To the casual observer, no matter what the doctors said or what measures they tried, yellow fever broke out; perhaps not every year in every place, but often enough. There was no reason for city leaders to create panic and risk financial collapse by implementing quarantine or other public measures before yellow fever was firmly and clearly established. After all, part of a city's reputation was built on its ability to provide a healthful environment—both physical and commercial. This was as true on the Atlantic Coast as on the Gulf Coast.

The battle to capture commercial trade between the mid-Atlantic cities was, as one writer said, "bitter and intense."[13] The press was often used as a tactical weapon. Newspapers, which had a vested interest in the economic success of their community through increased advertising dollars, readership, and the less tangible but still important bragging rights, exposed the weaknesses of their competitors and played up the strengths of their hometowns. Health was the key determinant in the war for prominence.

In 1855, Norfolk, Virginia, was marketing itself as Virginia's preeminent market town and port city. Home to about sixteen thousand people, Norfolk sat on the eastern shore of the Elizabeth River, near the mouth of the Chesapeake Bay. The city was across the York River, just south of the Gloucester County cottage where Walter Reed had been born four years earlier, and was well situated for both oceangoing trade and the movement of goods to and from the interior. City officials encouraged new construction, paved the streets, installed gas lamps, and sought immigrants. "Progress," declared a local merchant "is the motto of our people."[14]

Needing repairs, the steamship *Ben Franklin* arrived outside Norfolk while en route from the West Indies to New York in June 1855. The ship was ordered to quarantine and inspected by the port doctor. Unaware that two seamen had died of yellow fever during the voyage, he reported the ship free of disease. After twelve days, it was permitted to tie up at the city's docks for repair.

When the first cases of yellow fever appeared in the neighborhood near the *Ben Franklin*'s anchorage, local leaders and the press denied its existence. They called it Upshur's fever for Dr. George Upshur, who reported the first sixteen cases to the board of health. Upshur was accused of fearmongering and threatening the city's commercial interests. Finally, after more than a month, no longer able to fool themselves or the people of Norfolk, the board of health admitted to the presence of yellow fever.

The epidemic continued until the end of October. Ten thousand were stricken, and two thousand died. The economic impact was devastating; coffins became the leading commodity being unloaded at docks where other goods once arrived. The Norfolk and Petersburg Railroad went bankrupt. Newspapers, which months earlier had touted Norfolk's healthy business climate and public health improvements, halted publication. The presumptive "Queen of the Chesapeake" was dethroned. The *New York Sun* printed this doggerel in honor of Norfolk's and nearby Portsmouth's fall:

> Norfolk and Portsmouth! Cities doomed!
> Your streets were stilled, your people tombed;
> For the death angel rode the blast,
> And broke his vials as he passed.[15]

Norfolk's decline was not unique. Many southern towns feared the disease and its social and economic sequelae. Attracting newcomers to the southern cities in the yellow fever zones of the Atlantic and Gulf coasts continued to be a significant challenge for any town promoting growth and commercial opportunities. Epidemics like the ones in Norfolk and two years earlier in New Orleans only reinforced northerners' negative views of the South.

Six years after the 1855 Norfolk epidemic, the American Civil War began and the strained relations between South and North erupted into a four-year-long bloodbath. Epidemics of yellow fever among Union soldiers were one of the great concerns of commanders and doctors as the Civil War began. The Union army wisely prepared for battle with the disease by directing the U.S. Sanitary Commission to prepare a study of yellow fever. The 1862 Sanitary Commission's report, intended as a handbook for field surgeons, opened with this warning: "It will probably fall to the lot of many Army Surgeons to treat this disease during the occupation of the Southern territories by the Union Forces."[16]

The report was a comprehensive summary of the accumulated medical knowledge about yellow fever up to the 1860s. The commission addressed the origin, epidemiology, clinical features, prevention, and treatment of the disease. High ambient temperatures and humidity favored an outbreak, they noted. Frost ended an epidemic. Outbreaks skipped around cities, neighborhoods, and even ships. Men more than women were likely to become ill. Blacks got the disease less often than whites, and when they got it, blacks had milder cases. The more white blood someone carried, the sicker that person was likely to be. Soldiers and sailors suffered the most, and yellow fever fatality was very high among prostitutes—the reason for this, according to the commissioners, was that "excessive indulgence in sexual intercourse" was especially dangerous.[17] In "healthy years," only strangers took ill, and lifetime immunity following an attack was very likely. Yellow fever was a miasmic fever, but it was clearly different from malaria. Person-to-person transmission was rare, but clothes, bedding, merchandise, and other fomites conveyed the disease. The commission warned doctors that "to abandon quarantine restraints against yellow fever, is to put a price on human life and barter it for trade."[18] As to treatment, the authors stated, "We are without a specific plan for the cure of this most grave malady."[19]

The feared epidemics never came, probably due to the Union blockade of southern ports that greatly reduced trade with the Caribbean and South America. The only significant outbreaks occurred in Key West and North Carolina, and the disease played a minor role in the war. Of 233,786 disease deaths among Union troops, only 436 were officially reported as due to yellow fever.

New Orleans fell early in the conflict, and Union commanders and soldiers expected devastating yellow fever outbreaks in the occupied city. In April 1862, the Union navy sailed through a series of heavily armed Confederate choke points on the lower Mississippi River on their way to the Crescent City. Marines seized the city and raised the Union flag over New Orleans's public buildings. Within days, General Ben Butler took command of the town. Butler famously attacked southern womanhood by ordering that New Orleans women who spoke out against the Union were to be treated as common streetwalkers, and he became the most hated man in town, earning the moniker "Beast" Butler.

Butler was a Boston-bred politician-soldier whose privateer father died of yellow fever in the Caribbean before his son's birth and who studied every report of the devastating 1853 New Orleans epidemic. He used the knowledge to launch an attack on the disease in the city he was now responsible for. Despite the challenge of maintaining order in the occupied and still rebellious city, Butler and his successor, General Nathaniel Banks, greatly reduced and nearly eliminated yellow fever during the period of Union control. Butler's first action was to establish a quarantine grounds some seventy miles south of the city. Ships with perishable cargoes could be released in less than the required forty days, but only with a permit issued by the general himself on the advice of the quarantine doctor. The doctor knew that intentionally passing a diseased ship could mean a trip to the gallows.

While the Beast ruled New Orleans, yellow fever appeared only once, killing two. The disease was carried in by a ship loaded with coal. It had traveled from New York via the Bahamas. Butler personally approved the ship's release from quarantine without consulting the quarantine doctor. Physicians in the city quickly isolated the cases, and no one else became ill.

While quarantine could be imposed by fiat, sanitation required the cooperation of the occupied city. Union commanders employed legions of soldiers and locals to scrub the city clean and to make significant sanitary improvements. Unlike in many northern cities, there were no sewers or underground drains in New Orleans in 1862. Raw sewage ran in culverts through the streets to the canals and surrounding bayous. In early May, Butler reported, "the streets were reeking with putrefying filth, and the smells from the decomposing matter were, to a Northern nose, unbearable."[20]

The absence of yellow fever during the Union occupation was a source of great disappointment to some residents of New Orleans. According to General Butler, the inhabitants of New Orleans "relied with great confidence [on yellow fever] as an element to conquer our armies."[21] He reported that prayers were offered in the city's churches, where each Sunday the pious called on the Almighty to send an epidemic against the northern troops. After all, wrote Butler in an 1888 memoir, "*We were the unacclimated.*"[22] (The italics are Butler's.)

If divine intervention wasn't forthcoming, a farmer proposed a backup plan—germ warfare. He suggested carrying the dead bodies of yellow fever victims and their contaminated clothes to New Orleans in an attempt to infect the Union troops. The biological attack probably never happened. A southern sympathizer in Bermuda carried out a similar plan that targeted Abraham Lincoln and the populations of northern cities. Dr. Luke Blackburn shipped yellow fever–exposed clothes to Union ports. To President Lincoln he planned to send several diseased dress shirts. The attempt was discovered and the doctor fled to Canada.

In New Orleans, much to the dismay of the rebel supporters, the Union occupiers escaped completely unscathed. When asked why the city was free of yellow fever, one wag, as reported in the *New Orleans Picayune*, said, "You no believe in God? You no believe zere is mercie? Yellow fever and G-e-n-e-r-a-l Butler at the same time!!!"[23]

Chapter 5

The Nation Threatened

W HILE THE SOCIAL UPHEAVALS THAT ACCOMPANIED CON-
flicts seemed to drive yellow fever mortality to epidemic levels in
the Caribbean, they had the opposite effect during the American Civil War.
With a few exceptions, the war years passed without any significant yellow
fever outbreaks. An epidemic, carried in by blockade runners, struck Wilmington, North Carolina, in 1862, taking almost 450 lives. The next year, a
blockade runner delivered the disease to Galveston, Texas, where 265 people died. The battles against yellow fever that the Union army expected and
planned for did not occur. Among the northern troops, there were only two
significant encounters with the scourge. In Key West in 1863, 71 troops
were lost. An 1863 yellow fever attack on the Union army at New Bern,
North Carolina, was the worst; 700 soldiers lost their lives.

By 1866, peace was returning and Reconstruction was getting under
way. The federal government was pulling back from managing southern
cities. A relatively small outbreak of yellow fever struck New Orleans
shortly after responsibility for health and sanitation was transferred from
the Union army to the Louisiana State Board of Health. The two hundred
deaths it caused were not considered an epidemic by New Orleans standards, but they were far more than the eleven deaths reported during the
four years under Union occupation.

In all likelihood, the disease took advantage of a return to New Orleans's
historically lax sanitary practices. Jo Ann Carrigan, the author of *The Saffron Scourge: A History of Yellow Fever in Louisiana*, noted, "Without the
incentives provided by bayonet and military arrest, sanitary regulations were
ignored by officials and citizens alike, and New Orleans reverted to its customary state of filthiness."[1] Other factors must have also contributed to the
disease's return. The resumption of regular trade, especially with the
Caribbean, along with a relaxation of quarantine rules, opened the door to
yellow jack. Northern troops who remained in the city, Reconstruction-era
carpetbaggers, and other nonimmunes were available to feed the fever.

In 1867, yellow fever arrived in New Orleans on a sugar ship out of Havana. Before the disease left town that fall, the city surrendered 3,000 lives to it. Upriver, in Memphis, the disease took about 250 lives. It was the first occurrence of yellow fever in the Tennessee city since 1855, and it most likely originated in New Orleans.

Despite living in a city far south of Boston, New York, Philadelphia, Baltimore, and Norfolk—all of which had been stricken by yellow fever— Memphis's doctors had until 1855 convinced themselves that their town was too far north to support the disease. As a result, the city routinely welcomed refugees and the ill from stricken cities and towns below it along the Mississippi River. The sick were unloaded from riverboats and carried through town to the Memphis Hospital. The outbreak of 1867 and another one in 1873, which swept away more than two thousand residents, corrected the local doctors' misconception forever.

With the exception of 1867 and 1873, yellow fever was less prevalent across the postwar South than during the antebellum period. By the mid-1800s, New Orleans and other cities and towns where yellow fever was a common summer visitor had developed a fatalistic attitude about the disease. Where visitations were less common, the approach of summer sometimes engendered great apprehension. In those places, doctors and laypeople alike looked for the signs that could predict a coming plague. One sure predictor was the level of yellow jack activity in the Caribbean. In the spring of 1878, the level was high.

In March, the Louisiana Board of Health ordered all ships from yellow fever–infected ports to be detained at the quarantine stations, inspected, and fumigated before being allowed to dock in New Orleans. Quarantine was always a balancing act between commercial and public health interests, and despite the fears of admitting a virulent disease, an exception was made for steamers transporting fruit. Fruit importers threatened to sue the Board of Health for lost profits if their shipments rotted while in quarantine.

On April 29, 1878, President Rutherford B. Hayes signed the Quarantine Act of 1878 into law. It had taken southern legislators five years to accept the bill. After the 1873 epidemic, which was accompanied by cholera, the Louisiana Board of Health requested the state's congressional delegation to lobby for a federal takeover of quarantine operations. Soon, five other recently rebellious southern states joined with Louisiana in seeking protection by

Washington. The Quarantine Act gave the Marine Hospital Service, whose main function was providing health care to sailors, the responsibility for stopping the importation of disease via shipping. Even if the Act were not both toothless and unfunded, it was too late to save the South from the yellow fever already probing the defenses along the Mississippi River.

Between February and May, quarantine officers on the Mississippi River south of New Orleans learned of at least four deaths on coffee carriers sailing from Rio de Janeiro. The ships, their cargo, crews, and passengers were inspected, disinfected, and sent on their way. Meanwhile, in Cuba, a particularly virulent yellow fever raged. The Spanish colony was emerging from its first serious attempt at independence, the Ten Years' War. It ended with the Spanish remaining firmly in control of the island. Thousands of refugees were fleeing north, many to New Orleans. Evidence was mounting that 1878 could be a bad fever year.

In Memphis, the threat of yellow fever was recognized early. In May, the Tennessee Board of Health president Dr. Richard Brooke wrote Dr. Samuel Choppin of the New Orleans Board of Health, requesting he keep him informed of any yellow fever cases in the Crescent City. Dr. Choppin promised to do so, and he told Dr. Brooke of six yellow fever cases on the *Borussa*, which was held in quarantine after a voyage from Liverpool via Havana. As promised, he began sending weekly health reports. The weekly reports would never mention any yellow fever cases in the city.

No one knows how yellow fever slipped into New Orleans in the spring of 1878. When a special commission investigated the attack and reported on its cause, the crew of the steamship *Emily B. Souder* got the official blame. The ship arrived at the quarantine station on May 21 or 22 en route from Havana to New Orleans by way of Key West, carrying twenty-nine crewmen and nine passengers. One crew member reported being ill. He was diagnosed with a malarial fever and removed from the ship. Another crew member, ship's purser John Clark, had a funny look on his face, the quarantine physician later recalled. Clark claimed he had a "facial neuralgia" and was allowed to stay with his ship.[2] The *Souder* was fumigated, disinfected, and cleared on to New Orleans, where it docked at the foot of Calliope Street.

Clark took ill the night his ship docked and was transported by Dr. Emmanuel Drew to the home of a mulatto nurse at 65 Claiborne Street. In the very early morning of May 25, Clark died. Dr. Drew listed the cause of death as an intermittent bilious fever. Others reported that Clark had yellow fever. Four days later, the ship's engineer, Thomas Elliot, died. His attending physician ordered an autopsy. His skin, it was reported, was a "bright canary yellow" and his kidneys and liver were congested.[3] The diagnosis made in May was intermittent fever, but the doctor performing the autopsy later claimed he knew the illness was clearly yellow fever. The city's actions in May, however, were based on the disease they uncovered but refused to acknowledge—officials ordered the disinfection of the neighborhood where Clark and Elliot had lodged.

When the *Souder* left New Orleans on June 1 to return to Havana, the tug *Charles B. Woods* took its berth. Over the next six weeks, every member of the *Woods'* captain's and engineer's families took ill. A young woman neighbor living on Constance Street also became ill. On July 16, a doctor was called to her home to treat a four-year-old child. A few days later, the child was dead. For the first time in 1878—nearly two months after the *Souder* had docked—"yellow fever" was written on a death certificate in New Orleans.

Although the Memphis Board of Health did not know about New Orleans's yellow fever cases off the *Souder* or in the Constance Street neighborhood, it began preparing for the scourge. In early June, the newly appointed president of the Memphis Board of Health, Dr. Robert Wood Mitchell, recommended a quarantine be put in place from July 1 to October 1. On June 3, the board directed him to appear before the city's Common Council, where he would "present his views in regard to quarantine and to ask for additional money to be placed at the disposal of the Board of Health for sanitary purpose."[4] By the end of the month, the *Memphis Daily Appeal* was editorializing on the need for quarantine, while thirty-two Memphis physicians signed a petition against it. All railroad depots needed to be guarded, as well as river approaches, making an effective quarantine impossible, they argued. The doctors further claimed there was no real reason for one and that the money could be better spent elsewhere.

The request for quarantine was denied, and on July 11, Dr. Mitchell resigned as board president. He warned Memphis that if yellow fever returned, it would be "our own fault in not taking known necessary precautions against it."[5] Over four hundred citizens signed a petition calling on Dr. Mitchell to reconsider his resignation. But he held fast, and Mayor John Flippin named Dr. Dudley Dunn Saunders to replace him.

By the summer of 1878, the germ theory, expounded by Louis Pasteur in France and Robert Koch in Germany, was gaining widespread acceptance in the United States. Pasteur and Koch had both clearly demonstrated the association of a specific disease with a specific microorganism. Most physicians were convinced that a yet-to-be-discovered specific organism caused yellow fever. Along with traditional sanitary improvements, disinfection using carbolic acid became the standard response to the introduction of yellow fever and other diseases. "It was based on the hypothesis that the *materies morbi* of yellow fever consists of living germs, probably animalcular," stated an official report of the New Orleans Board of Health.[6] The report noted that the object was to attack yellow fever wherever it existed. Carbolic acid was thought to be an effective disinfecting agent. The city dispatched twenty-seven crews to spread the acid in the streets. Citizens were encouraged to purchase it to treat their homes, property, and privies.

Officials were confident they could ward off an epidemic. Other cities along transportation routes fanning out from New Orleans were less sanguine. Galveston, Shreveport, Pensacola, Mobile, and other communities threw up quarantines on all goods and passengers traveling from the city.

The fever continued to spread along with rumors of an epidemic. Panic set in. The rumors were confirmed on July 24, and soon one-fifth of New Orleans's population had left town. On August 10, following the diagnosis of 431 yellow fever cases and 118 deaths, the Louisiana Board of Health declared the outbreak an epidemic. As in the past, commerce came to a halt, the streets emptied, and ships sat stranded in their slips. The New Orleans *Picayune* noted, "Only our mosquitoes keep up the hum of industry."[7]

The first official word of yellow fever in New Orleans came in late July in a letter from Choppin to the Marine Hospital Service surgeon general John Woodworth. The correspondence found its way into the national press on July 26, two days after the New Orleans press had reported cases in the city. By that time, yellow fever was moving across the South and advancing on Memphis.

On July 27, the towboat *John D. Porter*, trailing barges and making its way to Pittsburgh, deposited two crew members with yellow fever, reported as sunstroke, at Vicksburg, Mississippi. That night, a third crewman died of yellow fever on the boat. Aware of the events on the *John D. Porter* while it was 250 miles south of Memphis at Vicksburg, Memphis's health officer prepared to meet it as it sailed north. He commandeered a boat, intercepted the *Porter*, and convinced its captain to bypass Memphis. The towboat continued on to Cairo, Illinois, where a replacement for one of the dead men took ill. He left the boat and boarded a train to return to Vicksburg, where he died of yellow fever shortly after arriving.

Meanwhile, with yellow fever closing in, the Memphis Board of Health called on the mayor to impose a quarantine, which he did on July 28. Three quarantine posts were established—one south of the city on President's Island in the Mississippi and two at railroad depots outside the city. Even in a river city like Memphis, the railroad was becoming the main mover of people and goods in and out of town. Two rail lines were blocked, the Memphis and Charleston Railroad, twelve miles from town, and the Mississippi and Tennessee Railroad, eight miles out. All goods bound for Memphis were off-loaded, disinfected, and held for ten days. A full-time quarantine physician was elected and given a salary of $300 a month. He immediately took up his post on President's Island. A week later, the Board of Health blocked all cargo from New Orleans and Vicksburg. The embargoed goods were ordered returned to their point of origin.

The longtime conflict between quarantine as a means to protect health and its detrimental impact on commerce—at least in the short term—flared up almost immediately. On August 2, a group of businessmen demanded the release of a train from New Orleans that was detained outside the city. The train carried $30,000 worth of sugar, coffee, and other commodities. The railroad had planned to send it back to New Orleans while residents near the siding where it was impounded threatened to burn it if the train did not leave soon. The merchants threatened a lawsuit to force the release of their commodities. With their city already on the verge of bankruptcy, Memphis leaders relented and admitted the shipments. Within two weeks, Memphis would abandon the quarantine, as it was so porous as to be meaningless.

On August 6, Memphis citizens learned of the first death from yellow fever in their city. A steamboat hand slipped through the quarantine and was admitted to the city hospital on August 2. He died three days later. A week after the sailor's death was reported, the increasingly anxious populace of Memphis learned of a devastating assault by yellow fever on the town of Grenada, Mississippi, about a hundred miles to their south. Correspondents reported one hundred cases in town. The local doctors were already overwhelmed and their medical supplies were exhausted. In telegraph messages, the leaders of Grenada pleaded with the citizens of Memphis for physicians and supplies. The city sent a small delegation that confirmed the disease as yellow fever. Physicians and others from New Orleans and Texas also came to help. The *New York Herald* paid a reporter $1,000 a day to report from the town. He lasted seven days before wiring his paper, stating that even $10,000 a day would not be enough to stay. The *New York Times* correspondent in Grenada reported, however, that the *Herald*'s man never entered Grenada, but filed his stories from a nearby burg. By the time the epidemic ended in December, the town of 2,000 recorded over 1,000 cases resulting in 350 deaths. Expressing the fears of many, a Grenada resident visiting West Virginia wrote to his wife, telling her that if yellow fever was in Grenada, it would "scatter all over the country."[8]

About the time the Grenada outbreak was being reported, Kate Bionda, who operated a food stand near the Memphis riverfront, died. Her death was the first official yellow fever death in a Memphis resident recorded in the city in 1878. Officials publicly acknowledged it on August 14, the day after she died. Also dying on the thirteenth was a policeman, James McConnell. Seven other yellow fever deaths were reported on the fourteenth. Yellow fever had arrived in Memphis.

Over the next five days, the roadways and railroads leaving the city were clogged with people fleeing the scourge. Along the roads, people on foot or on horseback and in buggies, goat carts, and carriages made their way to what they hoped was safety. A nun wrote, "On any road leading out of Memphis could be seen a procession of wagons piled high with beds, trunks, and small furniture, also carrying women and children."[9] Rail cars were filled until no space was left for passengers to sit or stand. Still, people tried to climb in or push loved ones through windows. The river played a smaller role in the exodus, since few boats were getting to Memphis; those that did were overwhelmed by terrified escapees. The refugees were "as mad as they were many," the *Daily Appeal* reported. "The ordinary courtesies of life were ignored; politeness gave way to selfishness and the desire for personal safety broke through all the social amenities."[10]

In a city with an estimated population of over 47,000 people, some 25,000 to 27,000 fled their homes and businesses as yellow fever infiltrated Memphis. About 5,000 settled in the rural areas of adjacent Shelby County. The remainder traveled north and east, either away from the river to places like Nashville, Louisville, and Chattanooga, or farther north out of the expected range of yellow fever to St. Louis and beyond. One writer estimated that 200,000 southerners heading north crossed the Ohio River in the summer of 1878. Detroit, Indianapolis, and New York all reported imported cases of yellow jack.

Louisville welcomed the refugees. The faculty of its medical college successfully convinced the population that the city was too far north and too clean to support yellow fever. Health authorities recorded sixty-four deaths in Louisville, but almost all were among the refugees.

The Memphis refugees were joined by tens of thousands of others fleeing the scourge as it spread through the Mississippi valley and beyond. Along the way, the refugees were often greeted with barricades and blockades. Many whose towns were free of yellow fever—and who planned on keeping them that way—threw up shotgun quarantines. Armed men were prepared to shoot anyone who doubted their resolve to protect their communities' health and businesses.

The residents of Holly Springs, Mississippi, about fifty miles south of Memphis, were told by their leading doctors that the town's elevation would protect them from yellow fever. It had never appeared there before. Aware of the plight of their neighbors, the town's people opened their city and their homes to refugees. Soon yellow fever was moving through the streets of Holly Springs, carrying off its Good Samaritans and their guests.

In Memphis on August 16, a group of concerned citizens met at the Opera House. Many of the city's leaders were among those fleeing, and the collapse of city government was approaching. As the people of Philadelphia had done eighty-five years earlier, they immediately formed a Citizens Relief Committee. Made up of leading businessmen and professionals and chaired by Charles G. Fisher, it took over the responsibility for aiding the poor, continuing city services, caring for the sick, and interring the dead.

In one of its first actions, the committee selected a refugee camp site south of the city. Other sites were soon secured. To supply the camp, a request was made to the War Department for rations and tents. The army depot at Evansville, Tennessee, responded quickly to the call and supplied the much-needed provisions. In New Orleans, a request in September for rations from army stores was also initially granted and two hundred thousand rations were provided. But a second issuance was halted by the secretary of war out of a growing uncertainty over the role of the federal government in providing welfare. The attorney general of the United States had called the distribution "an unlawful diversion of supplies voted for use by the Army."[11]

The committee was also faced with growing lawlessness, especially public drunkenness and looting in Memphis. They made a controversial decision to recruit blacks to augment the depleted city police force. The added manpower helped the city regain and maintain order.

As the epidemic worsened, support and assistance came from many sources, not just for Memphis but for stricken cities and towns across the

South. Southerners and northerners collected cash, food, clothes, and medical supplies. Special trains delivered the donated goods. Some observers felt the generous charity received from cities north of the Mason-Dixon line did more to help heal the lingering rifts opened by the Civil War than any other action to that point.

There were those who did much more than send old clothes or cash; they traveled into the ravaged cities to provide care, physical and spiritual, to the sick, dying, and bereaved. Many became martyrs to yellow fever themselves. Religious organizations, especially the Catholic and Episcopal orders, served the people of Memphis and elsewhere. In Memphis, thirty-four Catholic nuns and twenty-one Catholic priests were lost; four Episcopal nuns and two priests also died.

One of the legendary martyrs of Memphis came from a very different vocation. Dubbed the Mary Magdalene of Memphis, Annie Cook was the proprietor of the city's most opulent brothel. She voluntarily turned her recently renovated brick mansion at 34 Gayoso Street into a fever hospital where she and one of her girls, Lorena Meade, nursed the sick.

A group called the Christian Women of Louisville sent Madam Cook a note on the morning after the newspapers reported the conversion of the house from bordello to infirmary. They praised her personal ministrations to the sick, writing, "An act so generous, so benevolent, so utterly unselfish should not be passed over without notice. History may not record this good deed . . . but every heart in the whole country responds with affectionate gratitude to the noble example you have set for Christian men and women."[12]

Madam Cook was stricken by yellow fever on September 5 and died six days later. She was eulogized in the *Memphis Daily Appeal* and the *Chicago Tribune*. Her grave at Elmwood Cemetery, however, went unmarked for over a hundred years. A monument was erected in 1979 by a local couple in cooperation with the Brothers of the Sacred Heart.

Caring for the sick also became the primary responsibility of the Howard Association. The first chapter of this volunteer benevolent organization was established in New Orleans in 1837. A Memphis chapter was organized in 1855 to aid in Memphis's first yellow fever epidemic. The association recruited doctors and nurses from around the country, collected donations of money and medical supplies, and managed infirmaries, many of which were set up in the city's public schools. Dr. R. W. Mitchell, who resigned his post as the president of the Memphis Board of Health in June over the lack of support for rigorous quarantine, served as the medical director of the Howard Medical Corps. At the peak of the outbreak in mid-September, when 200 victims were dying each day, Howard physicians were seeing 100 to 150 patients each. Of the 41 Howard Association members at the start of the epidemic, 25 took ill and 10 died.

Although quacks and other opportunists tried to take advantage of the disaster by marketing their useless medicines and therapies, the physicians of Memphis and other cities were generally united in the treatment of yellow fever. The war between heroic medicine, where the doctor fought the disease to the patient's death, and the gentler treatment espoused by West Indian physicians that characterized the great epidemic at Philadelphia was long over. Doctors knew there was almost nothing they could do that would change the outcome of the illness. Acknowledging his professional limitations, one Memphis physician wrote, "The skillful practitioner . . . in the treatment of this fever is nothing more than the well-informed and practical pilot, who is familiar with every obstacle and danger, and possesses an intimate knowledge of the channel along which he must guide and direct this human float."[13]

Another doctor, William J. Armstrong, recorded the despair and frustration—the utter helplessness—felt by the doctors of Memphis. Like Philadelphia's Benjamin Rush, Armstrong was a prodigious letter writer who corresponded with his exiled wife. He described the desolation of the city, his and his colleagues' pessimistic outlook, the unrelenting stream of patients, and his doubts of self-worth in the face of an unbeatable enemy. His letter of September 9 described the toll on a fellow doctor: "Old Sol [Solomon P. Green] was left all night last night entirely alone [in a hospital] and could get no one to hear his cries for help. This morning in relating his fearful loneliness, he cried like a baby."[14] Two days later, a cool night raised hopes that the epidemic might soon end. "No one knows but the weary doctor what a delight that would be. . . . Kiss the children for me."[15] Nine days later, Dr. Armstrong died of yellow fever.

When the Mississippi valley epidemic ended in late 1878, the death toll was staggering. In five months, 120,000 people had fallen ill with yellow fever; 20,000 of them had perished. The economic toll was put at 100 million dollars. Across the South and beyond, citizens, doctors, and public health professionals began searching for the cause and a way to prevent another disaster.

The United States was a smaller place in 1878 than in 1793, despite decades of geographic expansion. Improvements in rail service and shipping enabled the relatively rapid movement of people, goods, and the diseases they carried. News of disease and disaster also moved quickly. The Associated Press, founded in 1848, for example, distributed news across the country and around the world almost instantly on its wires. Correspondents for the larger northern papers were sprinkled throughout the South.

Politically, the United States had also changed since the end of the Civil War. It has been said that at the outbreak of the war, the "United States" was a plural noun—a reflection of its loose confederation of independent states under a weak central government. The Civil War, among other things, established the supremacy of the federal government, and the "United States" became a single term—transforming from the "United States are" to the "United States is." This change in thinking about the structure of the United States, as well as the shrinking of the country through advances in communications and transportation, helped shape the coming debates about and response to the 1878 pandemic.

As was true before the Civil War, yellow fever was blamed by some in the North on the unsanitary practices and conditions of the South, a view echoed by many in the South. The *Memphis Daily Appeal* editorialized on November 7, 1878, that "we have been prey to every excess of human passion, folly, ignorance, and incapacity."[16] The rapid spread of the disease across the South and the scattering of refugees to distant cities also demonstrated that yellow fever was no longer a southern problem. An 1879 American Public Health Association (APHA) report stated, "The time has come when the advent of a pestilence to a Southern city can no longer be viewed with indifference at the North."[17]

Medical professionals and laypeople recognized the risks of future pandemics, and there was a widespread appeal to the federal government to investigate the 1878 disaster and to establish a national public health agency to prevent future attacks. A Yellow Fever Commission was named by the Marine Hospital Service surgeon general John Woodworth to conduct an investigation. Woodworth selected three southern physicians to man the committee, with Dr. Samuel Merrifield Bemiss of New Orleans named as chairman. The panel gathered in New Orleans on October 6, 1878, then fanned out to visit the cities most affected by yellow fever. Woodworth directed Bemiss to have a report ready for presentation to a special session of the APHA in November.

At 7:30 P.M. on November 19, the APHA meeting was called to order in Richmond, Virginia's Mozart Hall. In his opening remarks, the association's president, Elisha Harris, offered thoughts that would have been appropriate for 1793 but seemed strangely out of place in postgerm-theory 1878. He stated, "These pestilences indicate the various deep seated wrongs and neglects, vices and sins, of the people. Whenever the human race is in such a situation as to lose its strength, courage, liberty, wisdom, [and] lofty emotion, the plague, cholera, and fever comes."[18] The authors of the commission's report took a more scientific approach.

The meeting was almost immediately roiled in controversy over the ongoing political battles between factions aligned with Surgeon General John Woodworth and those siding with John Shaw Billings. Billings was the curator of the Army Surgeon General's Library and an early advocate of the use of medical statistics in the United States to direct public health. Their differences were the direct descendants of the long-standing and unresolved issue of the origin of yellow fever. Woodworth, along with many southern physicians, believed yellow fever was imported. Billings and much of the association's membership were proponents of local origin. Woodworth, as head of the Marine Hospital Service, saw quarantine as the primary solution. Billings saw sanitation as the key to preventing epidemics.

Concerned about the reception the report would get from the meeting's delegates, someone in the Woodworth faction, perhaps even a member of the Yellow Fever Commission, leaked the report to the press the day before it was to be publicly read. This was a clear violation of an agreement the committee had with the APHA and widened the rift between the two camps. Despite the political infighting, Dr. Bemiss presented the report on November 20. It claimed to provide "direct and convincing" evidence of importation; no evidence of any outbreaks arising locally was found.[19] The committee also found that no effective drugs or therapy were available, disinfection was generally useless, and quarantine was the most effective method of prevention.

The findings surprised no one, given that Woodworth had named southern doctors to the committee. In general, the South favored quarantine while the North favored sanitation. Not unexpectedly, a report of the Louisiana Board of Health released shortly after the Yellow Fever Commission's report came to similar conclusions. It specifically recommended "absolute nonintercourse with the ports where yellow fever is indigenous from the first of April to the first of November of each year."[20]

The APHA Yellow Fever Commission named by Woodworth in 1878 did not satisfy Congress's need for more information and guidance to help it respond to the national outcry for federal action. In a joint session held on December 18, 1878, the Committee of the Senate and House of Representatives on Epidemic Disease created a Board of Experts Authorized by Congress to Investigate the Yellow Fever Epidemic of 1878. Surgeon General Woodworth was named chairman. Several leading physicians of the day filled out the membership.

The board was given until January 29, 1879, about six weeks, to report on Congress's key concerns:

> 1stly. The origin, cause and distinctive features of yellow fever and cholera, whether or not they are indigenous to any part of the United States; if not, how they are brought to this country, and the localities from which they come and if found to be indigenous and also imported, in what proportion and to what extent has their presence in the United States been [owing] to importations.

> 2dly. The season of the year and atmospheric conditions, when and in which they may be propagated.

> 3dly. The means to be adopted by which their introduction into this country from other localities may be prevented.

> 4thly. The method of preventing its propagation and spread, when once introduced into any part of the United States.

> 5thly. The number of deaths that have occurred in the United States during the present year, the expenditures and the injury to business resulting therefrom.[21]

The members, who got $10 a day and expenses when on duty, met in room 3 of Memphis's Peabody Hotel on December 26, 27, and 28. Some had already visited thirty-four of the affected towns and cities. Reflecting its bias, the board resolved to visit those places that escaped the "epidemic by strict quarantine." Among the specific questions they set out to answer was, "Have bags of coffee, fruit, hides, coal, cotton lagging, mail matter, etc, been known to convey the poison?"[22]

On January 29, 1879, John Woodworth reported to Congress. His strongest language was in the introduction of the written report, where he outlined the threat to U.S. commercial interests and public health. "Yellow fever," he wrote, "should be dealt with as an enemy which imperils life and cripples commerce and industry. To no other great nation of the earth is yellow fever so calamitous as to the United States of America." Yellow fever, the Congress was told, was no longer a local and state problem. It threatened the nation and was therefore the purview of the federal government. Woodworth also called for systematic, scientific study that "should be increasingly directed against this enemy until our weapons are so perfected as to destroy or to surely hold it in check."[23]

During its short existence, the committee produced ninety conclusions concerning the origin, cause, and prevention of yellow fever and cholera, although most addressed concerns about yellow fever. Nothing the committee said was really new. Most conclusions simply repeated what was widely accepted about the disease. For example, the members stated that fomites (clothes, bedding, furniture, and other objects touched by patients) were a major source of yellow fever, but person-to-person transmission and infected individuals were uncertain sources. Among the committee's other conclusions were a need for increased ventilation on ships, improvements in sanitation and hygiene, isolation of the sick, segregation or dispersal of the well, and disinfection or destruction of the poisons (doctors often called the disease agent a poison rather than a germ).

The members were clear on the importance of quarantine. The committee, like its predecessor, found that yellow fever was almost always imported; in eighty-eight major epidemics since 1693, evidence of introduction from a foreign source existed in seventy-one. It concluded that quarantine was a more important method of prevention than local sanitation. One member, Louis A. Falligant, dissented. In a published reproach to the committee, and speaking for the supporters of local origin, he wrote, "I hold the view that yellow fever may be developed by indigenous as well as imported poisons; nor can I express too strongly the conclusions to which this view leads me, namely that local hygiene is of equal import with quarantine in checking the spread of the imported fever and of absolute necessity to the prevention of that of domestic origin."[24]

Dr. Falligant's comments notwithstanding, the committee's most controversial recommendation was for a two-level quarantine system to keep yellow fever out of the United States. The proposed first line of defense was a U.S. medical officer who would be assigned to foreign ports known or suspected to be sources of disease. The officer would inspect and certify ships, passengers, and cargo prior to embarkation. The second line of defense was a medical officer who would man domestic quarantine stations "to suppress interstate travel and traffic from infected places in times of epidemic."[25] These were radical proposals. The first part called on the United States government to infringe on the sovereign rights of foreign nations. The second would give the federal government a greater role in controlling interstate commerce that Congress would later act on.

Meanwhile, the battle over the primacy of sanitation versus the primacy of quarantine continued beyond the life of the commission. Responding to calls for a national public health agency, the lawmakers struggled over a bill creating such an entity. A key issue was whether the national authority for protecting public health should be the Marine Hospital Service or some other type of organization such as the APHA. The association won the day, and on March 3, 1879, the House and Senate passed a bill creating the National Board of Health. The board, though ostensibly independent of the APHA, had close ties to the public health association. Congress guaranteed four years of funding for the board, which was not renewed. Eleven days after the congressional vote in 1879, John Woodworth died.

The reports of the various commissions set up to examine the 1878 epidemic, along with the findings of the National Board of Health's yellow fever investigations in Havana during 1879, led Congress to call for a gathering of representatives of all maritime powers whose ports were regularly visited by yellow fever. The goal of the meeting was to get these countries to accept American inspectors at their ports. More than forty countries sent delegates to Washington. Spain selected Dr. Carlos Juan Finlay of Havana to represent Cuba and Puerto Rico at the congressionally mandated International Sanitary Conference in Washington, D.C., on February 18, 1881.

Chapter 6

Yellow Fever's Odd Couple

IN THE TWENTY YEARS OR SO BEFORE WALTER REED AND HIS YELLOW fever board landed in Cuba to investigate the disease, two men helped select the paths their investigations would take. One was Carlos Juan Finlay, who toiled away quietly in Cuba on his often ignored, sometimes derided, theory that mosquitoes transmitted yellow fever. The other was the U.S. Army physician George Miller Sternberg, a self-taught bacteriologist who had earned the sobriquet "Father of American Bacteriology." Sternberg claimed to have discovered a yellow fever bacterium, and his thoughts on its spread helped shape international public health policy and debate.

Juan Carlos Finlay was born in Cuba on December 3, 1833, the second son of Edward Finlay and Eliza de Barrés. For some reason, Juan Carlos was always called by his second name and became known as Carlos Juan. His father was a Scottish-born physician who had emigrated to the West Indies. His mother, of French descent, was living in Trinidad when she met and married Edward. In 1831, the Finlays moved to Cuba.

Young Carlos spent much of his boyhood on his father's coffee plantation, Buena Esperanza, near Alquizar, about twenty-five miles southwest of Havana, where he enjoyed a healthy outdoor life. When not out and about on the plantation, he was being home-schooled. When he was eleven, he and his brother Edward were enrolled in a French school and sent to live with a relative in France. Illness soon brought Carlos back to Cuba in 1846. Chorea, a nervous system disorder that afflicted him, left him with a stutter. The speech impediment, though improved with time, plagued him for the rest of his life, but it did not dampen his quest for knowledge. He returned to France in 1848 and enrolled at the lycée at Rouen.

In 1851, a debilitating bout of typhoid returned him to Cuba again. His and his father's dream of him studying medicine in France evaporated. Instead, Carlos traveled to Philadelphia, where he enrolled in Jefferson

Medical College. He received his Doctor of Medicine degree on March 10, 1855, and considered staying in the United States. New York had a growing Spanish-speaking population, and he was told he could easily establish a prosperous practice serving the Latin community. Despite the strong encouragement to stay, he chose to return to Cuba.

After a yearlong medical expedition with his father in Peru, Dr. Carlos Finlay settled in Havana, where he set up a general medical and ophthalmology practice. He briefly returned to France from 1860 to 1861 to supplement his American medical education, at that time considered inferior to European training. After returning to his island home and settling down in Havana, Finlay married Adele Shine on October 16, 1865. Like his mother, she was from Port of Spain, Trinidad.

Finlay was by all accounts a dedicated physician, and his medical practice kept him busy. His son wrote that he treated medicine as one might treat the priesthood, noting that his father never let a patient's lack of means interfere with a call for his services. Moreover, Finlay coupled moral guidance with his medical prescriptions. A religious and charitable man, he was said to be very forgiving of others' shortcomings—perhaps due to his own speech impediment.

In Cuba, he devoted much time to research and scientific discovery. While his days were set aside for seeing patients, his nights were for investigation and study. As was the case with many physicians of the day, his scientific pursuits were cosmopolitan, ranging from chemistry to meteorology to physics and mathematics. He was also well read in history and philosophy and dabbled in the relatively new field of epidemiology, the study of the distribution and causes of disease in a population. During a local cholera epidemic in 1867 and 1868, Finlay correctly identified drinking water as its source and reportedly tracked the contamination of the water supply to a Chinese immigrant who had died near a spring.

In 1868, inspired in part by the American Civil War and taking advantage of political turmoil in Spain, Carlos Manuel de Céspedes freed the thirty slaves on his Cuba plantation. Other planters soon followed. These reform-minded landholders and freed slaves joined forces, and soon much of east Cuba was in rebellion against Spain. The rebels launched a guerrilla war against Spanish troops and interests on the island. For the next ten years, Cuba was in a continuous state of violence. As fighting intensified in advance of the 1878 armistice, yellow fever attacked the island and was carried north to the United States by fleeing refugees, most likely sparking the Mississippi valley epidemic.

The Finlay family left Havana at the start of Cuba's Ten Years' War but returned to its beloved home a few months later. It was about this time that Finlay turned his attention to yellow fever. Using the microscope that he had brought home with him from medical school in Philadelphia—and that he used throughout his life—he began searching for the elusive yellow fever germ.

In August 1879, the Spanish governor appointed Finlay to work with the United States' National Health Board Yellow Fever Commission when it traveled to Cuba that year. Through this appointment, he met and developed a long-standing friendship with George Miller Sternberg, who was beginning to establish his credentials in bacteriology and on yellow fever. After a three-month stay in Havana and travels to South America, the U.S. commission concluded, "Yellow fever is an epidemic, transmissible disease and the agent capable of transmitting the disease must be in the air."[1] Based on this conclusion and some microscopic slides he had prepared, Finlay began to think that the key to unlocking the mystery of yellow fever lay in the blood vessels. Working out the mechanism consumed the next two years of his life.

Following his assignment with the U.S. commission, Finlay was selected to join the Cuban and Puerto Rican delegations to the 1881 International Sanitary Conference in Washington, D.C. The focus of the meeting was not science but politics, an opportunity for lawyers and diplomats to explore the limits of sovereignty and maritime tradition against the backdrop of public health. Finlay was late to the gathering, and much of the legal wrangling was over by the time he arrived. In his presentation, he called for more scientific research into yellow fever, noting the failure of both the contagionist and anticontagionist theories. He then presented his own emerging thoughts on the spread of yellow fever.

There were three conditions that had to be met for the propagation of yellow fever, Finlay announced. First was the presence of a single case of yellow fever. Next was the presence of a susceptible person. And last, the need for "the presence of an agent whose existence is entirely independent of the disease and the diseased, but necessary to transmit the disease from an individual afflicted by yellow fever to a healthy person."[2] Destroying this transmitting agent, he claimed, was the only way to halt yellow fever. Supposedly,

Finlay carried mosquitoes in stoppered vials to the meeting and was prepared to unveil the tiny insect as his proposed agent but he didn't.

Whether Finlay's statements were understood or thought important by
the majority of the conference delegates is uncertain. In a U.S. delegate's
report written immediately following the conference, no mention is made
of Finlay's speech. The conference did, however, heed his call for more
research and passed a resolution calling for the creation of an international
sanitary commission to study the disease. Finlay returned home and spent
the next several months working on his hypothetical agent of transmission.

The Cuba that Finlay returned to from Washington was still trying to
recover from the Ten Years' War. While Spain retained the island, reforms
were being instituted and more were promised. The old Cuba, based on
slavery and aristocracy, was gone; its future was uncertain. In Havana, the
patina of prosperity was maintained. It was the largest and the most fes-
tive city in the Caribbean. Cubanos gathered in the Plaza de Isabel II to
listen to music, play games, and eat and drink at the terraced cafes. They
took rides to the Paseo de Tacon through the hibiscus and Carolina bushes.
Other pleasures could also be had. There were two hundred brothels in
Havana and many gambling houses. The Finlays preferred to patronize the
opera and socialize at their home.

Mingling with the fashionable upper classes of Havana were the ubiq-
uitous beggars and unfortunates. Schools were poor, the Catholic Church
corrupt, and overall health poor. Havana's mortality rates were higher than
those of rural Cuba and twice those of the major European cities. The high
rates were driven by epidemics of Asiatic cholera, smallpox, and yellow
fever. The 1879 U.S. Yellow Fever Commission reported, "Since 1761 yellow fever has prevailed certainly in Havana and probably in other places in
Cuba, not only every year, but also every month in the year."[3] The statistics compiled by the military and civil hospitals proved that during the 408
months from 1856 to 1879, there was only one month free from an officially recorded case of yellow fever.

Against this background, Finlay struggled to assemble a cogent theory
on the transmission of yellow fever. He spent much of his time studying
the biology of mosquitoes and the epidemiology and clinical features of
yellow fever, looking to find where the insect and the germ intersected with
each other. Although Finlay often denied it, Patrick Manson's discovery of
the transmission by mosquitoes of filariasis, a disfiguring disease of the

tropics commonly called elephantiasis, probably influenced Finlay to focus on the insect. Some historians claim that news of Manson's 1879 research would not have reached Cuba by 1880 or 1881. Others dispute this. Either way, Finlay never claimed that he was guided by Manson's work.

Perhaps the true antecedent of Finlay's theory was the work of the French physician Louis-Daniel Beauperthuy. Based on his observations of yellow fever while working in the West Indies and South America from 1838 to 1853, he explained the relationship between the striped-leg *Culex fasciata* mosquito (now called *Aedes aegypti*) and the illness. Beauperthuy connected the dots as no one before had done. He described the subcutaneous events that occur when a mosquito introduces its sucker under the skin, and how venom released by the insect damages tissues and increases blood flow. He noted the relationship between the rainy season and yellow fever. The local Indians, he reported, employed several practices to repel the "winged serpents."[4] They burned smoky fires at the entrances to their huts and applied fatty substances to their skin. When these practices were followed, mosquito bites, and thus yellow fever, were reduced. He also correlated the geographic distribution of disease and the *Culex* mosquito.

According to Beauperthuy, the agent of yellow fever that *Stegomyia* carried was not a germ but the effluvia of swamps. The mosquito, he said, was a vector of tiny pieces of decomposing organic matter that it injected under the skin. No one had yet adequately explained the role of animalcules or germs in disease, so Beauperthuy could be forgiven for ideas that in some ways were closer to Benjamin Rush's rotting coffee theory than to the eventual truths of yellow fever.

Did Finlay know of Beauperthuy's work, and if so, how much did it influence the evolution of his hypothesis? As with Manson's filariasis discovery, Finlay does not mention Beauperthuy. But there was a good chance Finlay was aware of it. Beauperthuy published his work in a Venezuelan medical journal in May 1854, and he presented his mosquito theory at an April 1856 meeting of the Académie des Sciences in Paris. The academy published his report later that year; at the time, Finlay was in Philadelphia. There is no reason to believe that word of Beauperthuy's presentation before the Académie des Sciences would not have made its way to Philadelphia, especially as it was a startlingly new and controversial thesis on a disease intimately associated with Philadelphia. Even if the news didn't get to Philadelphia, Finlay's sabbatical to France during the early 1860s would have allowed him to hear of Beauperthuy. It is hard to believe that a physician from a yellow fever–endemic country would not have exchanged views on the origin and spread of that much-feared illness with his French colleagues.

Finlay wrote in 1902 that he was inspired toward his mosquito theory by the description of a plant fungus's life cycle in Philippe E. L. Van Tieghem's *Botanique. Puccina graminis* is a very destructive parasitic fungus of corn. It requires an intermediate host, the common barberry plant, to grow and multiply before moving to corn. When barberry is removed from around a cornfield, the fungus disappears. If this was Finlay's only source for his intermediate host theory for yellow fever, he made an extraordinary leap of logic from a plant pathogen to a human virus vectored by a mosquito. Still, whether Finlay had knowledge of Beauperthuy does not matter. Finlay saw value in the long-ignored theory and perhaps paired it with Manson's and Van Tieghem's work. He came to an understanding of how the mysterious ways of yellow fever could be explained if one replaced a plant fungus or swamp poisons with germs. Through his research and experiments, he proved to himself that the mosquito played an important role in spreading yellow fever. Proving it to others was the more difficult challenge.

By the summer of 1881, the seed planted earlier that year at the Washington sanitary conference had sprouted into a well-formed hypothesis. On the evening of August 14, 1881, Finlay stepped up to the podium at Havana's Academy of Sciences. He stood straight-backed in a black suit before about twenty of the forty academy members and began reading his lengthy paper, "The Mosquito Hypothetically Considered as the Transmitting Agent of Yellow Fever." The report demonstrated the many years of research and reflection Finlay had invested in developing this theory. He offered a detailed description of *Culex*'s morphology, biology, and ecology. Finlay described the intricacies of the mosquito's proboscis and the mechanism and effects of its bite. He correlated weather data and geographic features such as elevation and latitude with the known habits and habitats of the suspect mosquito and yellow fever.

In what he thought should clinch the argument, he presented case histories of five research subjects, four of whom he claimed to have gotten yellow fever through the bite of an infected *Culex* mosquito. He humbly noted, "These tests certainly favor my theory, but I do not wish to exaggerate in considering as fully verified something which still needs further proof."[5]

He then began to wrap up his speech by enumerating his conclusions. In the first two, he said the mosquito bites several times during its lifetime and that it could transfer the germ from person to person. The third addressed the four cases he presented, and here Finlay admitted a large hole in his experimental methods—the tests were carried out in an area with endemic yellow fever. It was possible, he admitted, that he had not actually caused all the cases through his experiments. Better controlled and more rigorous experiments were needed. Last, he noted, if the mosquito could conclusively be linked to yellow fever, the means of preventing the disease were evident—though he did not describe them.

He finished reading and stood before his fellow scientists and waited for their questions or comments. They responded with silence.

At the beginning of the nineteenth century, the Baltimore physician J. Crawford had explained what happened to those who permitted themselves thoughts that were clearly outside the mainstream of medicine. These non-conformists were "vilified, cruelly prosecuted or sunk into neglect."[6]

Crawford spoke from experience. In 1807, he suggested a mechanism for the transmission of yellow fever and malaria that fit with the anticontagionists' views. He observed parasitoid behavior in insects and drew an analogy about human disease. Parasitoid insects lay their eggs on or near hosts such as other insects. The hatching larvae feed on the host and kill it. Crawford reasoned that insect eggs could also sicken people. Diseases, he wrote, "must be occasioned by eggs insinuated, without our knowledge, into our bodies, externally or internally, or from eggs planted near our habitations."[7] He rejected the miasma theories of his day and, while he did not capture the true method of yellow fever transmission, his prescriptions for preventing the disease, if followed, could have averted some suffering and misery. He suggested avoiding insect breeding grounds and removing those infected from the area.

The silence that greeted Finlay as his stood behind the academy's podium may have been frustrating and disappointing but less hurtful than the "universal ridicule" his son said his father soon faced when defending and struggling to prove his mosquito theory.[8] He never was able to produce conclusive proof of his theory. According to his son, "crank" and "crazy old man" were a just a couple of the names applied to Carlos Finlay.[9] Only two people remained loyal to both him and his ideas on yellow fever during the nearly two decades he fought for their acceptance: his wife and his collaborator, Dr. Claudio Delgado.

Finlay realized that he could not conduct his experiments in Havana, a yellow fever hot spot. He began to work from an isolated Jesuit retreat farm called La Asuncion near Los Quemados. The farm had not had a case of yellow fever in eleven years and had no *Culex* mosquitoes. From the ninety-six inoculations performed in the fifteen years after presenting his theory, Finlay produced twelve cases that he or others diagnosed as yellow fever. In all likelihood, only one may have been yellow fever. That case was in a Jesuit father, the Reverend E. Urra, who was bitten on August 18, 1883, at La Asuncion. The other eleven cases were too mild to be definitively diagnosed. In addition, five of these cases later developed yellow fever. Since lifetime immunity follows a true case, those five men could not have been given yellow fever by Finlay.

Finlay pressed on. In 1894, at the Eighth International Congress of Hygiene and Demography in Budapest, he called for special measures to halt the spread of yellow fever. He prescribed protecting people from the stinging mosquitoes and destroying the insects. The report fell on deaf ears even in Cuba, where between 1885 and 1889, seven thousand yellow fever deaths were reported in Havana. In time, Finlay said that his main mission was to develop this natural vaccination against yellow fever. He tried one more inoculation in July 1900, after Walter Reed's Yellow Fever Board began its work; the volunteer remained well.

The second Cuban war for independence began in 1895. Although he sympathized with the pursuit of Cuban independence during the Ten Years' War and supported the second rebellion, Finlay was generally apolitical. His sons, however, actively supported the independence movement and his youngest son joined the rebel army. He escaped with only a severe case of malaria. When the United States declared war on Spain in 1898, the senior Finlay was in Tampa, Florida, with most of his family.

While Finlay was standing up to the Cuban and world public health community and getting slapped back down, George Sternberg was making great scientific strides in his studies and finding wide acceptance of his yellow fever work. By the mid-1880s, Sternberg was well on his way to solidifying his international reputation in bacteriology.

Sternberg was born on June 8, 1838, at Hatwick Seminary, New York, where his father was on the faculty. He was educated at the seminary and received his medical degree from the College of Physicians and Surgeons in New York City in 1860. He joined the Union army in the early days of the Civil War, and like many volunteers, he expected a short war followed by a return to the private practice of medicine. Instead, he served throughout the four years of the Civil War and never returned to his New Jersey practice. During the war, he received official commendations for courageous actions at the battles of Gaines' Mill, Turkey Bridge, and Malvern Hill. At the battle of Bull Run, Confederate troops captured him and briefly held him, but he escaped and evaded recapture, eventually making his way back to Washington, D.C. He remained in the army after the war, mainly serving at frontier posts and in the field with his troops. He provided medical care to wounded soldiers in the July 1877 battle of Clearwater against Chief Joseph and the Nez Perce Indians in Idaho. He also served at many different posts in the eastern United States.

In addition to his military credentials, his scientific accomplishments were significant. In 1881, he photographed and thus demonstrated, probably for the first time in the United States, the germ of tuberculosis discovered earlier that year by Robert Koch in Germany. He became an expert and national leader in the technique of photomicroscopy, publishing a how-to book of photomicrographs in 1884. He was among the first to identify the pneumococcus bacterium as a cause of pneumonia. While working at Johns Hopkins University, he demonstrated for the first time in this country the parasite of malaria in the blood of an active malarial patient.

A review of his bibliography, as compiled by the surgeon general's office and published in his wife's *George M. Sternberg: A Biography*, reveals that a significant portion of his career was devoted to chasing the cause of yellow fever. He wrote extensively on the epidemiology of the disease and on the theories of its etiology. His first medical paper, "An Inquiry into the Modus Operandi of the Yellow Fever Poison," published in the *New Orleans Medical and Surgical Journal* (July 1875), established him as the army's leading expert on yellow fever. Of Sternberg's 155 publications and presentations, 43 were clearly about yellow fever. Of the others, 38 addressed general bacteriology; 17, disinfectants; and 8, malaria. His quest to solve the yellow fever enigma spanned more than twenty-five years. During that time, he battled epidemics in New York City, New Orleans, and Ft. Barrancas, Florida, where he contracted a near fatal case. Survival meant he had lifetime immunity to the disease and could study it without fear of again becoming ill. While he made no significant breakthroughs in his studies of yellow fever, Sternberg investigated, tested, and struck down the discoveries of others. An historian of microbiology in the United States described Sternberg as "not a good mixer, rather stiff and unbending, distinctly egotistical, not one you would choose as a companion on a fishing trip."[10] Perhaps it was the perfect personality for the role he played in terminating scientifically weak yellow fever discoveries.

In 1879, yellow fever was again epidemic in the United States, and many feared a repeat of the 1878 disaster. In response to the outbreak, the Havana Yellow Fever Commission of the National Board of Health was established with Sternberg as secretary. Among the other members serving under Chairman Dr. Stanford Chaillé were Thomas Hardye, a civil engineer; and the Cuban physicians Drs. Juan Guitéras and Carlos Finlay. Their instructions directed them to examine the sanitary conditions at several Cuban ports, study the pathology of yellow fever, and report on its distribution in Cuba. Sternberg got a separate set of instructions that directed him to also undertake a study of the disease's nature and natural history.

Sternberg believed that the yellow fever bacteria would be found in the blood of its victims. He focused his work almost exclusively on the microscopic examination of blood. Blood drawn from patients in all stages of the illness made its way onto glass slides and then onto Sternberg's microscope stage. During his three months in Havana, he made an extensive photomicrographic record of his search, producing 105 photographs.

Although the commission failed to identify the cause of the disease or produce an effective control strategy, Sternberg began to build on his reputation as a leading expert in yellow fever and bacteriology. The 1880s were a remarkable era, as medicine moved from superstitions about the causes of some diseases to scientific proof that bacteria and other microscopic organisms were the true causes. Sternberg was an active player in this dramatic story as throughout the 1880s his work in the areas of disinfection and bacteriology continued and his reputation grew.

At the American Public Health Association's 1885 meeting, a resolution was passed calling for the appointment of a federal commission to study preventive inoculations being used in Mexico and Brazil. Congress would not vote the needed funds, so the commission never materialized, but President Grover Cleveland, in an executive action, directed Sternberg to make the inquiries. On May 4, 1887, Sternberg and his wife, Martha, sailed for Rio de Janeiro loaded down with a complete field outfit to carry out his bacteriological investigations. The ship, carrying mail, made stops at numerous cities as it sailed toward the Brazilian capital. Along the way, two German passengers developed yellow fever, and Sternberg feared he might be stuck in quarantine. But they recovered enough to walk off the ship in Rio de Janeiro and never were suspected by the Brazilian port authorities to have had the disease.

In Brazil, Sternberg was to verify the yellow fever germ of Dr. Domingo Freire. The doctor, however, was in France showing off his discovery when Sternberg arrived. That did not deter Sternberg. He set up his lab and began studying the blood and tissue of patients. He soon reported, "Having reviewed at length the claim of Dr. Freire to have discovered the specific germ of yellow fever, and to have transmitted this disease to certain lower animals by inoculation studies, [I have] arrived at the conclusion that his claims are without scientific foundation."[11]

Dr. Freire dealt with, Sternberg and his wife planned to sail from Brazil to Mexico, but when they arrived at Barbados, a quarantine prevented their travel from that Caribbean island to Mexico. Instead they sailed to New York, where Sternberg caught a train for Mexico. There he met with Dr. Carmona y Calle, who also claimed he had a suspect yellow fever germ. Sternberg made quick work of discrediting Dr. Carmona's bacteria and his attempts to produce a protective vaccine. While returning home, Sternberg was ordered to duty in Baltimore, which, his wife wrote, "was joyful news for both of us."[12] The bacteriologist could again enjoy the privilege of using the laboratories at Johns Hopkins University, where he was an honorary fellow.

During the winter of 1887–1888, Dr. Finlay sent his friend Dr. Sternberg several mosquito cultures harboring clusters of bacteria that Finlay thought could be the yellow fever germ. Sternberg was familiar with the organisms from his many studies of yellow fever cadavers and reported to his friend that it was a common bacteria often found in association with illness but not a cause of it. In April 1888, Sternberg boarded a ship for Havana to dash the hopes of Dr. Paul Gibier, a Frenchman with another candidate yellow fever germ. He returned to Cuba in 1889 to observe an epidemic in Havana.

As directed by an act of Congress, Sternberg summarized his many years of yellow fever work in an 1890 report on the "Etiology and Prevention of

Yellow Fever." He concluded in the 271-page manuscript, illustrated with twenty-one plates of his photomicrographs, that the germ of yellow fever had yet to been identified, but he was certain that it was a micro-organism that caused the disease. He went on to say that since the germ could not be found in blood and tissues, "it seems probable that it is to be found in the alimentary canal, as in the case of cholera."[13] Yet, he also conceded that the occurrence and distribution of the disease did not follow the patterns seen with cholera or typhoid, another disease carried in human waste. In the report, Sternberg, even after years of study, was clearly still struggling with yellow fever's most basic nature—its cause and mode of transmission. In the report's second to last paragraph, he halfheartedly stated, "The experimental evidence and the facts just stated seem to justify the recommendation that the dejecta [blood, feces, vomit, and urine] of yellow-fever patients should be regarded as infectious material" and should be disinfected before disposal. He ended the report saying that if this rule was followed, he believed the disease would never obtain "a foothold within the limits of the United States."[14]

Two years later, he published his nine-hundred-page *Manual of Bacteriology*, the first textbook on bacteriology published in the United States. It firmly established him as America's leading bacteriologist. With his strong military and extraordinary scientific credentials, not to mention his political contacts, Lieutenant Colonel George Miller Sternberg was appointed as surgeon general of the United States Army and promoted to the rank of brigadier general in 1893. He was selected over several more senior officers for the top job in the medical department, a position he held for a decade.

One of his first acts as surgeon general was to establish the Army Medical School in Washington, D.C. Despite the name, it was not a four-year medical school, as they are known today. The purpose of the new school was to teach doctors graduated from civilian medical schools about the practice of army medicine. He accomplished this without additional funding by reassigning talented officers to other designated positions in Washington and giving them additional duties to teach at his new school. Captain Walter Reed, Medical Corps, United States Army, was one of those who received orders to report to Washington, D.C., for duty as the curator of the Army Medical Museum with additional duty at the new Army Medical School.

Chapter 7

Walter Reed

W HEN THE CAREER MEDICAL OFFICER WALTER REED REPORTED
for duty at the Army Medical School in 1893, he was little more
than a frontier doctor. What separated him from the many other frontier
doctors then on duty in the army was a strong interest in the rapidly evolv-
ing scientific field of bacteriology. He had struggled to keep up with that
revolution in medical thinking, which was perhaps the greatest single
advancement in the healing arts. By 1893, during occasional postings to
Baltimore, Reed trained in the new field at Johns Hopkins University.
There his teachers were the leading and most progressive medical educa-
tors of the day. He demonstrated a willingness to learn and obvious aptitude for the new tools and techniques of scientific medicine, and that
caught the attention of George Sternberg.

Walter Reed was born on September 13, 1851, in Gloucester County,
Virginia. He was the fifth and last child of the Reverend Lemuel Sutton
Reed and Pharaba White Reed, who were both from North Carolina. The
small frame house where he was born was the temporary parsonage for the
Bellamy Methodist Church, where his father was the pastor. The owner of
the Belroi plantation was a member of the church and provided this home
while the parsonage was under construction. It was the custom of the
Methodist Church to move its ministers every two years. During Walter's
early years, the Reed family moved frequently.

During the year before the Civil War broke out, the Reeds lived in Lib-
erty, Virginia, on the eastern slope of the Blue Ridge Mountains in Bedford
County. Two of Walter's brothers, James and Thomas, would serve with the
Bedford Light Artillery, fighting for the Confederacy during the Civil War.
Although both survived the war, they were not immune to its personal
tragedy and hardships. James, a first sergeant, had his shattered hand amputated in a field hospital during the 1862 battle of Antietam. Half of
Thomas's unit was given furlough at one time under a scheme to keep the
men from going home at the end of their enlistment. It was wintertime, and

there was a lull in military activity. Despite the fact that he had no shoes, Thomas Reed walked seventy-five miles in the cold and snow to a railhead to catch a train home. An officer, in a history of Parker's Battery, wrote, "I might describe the barefooted men going home on furlough from East Tennessee. Tom Reed started through the snow with his feet tied up in rags, and when, after a tramp of many miles, he reached the cars at Bristol, they were bare and bleeding. A little girl, standing in a doorway, saw him, and burst into tears, and gave him a pair of socks."[1] Walter had his own Civil War adventure. As the war was winding down in 1865, Philip Sheridan's raiders swept through his town. He, his brother Christopher, and other town boys were sent by their parents to hide their horses. The Union troops, however, found them, seized the horses, and took the boys into custody. The boys were soon released, but the horses were taken.

During their childhood, Walter and his siblings received somewhat haphazard schooling, especially during the Civil War. After the war, their father asked the Methodist Church for reassignment to Charlottesville, Virginia, so his children could attend Thomas Jefferson's University of Virginia. Soon after the family arrived in their new home, Walter's mother died at age forty-nine; he was fourteen. At the age of fifteen, Walter was permitted to enter the University of Virginia because his two older brothers, James and Christopher, were students. After a successful year of studying Latin, Greek, and a course called History and Literature, he realized that his father could not support all three boys for the several years usually spent in earning the traditional Master of Arts degree. Because a medical degree could be attained more quickly, Walter presented the medical faculty with a sudden change in his plans. The formal faculty members may have taken pity on the naive but earnest young man, but they agreed—yes, he could receive an M.D. degree as soon as he passed all the courses. They hardly took him seriously, but he took himself very seriously. The primary subject of medical schools at the time was anatomy. Reed also studied chemistry, pharmacy, medicine, physiology, and surgery. He never saw a microscope, as they were not introduced to the University of Virginia until five years later, in 1874.

When he passed the examinations a year later, Walter Reed received his M.D. degree. He graduated at age seventeen, still over two months shy of his eighteenth birthday. He remains to this day the youngest graduate from the University of Virginia School of Medicine. As was common in those days, he sought further hands-on clinical training, going to Bellevue Hospital Medical College in New York City. His older brother Christopher went along to New York to study law. (Christopher Reed later served on the Kansas Supreme Court.) Reed earned his second M.D. degree at age eighteen from Bellevue, though it was not awarded until after he had turned twenty-one. He served in several positions in New York City and Brooklyn, where he received excellent training and built a splendid reputation.

Reed fell in love with a charming young woman, Emilie (she had changed it from Emily) Blackwell Lawrence, from Murfreesboro, North Carolina. He had lived in the town as a small boy and met Emilie when he visited his father, who was assigned there again. Reed was living and working in Brooklyn, where he held an appointment as a public health officer in the then independent city. Distance, time, and the cost of travel forced him to court her by mail.

In July 1874, Reed wrote Emilie that he was ready to leave Brooklyn. His duties at the Board of Health were becoming more demanding, and he had no time to establish a private practice. Moreover, after four years in the New York area, urban life had lost its fascination and, much to his own surprise, he had grown tired of the lifestyle. "To live in any other place than New York or Brooklyn never entered my head, and if a person had advised me to go to some small town, I would have certified his insanity," he wrote. "I have been unable to discover the great advantages of living in Metropolitan Cities, except it be in the 'wear and tear.'"[2]

He wanted to leave Brooklyn, yet knew that it was nearly hopeless to try to earn a living practicing medicine in any of the southern states during the disruptions following the Civil War. Returning home was not a viable option. Reed told Emilie that he had "about made up my mind to make a strenuous effort to enter the Medical Corps of the U.S. Army." Should he pass and establish himself as a successful army doctor and could "find some damsel who was foolish enough to trust me, I think I would get—married," he wrote.[3]

Reed spoke with the recorder of the Examining Board in early August 1874 and discovered just how difficult the Medical Corps examinations would be: "To my utter astonishment he informed me that the candidates must stand an examination on Latin, Greek, Mathematics & History, in addition to medical subjects." A somewhat distressed Reed wrote Emilie, "Horror of Horrors! Imagine me conjugating an irregular Greek verb, or telling what x + y equals or when Rome was founded, or the battle of Marathon fought—why this thing is impossible—I shall utterly fail."[4]

Beginning on February 8, 1875, Reed stood for the thirty hours of questioning spread over five days. One of the essay questions he was given was on the topic of hygiene, and it concerned yellow fever. He noted that the disease was endemic in Havana and addressed the conditions necessary for its propagation. In neat handwriting, but a somewhat awkward syntax, he said the disease was carried from its places of origin "by land & water— Either by germs clinging to clothing or in cargo of ship [sic]—or by a person who is is [sic] at the time sick of the disease being transported to a non-infected [locality]."[5] Sanitarians, he noted, thought filth and drainage had an effect on the spread of the disease.

Despite his anxiety, he passed the examinations. Another worry appeared. There was some danger that Reed would miss out on being commissioned an assistant surgeon with the rank of first lieutenant because Congress was reducing the total number of assistant surgeon positions— Medical Corps slots filled by first lieutenants and captains. That danger passed. While Congress lowered the number from 150 to 125, Reed got his commission and entered the army, filling slot number 112.

His commission assured, Reed proposed to Emilie in a March 24 letter. His heart, he wrote, had been captured by the beauty of her character, her womanly worth, the purity of her Christianity, and the charm of her intellect. He offered her "a true heart and a true hand" for her acceptance or rejection.[6] Emilie didn't immediately accept. There is no evidence until a June 1 letter written by Reed while at his sister's home that Emilie agreed to marry him.

Walter Reed accepted his commission on July 2, 1875. His first year's assignment was to the fort at Willet's Point on the north shore of Long Island at the mouth of the East River near the present-day Throgs Neck Bridge. The army had established the fort, later called Fort Totten, as a major component of the defensive network of fortifications guarding New York harbor in 1857. It was a pleasant, undemanding post—one of the most desirable in the army. Reed was very pleased with the assignment and hoped to stay several years. He told Emilie about his day: "I rise in the morning at 6:30 o'clock & and attend the 'sick-call.'" Later in the morning, he did his hospital rounds: "The number of sick are very few." After lunch, "I have nothing to do—in fact nothing else during the entire day," Reed reported.[7]

In August 1875, Emilie sent her fiancé Reed a caricature of himself at Willet's Point. Mosquitoes must have been a problem for the men at the post, since they seem to have been the center point of the drawing. Reed, with tender humor, wrote back, "The [mosquito perched] on the fence, I recognized at once! How could I ever forget one who had been so very *near* to me! My tears I could not restrain! After wrapping my mosquito netting securely about my head I sat & watched him through the meshes for quite some time—And as I beheld his calm, honest brow, my tears fell thick and fast—So strongly does friendship sway our better nature."[8]

Willet's Point was too good to last for such a young and inexperienced medical officer. In early 1876, Reed's next assignment, this time to an army post on the western frontier, came unexpectedly. He asked his beloved Emilie if she would consider moving up the wedding day; she did. Walter Reed and Emilie Lawrence were married on April 25, 1876. His father performed the ceremony in Murfreesboro in the very church where Reed first saw Emilie. After a brief honeymoon in Harrisonburg, Virginia, First Lieutenant Walter Reed, now twenty-four, was assigned to Fort Yuma, Arizona Territory.

As with military families today, the soldier reported to his assignment first; his wife joined him later. In the fall of 1876, just seven years after the completion of the transcontinental railroad, twenty-year-old Emilie Reed rode the train, alone, across the country, experiencing a blizzard and train wreck en route. Reed journeyed to San Francisco to meet her. He sported a new mustache, one he would wear for the rest of his life. From there, they traveled by steamer to San Diego and then endured a twenty-three-day buckboard ride over five hundred trackless miles to Reed's next assignment at Camp Lowell, Arizona Territory, near Tucson. Reed's caseload included malaria, typhoid, and dysentery in addition to the many illnesses and injuries common to military service. Adding to the difficulties of life on the frontier was the fact that the Congress did not pass an army appropriations bill for 1877, and for the first eleven months of that year, no one in the army was paid. The proud young couple had to borrow from their families to get by.

Reed was the only doctor for as many as two hundred miles around, and he cared for soldiers, family members, civilians, and Indians. His third posting in Arizona, Camp Apache on the White Mountain Apache Reservation, was located on the south bank of the White River in east-central Arizona. According to his friend Lieutenant Thomas Cruse, Reed was "the instigator of many humorous and boisterous table conversations" while dining in the officers' mess.[9] Cruse, who retired as a brigadier general in 1918, said that Reed "was at that time the greatest wag and joker that I ever saw."[10] Cruse also said that if anyone at their mess was destined for future greatness, no one would have guessed it would be Reed.

While at Camp Apache, he cared for a little Indian girl named Susie who had been badly burned in an accident and abandoned by her family. As she was only four or five years old and had no one to care for her, the Reed family took her in. She lived with them for about fifteen years before she returned to the West and lost contact with the Reeds. Over the next eighteen years, Reed and Emilie moved about fifteen times throughout the western frontier interspersed with assignments back East.

Their son, Walter Lawrence Reed, was born in 1877 at Camp Apache, Arizona, and several years later, in 1883, their daughter, Emilie Lawrence Reed, known throughout her life as Blossom, was born in Omaha, Nebraska. On these isolated postings, there was usually only one doctor; undoubtedly, Walter Reed delivered both of his own children.

In between the assignments in Arizona and Nebraska, the Reeds had several short assignments in the East, including one at Fort McHenry in Baltimore and another at Washington Barracks in the District of Columbia. While in Baltimore, Reed was first introduced to Johns Hopkins University, where he attended some lectures in 1881, but their formal courses in bacteriology and pathology had not yet been instituted.

Between 1882 and 1887, the Reeds were assigned to three different locations in Nebraska—Fort Omaha, Fort Sidney, and Fort Robinson. His experiences at Fort Sidney are described in a 1973 article by Gordon Chappell published in the quarterly journal, *Nebraska History*. Fort Sidney was called by one Reed biographer "a hell raising railroad town," and Reed had the responsibility of being surgeon in charge.[11] Again, he provided care to everyone, including soldiers, family members, civilians, and Indians. He treated the usual illnesses, delivered babies, performed minor surgery, cared for children—including one who probably had acute rheumatic fever—and handled the more difficult cases of typhoid, erysipelas, and bacterial pneumonia. He also performed induction physicals and medical exams for fitness for military duty. He determined the degree of soldiers' disabilities and also determined if the injury or illness had been incurred in the line of duty. He later used some of the cases of erysipelas that he saw at Fort Sidney in his first scientific publication. "The Contagiousness of Erysipelas" was

published years later in the *Boston Medical and Surgical Journal*, the predecessor of the *New England Journal of Medicine*.

Fort Robinson, the Reeds' next assignment, was in the sand hills of the
far northwest Nebraska panhandle, a desolate place with bitter cold winters and miserable hot summers. In the fall of 1884, Jules Sandoz, a twenty-
seven-year-old Swiss granger, was brought to the post hospital after being
found on the side of a wagon trail with his left ankle badly fractured and
his leg swollen and putrid with infection. Jules had fallen about sixty feet
into a well he had been digging, fracturing his ankle. His helpers rescued
him from the well but, shortly after, abandoned him to live or die on his
own. He attempted to care for himself, but after several days he dragged
himself to the wagon trail and eventually was found by soldiers from Fort
Robinson. Reed, the post surgeon, operated on him and later wrote a clinically detailed letter to Jules's parents in Switzerland:

> His injury was a very severe one—being a compound, comminuted
> fracture of the left ankle-joint, with dislocation. He was admitted
> to hospital on 18th day after receipt of injury, & had a truly hor-
> rible joint. I at once placed him under ether, removed the astragalus
> entire & a part of the os calcis and int malleolus. Drainage tube
> was then carried through joint & wound dressed antiseptically &
> placed in plaster of paris splint. I may say that had I been permit-
> ted to fully exercise my judgment, I should have amputated at the
> ankle-joint, but your son would not consent. The wound is nearly
> healed, & I anticipate that he will yet have a useful foot. You may
> rest assured that he shall have my best attention.[12]

Despite the lack of antibiotics, Jules miraculously survived but with a significant lifelong limp. He lived the remainder of his long life in western
Nebraska, where he died in 1928 at age seventy-one. His daughter, Mari Sandoz, who became an award-winning writer of Nebraska and the American
West, memorialized her father in her first book published in 1935, *Old Jules*.

From 1887 to 1890, the Reeds were assigned to Mount Vernon Barracks, Alabama. During this assignment, one of Walter's responsibilities was
providing care to almost four hundred Apache Indians who were being held
there, including the great chief, Geronimo. Reed wrote an article entitled
"Geronimo and His Warriors in Captivity" that was published in the
August 16, 1890, issue of the *Illustrated American*. The article briefly

recounted the history of the Apache Indians, their struggles with the government, and their eventual surrender to the U.S. Army in 1886. Members of the tribe were sent to various posts in the South, and in 1887, many were at Mount Vernon Barracks. Reed also addressed their traditional culture and how they dealt with being forced to adopt another culture under the direction of the U.S. government. The closing sentence of the article gives an interesting glimpse at Reed's sense of humor. It addresses a cultural practice of the Apache and reads, "Further, when it is remembered that a man is not allowed to speak to or even look at his mother-in-law under any circumstances, who can say that the Indian is altogether behind the Caucasian in civilization?"[13]

As he neared the end of his tour at Mount Vernon Barracks, Alabama, Walter Reed was also approaching a crossroads in his career. Now almost forty years old with fifteen years in the army, he was still several years away from promotion to major. His family and home life were going very well. His dedicated wife and children were healthy and supportive of his chosen career despite the difficulties, frequent moves, and, on at least one occasion, no pay for almost a year. Professionally, however, Reed was yearning to become more involved with the revolutionary changes sweeping through science and medicine. He was in danger of missing out on the new field of bacteriology, with its discoveries of the causes of diseases that had been mysteries for centuries.

Walter Reed, the veteran of Indian forts and isolated army posts, had witnessed from the sidelines the remarkable transformation of medicine from a profession practiced with little scientific basis to one in which science was becoming the basis for the practice. His brief chance to attend some lectures at Johns Hopkins University during his earlier assignment to Fort McHenry in Baltimore had been almost ten years before. Those ten years were exciting times in the world of medicine, as new causes and treatments of old diseases were being discovered. In the early 1880s, Carl J. Eberth discovered the typhoid bacillus; the French army physician Charles Louis Alphonse Laveran identified the parasite of malaria; Robert Koch isolated the organisms of tuberculosis and cholera; Edwin Klebs discovered the agent of diphtheria; and others found the organisms of pneumonia, tetanus, erysipelas, and cerebrospinal meningitis.

Reed tried to keep pace with his changing profession. His request for leave to again study at Hopkins coincided with the arrival of a new surgeon general, Jedediah Hyde Baxter. Baxter, a physician with a law degree, had worked to institute what is now called continuing medical education. Reed's request was approved and strengthened by his assignment to a Baltimore recruit examination station. This gave him his army salary and time to complete the full seven-month course in pathology and bacteriology.

In the fall of 1890, when Walter Reed walked into the new Johns Hopkins Hospital, opened just the year before, he knew he had been given the opportunity of a lifetime. He was wise and energetic enough to take full advantage of it. John Shaw Billings, the curator of the Army Medical Museum and the librarian of the Surgeon General's Library, had selected William Henry Welch to be the dean and professor of pathology for the new medical school that was to open soon. Together they had recruited what was to become one of the most outstanding faculties in the history of U.S. medical education. Known as "The Big Four," they were Welch, William Osler, William S. Halsted, and Howard A. Kelly. Reed was exposed to them all, but Welch and Kelly had the greatest influence on his career. "I well recall with what eagerness and enthusiasm he turned his attention to the new fields of scientific medicine, thus first opened to him," Welch would write after Reed's death. "[He] possessed unusual aptitude for the work that he had undertaken [at Johns Hopkins], and . . . he combined with excellent natural endowments of mind a sincere, manly and winning personality."[14]

Not long into the course, the army again called, and just before Christmas 1890, Reed was sent on temporary duty to Fort Keogh, Montana. There he cared for those wounded in the battle of Wounded Knee. After about a month, he returned to Baltimore and completed his course. As army officers have done for years, he began to look for his next assignment. Not wanting to waste his newly acquired knowledge and laboratory skills, he approached the intimidating John Shaw Billings. Billings offered little, if any, help.

Reed must have been very disappointed and probably even discouraged to be ordered back to the western frontier, this time to Fort Snelling, Minnesota. In contrast to some of his previous assignments, Fort Snelling was in the vicinity of Minneapolis and thus less isolated. Instead of withdrawing into his disappointment after he arrived in November 1891, Reed quickly reached out to the local medical community. He was made an honorary member of the Ramsey County Medical Society. Reed worked with Louis Wilson, a local high school biology teacher. Wilson, later the director of the Mayo Foundation, assisted Reed in setting up a bacteriology laboratory and in processing throat cultures for the purpose of diagnosing diphtheria. It was while at Fort Snelling that Reed's first scientific publication, "The Contagiousness of Erysipelas," appeared in print. Better late than never, but at forty-one he must have wondered if he would ever get that big break necessary to give him his chance to really make his mark and to make a difference.

In the spring of 1893, George Miller Sternberg's selection as surgeon general turned out to be a watershed in Walter Reed's career. Reed was recalled to Washington to join the faculty of Sternberg's new Army Medical School. One of the factors in Reed's getting the assignment was geography. He lived closer to Washington (Minnesota) than the other candidate (California) and it would cost the army less to move him.

Reed was promoted to major, and in an ironic twist, he replaced John Shaw Billings as the curator of the Army Medical Museum. He was given additional duties as a professor of clinical and sanitary microscopy at the new Army Medical School. Reed had no experience as a teacher, but he had a wealth of experience in the field environment, which Sternberg knew would be needed as the fledgling school tried to turn civilian doctors into Medical Corps officers.

The Reeds lived in Georgetown in the 3000 block of Q Street, NW. The Army Medical School was housed with the medical museum at 7th and B Streets, SW, a good half-hour walk. Lawrence, their oldest child, had attended school away from home during the family's assignments in the West. He was now able to stay at home to attend high school.

Reed began to increase his skill in bacteriological techniques. Soon he was doing original studies on various bacteria and bacterial diseases. Quietly, unobtrusively, he got things done. Reed's work and writings showed accuracy and originality. His military experience and excellent judgment made him a particularly valuable asset in investigating epidemics and in making sanitary inspections. Over the years, he became a trusted troubleshooter for General Sternberg.

During this time, he renewed his association with Dr. James Carroll, whom he had earlier met and worked with at Johns Hopkins. Despite his medical degree, Carroll remained a sergeant in the army. Reed worked with Carroll both to strengthen their own laboratory skills and to develop medical school courses in pathology and bacteriology. Born in England in 1854, James Carroll had immigrated to Canada in his early teens. There he worked as a woodsman for several years before coming to the United States and enlisting in the U.S. Army in June 1874. He served as a private, corporal, sergeant, and hospital steward with numerous assignments on the western frontier. During his third enlistment, at age thirty, he became interested in the field of medicine and began a quest that culminated seven years later in his being awarded an M.D. degree from the University of Maryland in April 1891. While doing postgraduate work in bacteriology at Johns Hopkins Hospital, Carroll worked under Dr. William Welch and assisted Walter Reed, another Welch pupil, in his laboratory work. In 1895, he was assigned to the Army Medical Museum in Washington, D.C., to work with Reed. Unknown to Reed and Carroll at the time, this was the beginning of what would define their life's work.

Reed's time in Washington was filled with many endeavors. He became a member of the Medical Society of the District of Columbia and frequently took an active part in the public discussion on new medical discoveries. In 1895, he was invited to join the faculty of the Columbian University Medical School, now George Washington University. There he taught night classes to supplement his army income. During that same year, he was involved in his first epidemiological study, evaluating an outbreak of malaria in the nation's capital at Washington Barracks, now Fort Lesley J. McNair, and at Fort Myer across the Potomac River in Virginia. He defended the Army Medical School against antivivisectionists' claims that the school abused and mutilated animals in its classes and experiments. He became a delegate to the American Public Health Association. Needing to escape the hubbub of Washington and its unbearably hot and humid summers, the Reeds spent their annual summer leave at a mountain cabin they had purchased near Blue Ridge Summit, Pennsylvania. Possibly in honor of their time on the western frontier, their cabin was given the Indian name Keewaydin, meaning "west wind."

In the summer of 1896, Reed was sent to Key West to investigate a smallpox epidemic. There he met and befriended another medical officer, Jefferson Randolph Kean. A great-grandson of Thomas Jefferson, Kean, like Reed, was a medical graduate of the University of Virginia and a career Medical Corps officer; they became fast and lifelong friends.

The school year of 1896–1897 was busy and hectic, as was becoming the norm for Reed. He wrote his father in late 1896, "I have never been so busy in all my life, & I sometimes get so weary that I want to lie down and die!"[15] Reed offered his resignation as museum curator in early 1897 to devote more time to his teaching duties, but the offer was denied. Life was about to get more hectic for Reed.

The Italian scientist Giuseppe Sanarelli, working as the director of the Institute of Experimental Hygiene at the University of Montevideo, Uruguay, claimed that a bacterium he had identified, *Bacillus icteroides*, was the specific causative agent of yellow fever. His startling announcement was in the July 3, 1897, issue of the *British Medical Journal*. Sanarelli reported that he had found the microorganism in the bodies of yellow fever victims during life and after death; he had also found that it caused significant illness and even death in almost all domestic animals. Going further, Sanarelli had given *Bacillus icteroides* to five human beings, causing what he called "typical yellow fever, accompanied by all its imposing anatomical and symptomatological retinue."[16] Sanarelli's discovery, touted by the Pasteur Institute in Paris and translated into several languages, caused a sensation in the scientific world.

The army surgeon general George Miller Sternberg was obviously very interested in this announcement, as he had spent a large part of his career in pursuit of the yellow fever agent. In the fall of that same year, he published a paper touting his "*Bacillus X*" as the causative agent. This publication drew the battle lines and set the stage for several years of bitter scientific haggling. Sternberg, who had disproved a number of researchers' claims of finding the germ of yellow fever, was convinced that *Bacillus icteroides* did not cause the disease. Included in his reasoning was the fact that in his many years of searching, he himself had not found it. He had more than enough faith in his own scientific abilities to believe that if a bacterium was responsible for yellow fever, it would not have escaped his culture techniques or his microscope. Notwithstanding the fact that he was considered one of America's leading bacteriologists, Sternberg was unwilling to simply say, referring to the causative bacteria, "If I could not find it, it must not exist."

Therefore, he ordered Walter Reed and his laboratory assistant, James Carroll, to get to work evaluating the Sanarelli bacillus and to determine if it bore any relationship to the *Bacillus X* that Sternberg had discovered in the bodies of yellow fever victims ten years before. Reed stated that he hoped to confirm Sanarelli's work, but his and Carroll's findings did not support any such confirmation. Instead, after over eighteen months of work that included animal experiments and bacteriologic studies, they found *Bacillus icteroides* to be a variety of *Bacillus cholerae suis*, the common hog cholera bacterium, and not causally related to yellow fever. They determined that if it was present at all in yellow fever patients, it was a secondary invader, and they published a brief two-page article in the April 29, 1899, *Medical News*. They also determined that it bore no relationship to Sternberg's *Bacillus X*.

Sanarelli replied four months later, in a long, stinging, six-page article in the same journal, that a "personal element has obtruded itself into the controversy which followed the appearance of my articles on the etiology of yellow fever." Sanarelli, just thirty-three years old, directly attacked the integrity of Sternberg by saying, "I cannot understand, however, his obstinate unwillingness to concede that another has succeeded in solving the problem which proved unsolvable to him." Unwilling to stop there, Sanarelli questioned Sternberg's professionalism and integrity: "If it is true, however, that the man of science labors for the good of humanity and not for the sake of any personal satisfaction, or for self-glorification, then every laborer in the field of bacteriology can only rejoice sincerely at the successful issue of my studies. Unfortunately, this is not the case."[17] This attack was all the more staggering because Sternberg, who was almost thirty years older than Sanarelli, was the current surgeon general of the United States Army as well as the immediate past president of the American Medical Association and considered the leading bacteriologist in the United States.

After blasting Surgeon General Sternberg, Sanarelli pointed his cannon at Reed and Carroll, accusing them of faulty laboratory techniques. "I find it impossible to give any serious consideration to the strange position taken by Drs. Reed and Carroll. It is evident that their conclusion has no other significance than a gross and deplorable error was made in their laboratory and that somehow the cultures of the two micro-organisms being experimented with got mixed for want of sufficient attention." Sanarelli closed his long diatribe with the following: "I am inclined to doubt if those who find it so easy to criticize are in a position to treat the bacteriological and pathogenetic questions of the infectious diseases with as much experience and authority, for these can only be acquired after many years of practical study at the bedside of the sick, in the autopsy-room and in the laboratory of comparative experimental pathology."[18]

Reed and Carroll vigorously defended themselves and their work with a published response the next month in the September 9, 1899, issue of *Medical News*. The following week, the *Journal of the American Medical Association* addressed the controversy and what it called "Sanarelli's remarkable attack." The editorial read, "Drs. Reed and Carroll fearing that silence on their part might be construed by the general public as an admission that they had followed faulty technical methods in their work, made a vigorous and, it seems to us, wholly successful defense of their methods in the investigation which led them to announce the rather startling view that the *Bacillus icteroides* should be regarded as a variety of the hog cholera bacillus."[19]

It continued, "On the whole Reed and Carroll have strengthened their position in holding the opinion that *Bacillus icteroides* is a variety of the hog cholera bacillus." The editorial concluded that "the methods followed in the laboratories of the Army Medical Museum are above all suspicion. His [Sanarelli's] aspersions on the scientific spirit of the workers in the laboratory are certainly nothing more nor less than contemptible."[20]

As Sternberg and Reed publicly debated Sanarelli, two officers with the U.S. Marine Hospital Service (later the U.S. Public Health Service) published a report that could be considered the official U.S. position on the origin, spread, and control of yellow fever. Fueling the flames of the now roaring academic and personal battles over the etiology of disease were Eugene Wasdin and H. D. Geddings. The surgeon general of the Marine Hospital Service had sent them to Havana in late 1897 to study Sanarelli's *Bacillus icteroides*. An abstract of their July 1899 official U.S. government report was published in the *New York Medical Journal* in August 1899, directly in the midst of the dueling articles being published by Sanarelli, Sternberg, and Reed and Carroll. Their investigations, they noted, were "detailed by authority of the Secretary of the Treasury and the President as a commission to investigate in Havana the nature of yellow fever."[21] Wasdin and Geddings unequivocally declared Sanarelli's bacterium as the cause of yellow fever. They said they had found the Sanarelli organism in the blood of fourteen of fourteen cases that were diagnosed as yellow fever, but not in any patients who were ill with other disease. They also reported that "infection takes place by way of the respiratory tract," that yellow fever was "naturally infectious to certain animals,"[22] and that disinfectants were effective at controlling the disease. The Marine Hospital Service surgeon general said the report eliminated the many incorrect conclusions about yellow fever. He praised the work of his officers, calling their findings "a notable achievement in medical science and one of the greatest practical value to the people of the United States and other countries infected, or liable to be infected."[23]

Chapter 8

Spanish Bullets
and Yellow Fever

IT WAS "AMERICA'S SPLENDID LITTLE WAR." AND AT ITS END, THE United States, which had only recently tamed its own wild frontier, was a world power with overseas possessions. In just a few months of fighting, the United States took from the Spanish crown Cuba, Puerto Rico, Guam, and the Philippines—a country so remote to Americans that even President McKinley reportedly had to search a globe to find it. The new territories presented many challenges. Among them was managing the tropical diseases prevalent on these islands, especially yellow fever in Cuba. American doctors could now confront the scourge on its home field.

Late in the evening of February 13, 1898, a massive explosion tore apart the battleship USS *Maine* while it was at anchor in Havana harbor; 268 U.S. sailors and Marines were killed. A navy court of inquiry concluded that a submarine mine was responsible for the ship's destruction. And while the court admitted it could not affix blame to any person or persons, the Spanish government was the presumed culprit.

For years, expansionists and a few newspapers had been preparing the American public for a Cuban war. "You furnish the pictures and I'll furnish the war,"[1] William Randolph Hearst, the publisher-editor of the New York *Journal*, famously cabled his artist Frederic Remington in Cuba. After the sinking of the *Maine*, that war, the natural end to a century-long fascination with Cuba, was inevitable. In 1823, Thomas Jefferson had told President James Monroe, "I candidly confess, that I have ever looked on Cuba as the most interesting addition which could ever be made to our system of States."[2] Throughout the 1800s, the United States continued to covet

Cuba. Several presidents entered negotiations with Spain in an attempt to buy the island. Since the end of the Ten Years' War in 1878, economic ties between the Spanish colony and its northern neighbor had grown tighter. Increasingly, Americans bought sugar and tobacco plantations and invested in and traveled to the island. By the start of the second rebellion against Spain in 1895, the United States was Cuba's largest trading partner.

In the spring of 1898, the U.S. military was not ready for a foreign war. That was especially true of the army and even truer of its Medical Department, which was underfunded and undermanned even in peacetime. Surgeon General George Sternberg found himself asked to do the nearly impossible—equip, train, man, and field a wartime medical department that could support an army fighting on foreign soils—while at the same time he was to protect the troops from the tropical diseases that had plagued, if not destroyed, nearly every foreign force that ever set foot in the West Indies. On the eve of war, there were 177 commissioned medical officers in the entire Army Medical Department. Fifteen who had recently been released for budgetary reasons were quickly recalled, making a grand total of 192 regular army medical officers.

Several weeks before the declaration of war, Walter Reed had applied to Sternberg for field duty, asking that he be assigned to Captain William T. Sampson's squadron. "To all of which the [Surgeon General] turned a deaf ear, while thanking me for my offer," Reed wrote his friend Jefferson Kean.[3] Meanwhile, Reed's twenty-year-old son's attempt to receive a commission likewise was denied. Undeterred, Lawrence Reed joined up as an enlisted soldier anyway. He eventually ended up in Cuba but after the fighting was over.

According to Reed, the surgeon general was determined to keep all nonimmune regular Army medical officers out of Cuba. Despite that, Reed had found out that Kean's once-denied request for field duty was being reconsidered. Should Kean get to Cuba, Reed had a piece of advice for him. In keeping with Sternberg's theory of yellow fever transmission, he warned his friend that the germ was probably inhaled, "hence [a] plug of cotton in nostrils would be advisable."[4]

To help staff the Army Medical Corps, a call went out for civilian doctors to sign on as contract surgeons. Among the applicants was Carlos Finlay. He and his family had left Cuba and were living in Tampa, Florida. The sixty-five-year-old exile contacted Sternberg requesting a commission in the U.S. Army. Instead, the surgeon general offered him a position as a contract civilian physician. Finlay accepted the contract and was assigned to Santiago.

Cuba was widely recognized as a breeding ground for malaria and yellow fever. While the exact numbers were yet to be tallied, the War Department knew the devastating toll these diseases were taking on Spanish soldiers deployed to the island to put down the rebellion. The geographic proximity of Cuba to the United States and the many Americans who lived or traveled there provided the U.S. government with multiple sources of intelligence. The United States had been collecting information on the Cuban conflict since its outbreak in 1895. Between 1895 and 1898, an estimated 16,000 Spanish troops succumbed to yellow fever. In 1898, of an army of 230,000, only 55,000 were available to fight. And of 18,000 Spanish troops garrisoned at Manzanillo, 6,000 were in fever wards. The Cuban rebels had adopted a strategy to let yellow fever and other diseases do much of their killing

An epidemic of yellow fever among the troops was the U.S. military planners' greatest fear. Like many citizens, they attached to the disease a superstitious terror far in excess of its true effects. Over two hundred years of experience with the disease in the Caribbean had taught them that they couldn't prevent it, they couldn't cure it, and they had no idea where it came from. What was undisputed was the correlation between yellow fever and the rainy season. But as the war council developed and reviewed its plans, it became clear that the earliest that U.S. soldiers could land in Cuba was at the start of the rainy season.

Surgeon General Sternberg was particularly worried, and he took his concerns directly to President McKinley, imploring him not to invade Cuba during the wet months. Invasion at that time, he predicted, would mean death and disaster for the army. On April 20, 1898, the commanding general of the army General Nelson Miles and Fifth Army Corps Commander General William Shafter met with President McKinley and his secretaries of war and the navy at the White House to plan a war strategy. The role of yellow fever was a central topic of discussion. Miles told the president that the army would not be ready to invade before the end of June and the start of the yellow fever season. Echoing Sternberg's warnings, he stressed the need to delay the invasion until the fall. McKinley agreed and worked up a plan that called for an immediate naval blockade of Cuba along with small raids on the island throughout the summer. In the fall, when the danger of yellow fever had passed, the army would launch a major land campaign.

On April 23, as Spain declared war against the United States, McKinley issued a call for 125,000 volunteers. Two days later, the U.S. Congress, at the request of the president, voted a declaration of war against the kingdom of Spain. The declaration was made retroactive to April 21. On April 27, a U.S. Navy squadron already positioned off the northwest coast of Cuba began a bombardment of the city of Matanzas.

The war plan agreed to at the White House soon collapsed. Infighting between the regular army and state militias forced a summer invasion. The militias and volunteer regiments being organized to join the adventure needed about six months to become war ready, just in time for the planned fall invasion. The regular army, which wanted to keep as much of the glory to itself, therefore lobbied for a June invasion. They got their wish. On June 22, after a short naval bombardment, the Fifth Army Corps of sixteen thousand men, under the command of General William Shafter, went ashore at Daiquiri, on the southeast coast of Cuba, the first stop on the road to Santiago. The First U.S. Volunteer Calvary, popularly known as the Rough Riders, pushed ahead of regular army units and were among the first troopers on the beach. They were immediately dispatched to tear down a Spanish flag waving over an abandoned blockhouse. As they tore down the Spanish colors and hoisted the Stars and Stripes, the soldiers on the beach, and even those still in the landing boats, responded with a fifteen-minute celebration of shouts and songs followed by a band playing "The Star Spangled Banner."

Within two weeks, the expeditionary force had battled Spanish troops at Las Guasimas, El Caney, and San Juan Hill. The army quickly approached Santiago, where the navy had the Spanish fleet blockaded. On July 3, as the fleet attempted to escape the harbor, U.S. warships attacked and the enemy ships were destroyed. The Fifth Army, camped on the outskirts of town, dug in around the besieged city as negotiations for its surrender began. On July 11, the last soldier killed by Spanish guns at Santiago fell. A new enemy was already in place. The first case of yellow fever appeared at Siboney on July 6. While it caused some anxiety, for the next several weeks the real foes were malaria and dysentery.

It was not until the twentieth century that battle wounds began to replace disease as the leading killer of wartime soldiers. Although yellow fever was the most feared of all the illnesses threatening the Cuban invasion force, cases in mid-July were sporadic. Other tropical and camp diseases became epidemic in the stalled Fifth Army Corps. General Shafter understood the effects of the diseases on his men. Disease, he admitted, was a "thousand times harder to stand up against than the missiles of the enemy."[5]

Slowly, yellow fever was infiltrating the Fifth Army Corps. Shafter told his superiors in Washington of three cases of the illness in a Michigan regiment in a July 9 dispatch. Among the officers and doctors, there was a perception that yellow fever–infected buildings in the town of Siboney were the source of the outbreak. With the support and recommendations of U.S. Army physicians and the Cuban consultant Dr. Juan Guitéras, General Miles ordered Siboney evacuated and burned to the ground on July 11.

The next day, Colonel Theodore Roosevelt reported that only 350 of his 600 Rough Riders were well enough for duty; but still, yellow fever was not the disabler. The effects of dysentery were evident in the encampment. Private Charles Post of the 71st New York U.S. Volunteers described shallow latrines that "were spattered with blood, ample evidence that dysentery was crowding upon us." He reported that the usual honors for fallen soldiers were suspended: "Volleys and taps had been stopped by official order from headquarters lest their frequency might demoralize us! Soldiers were buried in silence but for the chaplain."[6] The silent burials could not hide the files of men with picks and shovels carrying stretchers covered with blankets or ponchos who, along with a chaplain, headed out to the burial grounds several times a day. On July 13, General Miles wrote the secretary of war, "There are 100 cases of yellow fever in this command, and the opinion of the surgeons is that it will spread rapidly."[7] Despite the fact that other diseases were decimating the army, Shafter, Miles, and the McKinley administration began focusing on the relatively few yellow fever cases. Yellow fever camps and hospitals were set up away from the main troop concentrations to isolate the sick and prevent the spread of the illness. Regiments of presumed immune soldiers, including black regiments, were assigned to these facilities.

While Shafter should have been more accurate in his reports to Washington about the health of his army, any action that revealed the presence of the disease or the increasing enfeeblement of the troops had to be avoided. Negotiations for the surrender of Santiago and the Spanish forces in the area were still in progress. Political and military leaders in Washington believed that if the Spanish commander, General José Toral, learned of the sicknesses sweeping through the Fifth Corps or sensed any panic or demoralization among the U.S. troops due to the appearance of yellow fever, the talks would be broken off. Disease was now the Spaniards' ally. The secretary of war, Russell Alger, promised Shafter that once the enemy capitulated, troops could be moved into positions around Santiago and to the high ground above the yellow fever belt. "Experts here say this can be done," he cabled Shafter.[8]

Toral surrendered his army and the city on July 17, effectively ending the Cuban campaign. Immediately, preparations were made to begin moving troops to what was believed to be safe camps. From Shafter on down to the lowest enlisted man, the "expert's advice"—assumed to be from Sternberg—was thought logistically impossible to implement. Private Post reported, "Surgeon General Sternberg was capable of almost anything; for it was he who said of us, in the trenches, that we should be moved back some twenty or so miles where it was healthier! They couldn't get sufficient food into the trenches when the trenches were only two or three miles out of Santiago—and how would they get it out twenty miles or more, without roads, and with the rainy season on!"[9]

Although there was great concern in Washington about yellow fever attacking the troops around Santiago, Secretary of War Alger was still being misled with generally good reports about the overall condition of the army. Even after the surrender, Shafter did not communicate the full extent of his command's collapse from malaria, typhoid, and dysentery. As to yellow fever, despite his doubts, Shafter was telling Alger that he could move his men to higher ground as recommended. Meanwhile, Alger began planning for the return home of the Fifth Army Corps.

The generals in Cuba did not regard yellow fever as having a major effect on their army, yet. Their real concern was that a devastating epidemic awaited the troops if they stayed on the island much longer. While his medical staff was reporting an alarming increase in the number of fever cases—some fifteen hundred throughout the Fifth Army Corps, many attributed to yellow fever—Shafter and others questioned the accuracy of the diagnoses. Distinguishing between typhoid, yellow fever, and malaria was sometimes difficult in the best of circumstances; for army surgeons in the field, it was significantly harder.

Theodore Roosevelt in his history of the Rough Riders wrote that whenever a man was sent to the rear, he was decreed to have yellow fever, whereas if he was kept at the front, it always turned out that he had malarial fever, and after a few days he was back at work again. "I doubt if there were ever more than a dozen genuine cases of yellow fever in the whole cavalry division," said Roosevelt. "But the authorities at Washington, misled by the reports they received from one or two of their military and medical advisors at the front, became panic-struck, and under the influence of their fears hesitated to bring the army home, lest it might import yellow fever into the United States."[10]

The importation of yellow fever from the front in Cuba to the United States was a real concern. There was little question among pubic health doctors and the public that Cuba was the source of many devastating American epidemics. To reduce the risk of bringing the disease home with the army, a reception center for soldiers was planned on the New England coast. Hearing of the center, several prominent New England senators called on Secretary of War Alger to express their concerns, and planning halted. Still, the troops had to arrive somewhere.

Toward the end of July, Shafter's reports home began to provide more details about the true condition of his army. On August 1, he cabled Alger, "Total sick, 4,255; total fever cases, 3,164; new cases of fever, 653; cases of fever returned to duty, 722."[11] Perhaps more significantly, soldiers' letters home detailed the deplorable condition of the U.S. forces in Cuba. Some of these reports from the troops made their way into newspapers. Political pressure was building to repatriate the army. On July 28, the War Department leased five thousand acres of land near Montauk Point, Long Island, to serve as a reception and quarantine camp for the returning troops. The location had been chosen by Sternberg on July 26. Named Camp Wikoff for an officer killed at San Juan Hill, the land was in a sparsely populated area of far eastern Long Island, about a hundred miles from New York City. Alger recommended to Shafter that he tell his command that they would soon be coming home and ordered him to send a contingent of dismounted cavalry to Montauk Point on August 1. The next day, Shafter emphasized to Alger his and his advisers' concern that a yellow fever epidemic was likely, and that the War Department should order his entire force out of Cuba "as rapidly as possible."[12]

In a cablegram received by Alger on August 3, Shafter finally detailed the deplorable conditions of his army. He told the secretary that moving his soldiers to higher ground was impossible and he described the toll taken by malaria, typhoid, and dysentery. Alger was greatly surprised by the report. He immediately ordered the general to "move to the United States such of the troops under your command as are not required for duty at Santiago."[13]

Also on August 3, Theodore Roosevelt openly handed the Associated Press correspondent with the Fifth Corps a letter to Shafter that he alone had authored. He predicted the "destruction of thousands." And while he admitted that yellow fever was not then a significant problem, the command was "so weakened and shattered as to be ripe for dying like rotten sheep." In the closing paragraph, Roosevelt gave his reason for writing the letter: "I cannot see our men who have fought so bravely and who have endured extreme hardship and danger so uncomplainingly, go to destruction without striving so far as lies in me to avert a doom as fearful as it is unnecessary and undeserved."[14]

According to an Associated Press reporter in Cuba, Roosevelt urged his fellow officers to prepare a similar letter for General Shafter. Dubbed the Round Robin letter, it laid out the views and concerns of the general officers of the corps. They echoed Roosevelt's fears and admitted that yellow fever was only sporadically appearing among their men, but warned that "the army is disabled by malarial-fever to such an extent that its efficiency is destroyed, and it is in a condition to be practically entirely destroyed by the epidemic of yellow fever sure to come in the near future."[15] The army, they said, must be moved at once or it would perish.

Like Roosevelt's letter, the Round Robin letter was also given to the AP reporter in Santiago, and he incorporated the two letters into a story he wired to New York. The next day, newspaper readers across the United States read of the impending doom of the Fifth Corps. The president was furious. He and Alger felt betrayed by their own officers. Shafter most likely leaked the Round Robin report, possibly through Roosevelt. Perhaps he was truly convinced that his weakened troops would be slaughtered by a yellow fever epidemic; perhaps the threat of yellow fever was a red herring to force the War Department to bring the troops home or reassign them to Puerto Rico. The end of combat was a great emotional letdown for the troops, and few saw any reason to stay in Cuba. Either way Shafter, like Roosevelt, must have felt that Alger needed the weight of political and public opinion to carry out his promise to withdraw the army from Cuba. Alger called the incident "a gross breach of army regulations and military discipline" that revealed sensitive information to the enemy.[16]

Although the War Department was already preparing to withdraw the soldiers, the letters may have accelerated the process. The Fifth Corps was quickly pulled out of Cuba and transported to Camp Wikoff. The camp was incomplete and far from ready to receive the corps and other units arriving there. Yellow fever and the fear of yellow fever came with the troops, and a quarantine hospital was constructed on a little plateau that rested on top of a high hill overlooking Fort Pond Bay. Private Charles Post became a patient there but had no confidence in the contract surgeons who were rushed into service. He sarcastically noted that they must have completed only two years of a four-year medical course of study to qualify: "I swallowed the quinine pills [they gave me] but threw away the blue mass, a sort of compound cathartic made from mercury, I believe, and a very popular [yellow fever] remedy nearly a century ago."[17]

When the victorious Fifth Army Corps mustered out of service at Camp Wikoff on October 3, 1898, it had listed 243 men killed in action and 1,445 wounded; 771 were lost to disease. Overall, during the Spanish-American War, fewer than 400 men had been killed in action or died from wounds, while over 2,500 had died of disease. The fact that most of the disease deaths occurred in troops who never left the relative safety of the United States was a scandal.

Among the doctors who served with the Fifth Corps in Cuba was Dr. Victor Vaughan. He had been the dean of the University of Michigan Medical School when he enlisted as a surgeon in the U.S. Volunteers at the start of the war. He was struck by yellow fever at Siboney. He recovered but returned home 60 pounds lighter than the 210 pounds he had carried when shipped to Cuba. Waiting for him in New York was an order from the surgeon general. Vaughan was directed to join another volunteer physician, Major Edward Shakespeare, an ophthalmologist from Philadelphia, and Chairman Major Walter Reed on the U.S. Army's Typhoid Board.

Reed had spent the short war in Washington mainly looking for the elusive yellow fever germ. Now that the conflict was winding down, and the scandalous conditions of the army training camps had come to the forefront, Reed was given charge of a large field investigation—his first such assignment. As they searched for answers to the typhoid problem Reed,

Vaughan, and Shakespeare would also be working under a microscope of sorts themselves. There was great public and political interest in the horrendous camp conditions.

Beginning in August 1898, the Typhoid Board began a study of one of the great disgraces of the Spanish-American War. When the war was declared in the spring of 1898, the regular army counted twenty-five thousand men—completely inadequate to fight an overseas war. State governors hastily threw together regiments of U.S. Volunteers. Regimental surgeons were chosen by politically appointed regimental commanders. Many times they were without either experience or true interest in the military, save for the expected adventure. It was a prescription for disaster that quickly came. Thousands of volunteers from all over the country flooded into training camps located mostly in the Southeast. The surgeon general issued directives for the medical officers to keep the posts as sanitary as possible, but many commanders regarded the efforts as unreasonable or even ridiculous. Within a few short months, 90 percent of the regiments had typhoid fever.

More U.S. troops died of typhoid fever in these stateside camps than died in battle in Cuba, Puerto Rico, and the Philippines. Among the first 171,000 troops called to service—mostly volunteers and National Guardsmen, many unfit and ill-prepared for army life—20,700 contracted typhoid and over 1,500 died. In at least one division, illness rates approached 10 percent. Medical personnel, supplies, and facilities were stretched beyond their breaking points. The Medical Department faced searing public outrage over the conditions of the camps, much of it directed at Sternberg. But the majority of the fault was not the surgeon general's; it largely belonged to the soldiers themselves and their officers, who failed to follow even the most basic commonsense rules of camp hygiene. The board would report that the ground at Camp Thomas in Chickamauga, Georgia, was so fouled with feces that one could not take a step without landing in some.

Ignorance of the basic principles of camp sanitation and preventive medicine led to tragedy, but also to an opportunity to study the cause and spread of typhoid, long a devastating disease in army camps. For several months, the Typhoid Board visited every U.S. training camp, set up laboratories, identified and confirmed typhoid cases, mapped out the camps and occurrence of cases, and interviewed medical and nonmedical personnel looking for answers as to why typhoid had been allowed to ripen and run rampant through the camps. They then spent many more months organizing and tabulating their data.

Both Reed and Shakespeare died before the board's full report, edited by Vaughan, would be published in 1904. An abstract of their findings was issued in 1900 while Reed was working on yellow fever in Cuba. The board produced an extraordinarily well-researched and documented account of the conditions that allowed typhoid to take hold in the camps. Reed and his colleagues established the importance of human contact and flies in the epidemiology of typhoid fever, developed the concept of the typhoid carrier state in healthy individuals, and eliminated the diagnosis of typhomalaria as a disease entity. Most important, they focused the bright light of science on the responsibility of the military commander to protect the troops from disease.

The report helped deflect some of the blame from the regular army's medical corps and its leader. By demonstrating that sanitation was essential for the effectiveness of the troops, the board assigned responsibility for his soldiers' health, first and foremost, to the military commander. There can be little doubt that Reed's leadership, both administrative and scientific, caused him to grow in Sternberg's esteem.

While the surgeon general and his medical department faced scandal and recriminations at home, the mission of the army in Cuba shifted from combat to occupation. With the raising of the Stars and Stripes over the governor's palace in Havana on New Year's Day 1899, the United States formally took control of Cuba. It took charge of a colony devastated by years of civil war and decades of Spanish neglect.

Uncertain of the coming challenges, the United States sent forty-three thousand troops to Cuba during the winter of 1899 to prepare to govern the island. As it became clear that there would be little resistance to the U.S. takeover, many of the soldiers began returning home. As the year went on, the number dropped to fifteen thousand men, mainly with the Seventh Army Corps left in Cuba.

The U.S. government planned a four-year occupation of Cuba. During this time, Cuban nationals would be trained and mentored to assume control of their own country. The U.S. Army was counted on to play the largest role in this interim government. The country was divided into districts, and numerous officers were appointed as military governors. A brigadier general in the U.S. Volunteers, Leonard Wood, was made the governor general of Santiago on the southeastern end of the island. He was both an army physician and a decorated officer who was awarded the Medal of Honor in 1898 for his actions during an 1886 campaign against the Apache Indians that led to the surrender of Geronimo. Wood was the White House physician when he met the deputy secretary of the navy, Theodore Roosevelt, in 1897. Wood's physical stamina was legendary, and Roosevelt, a great outdoorsman, was immediately impressed; the two became fast friends. During the many hours they spent together, they talked of great adventure and vowed not to miss the expected war with Spain. When the USS *Maine* was sunk, Roosevelt had the political clout to get them both commissions in the First U.S. Volunteer Cavalry, Wood as regimental colonel and Roosevelt as lieutenant colonel. When Wood was promoted to brigadier general, U.S. Volunteers, just before the climactic battle at Kettle Hill (popularly known as the battle of San Juan Hill), Roosevelt became the commander of the Rough Riders.

Wood and his counterparts faced significant challenges in rebuilding the former colony into an independently functioning nation. Schools were one of the challenges. Educating Cuban children had not been a Spanish priority, but education was essential to the long-term success of the island nation. Public health was even more urgent. Cuba was racked by diseases, and the death rate, especially in the cities, was closer to that of medieval Europe than late-nineteenth-century United States.

Cuba's cities were filthy; Havana was littered with dead animals, garbage went uncollected, raw sewage ran through the streets to the harbor, and puddles of stagnant water were everywhere. The city, an eyewitness said, was "practically untouched by real progress and . . . years behind in everything except natural and man-made beauty."[18] Conditions in Santiago and other Cuban cities were no better.

General John Brooke, the governor general of Cuba, on the advice of his chief surgeon, initiated an island-wide campaign to improve sanitation. In Santiago, the cleanup campaign began almost as soon as Spanish troops left the city. Recognizing the health threats in Santiago, the city's governor general, Leonard Wood, ordered it sanitized. Teams of inspectors and street cleaners under the command of his medical officers attacked the filth with a "vigor."[19] Within two months, they removed eleven hundred bodies—both human and animal—and carried off up to two hundred loads of trash a day. They began modernizing Santiago's antiquated and inadequate sewer system. Wood, along with his medical officers, personally visited each house to ensure that it was properly cleaned up.

In Havana, Chief Sanitary Officer Major William Crawford Gorgas believed, "as did everybody else," that yellow fever and most other diseases were "caused by filth, dirt, and general insanitary conditions."[20] Gorgas's life had been linked to yellow fever since his birth on October 3, 1854, near Mobile, Alabama. His father, Josiah, a graduate of West Point, was serving as an ordnance officer assigned to the arsenal at Mount Vernon barracks. His mother was the daughter of a former governor of Alabama and congressman. Attending his mother at the birth was Dr. Josiah Nott of Mobile. Although it had nothing to do with his birth, it is an interesting quirk of history, given the role that Gorgas was to play in the future of yellow fever, that Nott had published several years previously a landmark article on yellow fever.

At the start of the Civil War, Josiah Gorgas left the army and joined the Confederacy. He was appointed brigadier general and chief of ordnance by Jefferson Davis. After the Civil War, young Gorgas attended the University of the South at Sewanee, Tennessee, where his father was president. After studying law for a year, he entered Bellevue Medical College in New York City in 1876, graduating in 1879. At Bellevue, he worked with Dr. William Welch, who would play a very important supporting role in Gorgas's career, ultimately defending him before the president of the United States.

In 1880, Gorgas joined the army and began a series of assignments and moves throughout the United States. While at Fort Brown, Texas, he met his future wife, the daughter of his commanding officer, as she lay on what many thought was her deathbed, in the apparent final fatal throes of yellow fever. She recovered, and later Gorgas recovered from his own case of yellow fever. Because of his subsequent immunity, he spent many years at Fort Barrancas, Pensacola Bay, Florida, where yellow fever was common. Unlike with Walter Reed, there is no evidence that Gorgas received any further formal schooling or developed any specific scientific skills. As a yellow fever immune, he was sent to Cuba with the troops when the Spanish-American War broke out in 1898 and placed in charge of the yellow fever hospital at Siboney.

In 1898, Gorgas, like Wood, went to work cleaning city streets that were filled with garbage and rubbish accumulated over decades of neglect:

decaying vegetables, animals, and occasionally even a human corpse. Death rates began to fall, and during the first seven months of 1899, there were only sixty yellow fever cases in Havana and fourteen deaths—a relatively low number of cases and deaths for the city. General William Ludlow, the military governor of Havana, was confident that yellow fever had been controlled by the intense sanitary measures undertaken.

It did appear that the sanitary campaigns were working. Progress was being made in controlling the true filth diseases, such as typhoid and dysentery. Even malaria was being controlled. The recent discovery by Ronald Ross that the *Anopheles* mosquito transmitted malaria led U.S. Army Surgeon Major Jefferson Randolph Kean, who came to Cuba in December with the Seventh Army Corps, to recommend that the troops use mosquito netting. While the netting led to a decrease in the number of malaria cases, its effectiveness at preventing yellow fever would have been much less— the malaria mosquito is generally a night biter while the yellow fever mosquito is a day biter.

On June 21, 1899, the first yellow fever case appeared in Santiago. To protect the force, the doctors started moving troops from the city to safe points inland on June 30. They also began disinfecting the barracks, clothing, and the men themselves. Despite the sanitary improvements, by mid-July there were 158 known cases. Wood reported that the outbreak was confined entirely to the American residents of the city. No Cubans were known to be sick with it. Wood was away from Santiago as the epidemic took hold, and when he returned, he was not pleased with the little progress he saw toward controlling the disease. Feeling more should be done, he wrote, "I tied the whole place up with a cast-iron military order which is going to cause a great deal of kicking, but which I think will save a great many lives, and I hope soon to check the spread of the disease."[21]

General Wood ordered a quarantine of the city. Ships were blocked from docking in Santiago, and no Americans could enter the city without Wood's permission. He and his medical staff could not find a particular point of infection, but they assumed infected buildings were the source. When cases appeared in private homes, Wood ordered them fumigated with sulfur fumes or formaldehyde. Sanitarians spread a corrosive sublimate on the ground outside the infected buildings, then sealed the buildings for a week. No property could be removed from any infected home.

When the outbreak ended in late October, the medical authorities had recorded more than two hundred cases. One in five had died.

While yellow fever was parrying with the Americans in Cuba, a few small outbreaks of it occurred in the United States in 1899. The September 9, 1899, issue of the *Journal of the American Medical Association* carried some editorial remarks on the disease with specific mention of cases at Hampton, Virginia, and elsewhere. The editorial traced the few cases back to Cuba, even though the authors admitted that "but little of the disease seems to be prevailing there." They were hopeful that the cleansing of Cuba would eventually lead to yellow fever's demise:

> It has been expected and we have so claimed in these columns, that hereafter hygiene laws would be enforced, and the disease kept out or at least kept under control. We have no reason to change our views. A complete sanitary inspection of the island cannot be made in one season, nor can the requisite hygienic measures be carried out in a few short months. The rigid measures that have been adopted, and which are being extended throughout the island, will, it may be expected, completely wipe out the disease.[22]

Despite the authors' optimism, yellow fever continued to mystify and frustrate the army doctors charged with defeating it.

The sanitarians scrubbed Cuban streets and even sprayed them with disinfectants. A new one evaluated by Major William M. Black, U.S. Army Corps of Engineers, was called electrozone, a patented process by which disinfectant was made out of seawater. Walter Reed, who had already been to Cuba on an inspection trip after the end of the Spanish-American War, was sent back to Cuba in March 1900 to investigate the worthiness of electrozone before the army purchased any. He concluded that it was just as effective a solution as ordinary chloride of lime, but much more expensive.

Reed seemed to be enjoying his time in Cuba. Instead of indulging in the amenities and fine dining of a Havana hotel during his temporary duty in Cuba, Reed gravitated toward the familiarity and comradeship of the military post at Columbia Barracks. He stayed at the Bachelor Officers Quarters near the military hospital. Columbia Barracks, home to the Seventh Cavalry, was located on a plateau that sloped north toward the Gulf of Mexico about a mile away. Home to nineteen hundred soldiers and about the size of two city blocks, Columbia Barracks had been established as Camp Columbia six miles outside of Havana in December 1898 to garrison volunteer soldiers. In 1899, the original tents at Camp Columbia were replaced by new, more permanent buildings, and the name was changed to Columbia Barracks. The new buildings included field quarters, barracks, and a hospital compound. The buildings of the hospital compound formed a square surrounding a small parade field. These buildings included four or five medical wards, two barracks for the enlisted men, the officers' quarters, the operating room, and the laboratory. There were a few trees for shade and little or no shrubbery, but ocean breezes kept it reasonably cool except in the heat of the day.

While his investigation of electrozone was in progress during March 1900, Reed enjoyed the company of the young medical officers at Columbia Barracks. The Bachelor Officers Quarters with its wide wraparound veranda was washed by delightful breezes in the evening and was the center of after-hours activity. Despite the fact that he was almost twenty years older than most of the young doctors, a career regular army officer, and a very senior major, Reed was described as jovial, quickly putting everyone at ease. Many evenings were spent discussing the mysteries of the dreadful diseases they struggled to understand.

By early 1900, Walter Reed was already regarded as a leader of the Army Medical Corps and was well known for his work as the head of the U.S. Army Typhoid Board. Though not yet published, the findings of the Typhoid Board had made their way to Cuba. Based on the recognition of the typhoid carrier state and role of feces, filth, fingers, and flies in the transmission of typhoid, changes were being implemented among the troops garrisoned on the island. One key recommendation from the Typhoid Board had reached Columbia Barracks in July 1899. It concerned a new apparatus, an odorless excavator system for disposal of human waste. In July 1899, when the system was put into use, 42 of every 1,000 soldiers developed typhoid fever. By October, the rate was down to 10 per 1,000; and by February 1900, it had further lowered to 3 of every 1,000 soldiers. The admission rate to the Columbia Barracks hospital likewise dropped from 200 cases per month in October 1899 to 50 cases per month just four months later.

In addition to typhoid, the young medical officers at Columbia Barracks had treated smallpox, malaria, and other diseases during the past year.

In September and early October 1899, they had even experienced a brief epidemic of dengue fever—unknown at the time but caused by a virus similar to yellow fever's and carried by the same mosquito. As the art of diagnosis began to shift from the patient's bedside to the laboratory, Albert Truby, the post surgeon, had asked the War Department for a full-time physician to assist in the laboratory at Columbia Barracks. The contract surgeon Jesse Lazear, a Johns Hopkins University Medical School graduate from Baltimore with European training, applied to fill that position. At the time of his appointment, he was an instructor in clinical medicine and head of the clinical laboratories at Johns Hopkins' Medical School. Lazear arrived with his wife, Mabel, and infant son, Houston, in early February. He established himself as a quick study as well as a diligent, dependable, and skilled worker. During Reed's stay, Lazear was detailed to assist him. Reed visited his laboratory at Columbia Barracks and was impressed with his abilities and his work. Lazear was eventually put in charge of the hospital laboratory at Columbia Barracks.

During August and September 1899, there had been an outbreak of yellow fever during an epidemic at Cabaña Fortress in Havana and nearby Camp Ludlow, with twenty-three cases and eight deaths. There had been none at Columbia Barracks. Although yellow fever was not a significant clinical problem in early 1900, the threat of it was of great interest and concern. The young doctors were all acutely aware of the ongoing scientific debate over yellow fever among their surgeon general, Walter Reed, and James Carroll and the Italian scientist Giuseppe Sanarelli. They must have been thrilled to have one of its heavyweight combatants in their midst. During the evenings spent on the veranda of the Bachelor Officers Quarters, they undoubtedly asked Reed many questions about his research and where he thought the search for the yellow fever germ would lead. The army doctors surely debated the many theories as to the cause and mechanism of its deadly spread. Reed in turn grilled them on the clinical details of the cases they had seen while in Cuba. Despite his seniority and years of clinical experience, Reed had never seen an active, acute case of the fearsome yellow jack.

One of the young doctors Reed would have quizzed about the clinical aspects of yellow fever was his former laboratory colleague Aristides Agramonte. Agramonte was born in Cuba in 1868, but his family immigrated to the United States when he was three after his father, Brigadier

General Eduardo Agramonte, was killed in action on March 8, 1872, during the First Cuban War for Independence. He studied at the College of the City of New York and attended medical school at Columbia University, graduating with honors in 1892. One of his medical school classmates was Jesse Lazear, now his partner in the army's struggle against yellow fever. Agramonte remained in New York City, working in several different positions for the city and the health department. At the time the Spanish-American War broke out in April 1898, he was an assistant bacteriologist in the New York Health Department.

In May 1898, Agramonte was appointed as a contract acting assistant surgeon in the U.S. Army Medical Corps and worked for several months in the Army Medical Museum laboratory with Walter Reed and James Carroll. The three studied *Bacillus icteroides* and *Bacillus X*. Later in 1898, he was sent to Santiago de Cuba to study yellow fever. Although he had no recollection or knowledge of having had yellow fever as a child, he was thought to be immune to yellow fever because he had been born in Cuba.

For almost a year between December 1898 and November 1899, Agramonte worked on the question of the etiology of yellow fever while in Santiago and later in Havana. He autopsied numerous cases of yellow fever and found the presence of Sanarelli's *Bacillus icteroides* in less than a third of the cases. He also experimented with injecting blood from yellow fever victims into guinea pigs and rabbits; in contradiction to Sanarelli, he reported that it was "not possible to produce any disease even remotely similar to yellow fever."[23] He also undertook some rather frightening experiments by injecting serum for yellow fever patients under the skin of other patients sick with yellow fever. Fortunately none died from either the yellow fever or the injection. Whether they later became sick from the injection of the serum that could have been contaminated with any number of viruses is not known. The results of his research were published in the February 1900 *Medical News*. Several months later, in May 1900, Agramonte was placed in charge of the division laboratory at Military Hospital Number One in Havana, located next to the University of Havana on Principe Hill.

Major Reed returned to Washington in April 1900 and reported to his surgeon general. Although Reed's mission had been to study electrozone, General Sternberg was probably more interested in hearing about the health of the troops in regard to the many infectious diseases present in Cuba. Sternberg was the nation's leading bacteriologist, and yellow fever had been a lifelong academic pursuit. Although a senior administrator, he had been actively involved in the academic debates with Sanarelli, as well as the Marine Hospital Service officers Wasdin and Geddings. Reed, obviously aware of his boss's interest, most certainly pushed for the opportunity to return to Cuba to specifically study yellow fever. General Wood was concerned about the welfare of his troops and interested in seeing to it that yellow fever was brought under control. If Sternberg had any doubts, they were erased on May 19 when yellow fever broke out in Quemados de Marianao, a quiet little village that adjoined the boundary of Columbia Barracks. The first case occurred in the house at 20 General Lee Street, only a few hundred yards from the barracks hospital; other cases quickly followed.

The appearance of the disease at Quemados was not unexpected. The year 1899 had been a quiet fever period, but 1900 started ominously, and many believed it would be a "yellow fever year."[24] The reopening of Cuba to Spanish immigration in mid-1899 brought in large numbers of nonimmunes. Twelve thousand arrived between August and December. They, along with many nonimmune Americans, supplied the fuel needed for a new epidemic. By December 1899, there was a severe winter epidemic in full bloom, but it did not last through the winter.

Despite the new yellow fever cases, the doctors were confident that the cleansing of Cuba would hold the disease in check. Gorgas was particularly proud of his work in Havana. Sanitary conditions were greatly improved, and the falling death rate from all causes was evidence of his significant success. During 1900, the city was "as clean and in as good sanitary condition as it was possible for labor to make it," he said.[25] His wife later wrote that the streets were as clean and orderly as "New York's Fifth Avenue."[26] To his dismay, however, Gorgas noted that the improved sanitary conditions were having no effect on the occurrence of yellow fever. The Cubans, who watched the American sanitary campaign with amused interest, pointed out that the cleanest parts of the city had the most cases of yellow fever. These neighborhoods were home to many nonimmune Americans arriving in Havana. A frustrated Gorgas later wrote, "The health authorities were at their wit's end. We evidently could not get rid of Havana as focus of infection by any method."[27]

The new yellow fever cases in Cuba did not escape the notice of military leaders in Washington. On May 23, 1900, Sternberg issued a request for orders to the adjutant general of the army that would set into motion the most remarkable eight months of medical discovery and accomplishment in the history of the U.S. Army. He recommended that a board, headquartered at Columbia Barracks, Cuba, be established "for the purpose of pursuing scientific investigations with reference to the infectious diseases prevalent on the island of Cuba and especially of yellow fever."[28] There was no question in Sternberg's mind who would lead the board—Major Walter Reed, surgeon, U.S. Army, was the only choice. The other three members were no doubt handpicked by Reed. His trusted and capable assistant, Dr. James Carroll, was to be the second in charge. The other two members were chosen based on a combination of ability and, probably of equal importance, convenience. Drs. Aristides Agramonte and Reed's new acquaintance, Jesse Lazear, were already in Cuba. Reed had worked with Agramonte before and knew his abilities. To confirm his impressions of Lazear from his earlier trip to Cuba, Reed spoke to General Sternberg and learned that William Welch at Johns Hopkins had given Lazear a positive recommendation. Welch's report was all Reed needed to hear; Lazear was added to the team.

The orders were published on May 24 as paragraph 34, Special Order No. 122, naming the four doctors to serve on the board, but gave their instructions as "for the purpose of pursuing scientific investigations with reference to the infectious diseases prevalent on the Island of Cuba."[29] The words "yellow fever" did not appear in the official orders. It is possible the failure to mention yellow fever in the published orders was a political decision so as not to offend the Cubans, or to avoid arousing concern among U.S. government leaders or the public about the recurrence of more yellow fever and possible deaths in Cuba. Continuing deaths in an occupation army after the fighting was over did not sit well with anyone.

A few days later on May 29, Sternberg followed the formal orders with a letter of personal instruction to Reed. He was to report directly to Major General Leonard Wood, now the governor general of Cuba, to "inform him of the object of your investigation and the nature of your instruction."[30] Sternberg, despite being surgeon general of the army, was a staff officer and had no command authority over anybody or anything in Cuba. From his influential position, however, he could call upon the good graces of the local commanders to provide support for Reed and the board. Only two years before, Wood had been a captain in the Medical Corps and well below the surgeon general in rank and even junior in rank to Major Reed.

Despite his meteoric rise in the U.S. Volunteers, Wood was aware that the commission would expire and he would revert to his permanent rank of captain. It was entirely possible he would end up back in the Medical Corps of the regular army. Wood was also aware that any success of the board would reflect well upon him as governor general. He would most certainly be cooperative, but as governor general of all of Cuba, he had many competing priorities.

Reed was also authorized to "obtain from the Medical Supply Depot in Havana such articles as you may require, upon requisitions of the Chief Surgeon, Division of Cuba."[31] Sternberg's statement was further evidence that he and Reed would be dependent on the voluntary support of the local officers in charge. Reed knew well that without the clout of command authority, this voluntary support could take time. He thought the work in Cuba might require two or three years.

In the middle paragraph of the letter, Sternberg laid out the scientific mission: "You will naturally give special attention to questions relating to the etiology and prevention of yellow fever. As you are familiar with what has already been done by other bacteriologists in this field of investigation, I do not consider it necessary to give you any suggestions or detailed instructions. But it is evident that the most important question that will occupy your attention is that which related to the etiology of this disease."[32]

During their preparations before departing for Cuba, Reed and Carroll visited Leland O. Howard, the chief of the Bureau of Entomology, U.S. Department of Agriculture in Washington, D.C. Howard was considered one of the nation's leading experts on mosquitoes and welcomed them to the entomology offices to study the life cycle, habits, and anatomy of any possible disease-carrying mosquitoes.

Just as applied science was exploding within the practice of medicine, the discoveries that connected insects to the etiology of certain diseases were dramatically changing the disciplines of both entomology and medicine. In 1878, Patrick Manson had essentially founded the field of tropical medicine when he made a seminal discovery that the disease lymphatic filariasis, commonly called elephantiasis, was transmitted to humans by a mosquito. Between 1889 and 1891, Theobald Smith linked the carriage of the organism of Texas cattle fever to a tick. Major Ronald Ross of the British army demonstrated in 1897 and 1898 that the *Anopheles* mosquito carried malaria. Reed did not at this time believe that yellow fever was transmitted by mosquitoes, but he was aware that Dr. Carlos Finlay of Havana had theorized almost twenty years before that it was transmitted by the common *Culex*, later *Aedes*, mosquito. Reed wanted to be as prepared as he could possibly be for any line of potential study upon his arrival back in Havana.

Reed and Sternberg had a long conference to discuss the scientific work the board would undertake. Sternberg wanted, once and for all, to quiet the supporters of Sanarelli and his *Bacillus icteroides*. Reed was happy to comply, but knew that this particular part would be quick work and wanted to discuss the next step. He later told a friend, "(I) suggested to General Sternberg that it might be well to study the role of the mosquito in connection with the development of yellow fever, and to that General Sternberg said, 'No; that has already been decided to be a useless investigation.'"[33]

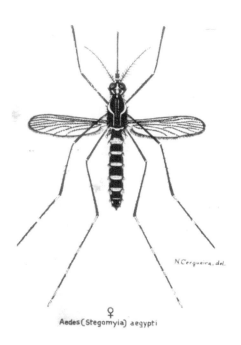

A female *Aedes aegypti*

Walter Reed and his daughter,
Blossom, circa 1900

Carlos Juan Finlay, 1900

The burning of Siboney to eradicate yellow fever, July 1898

Hospital personnel at Camp Columbia near Havana, Cuba, circa 1900

Las Animas yellow fever hospital in Havana, Cuba, circa 1900

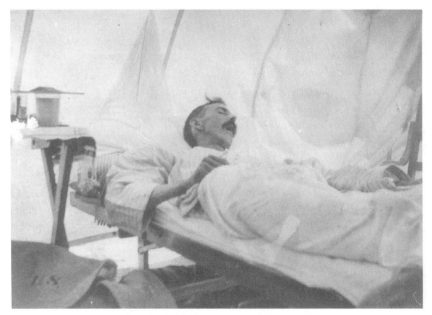

A yellow fever patient in Cuba, 1898

Henry Rose Carter, circa 1915

Walter Reed, circa 1900

James Carroll, circa 1900

Jesse Lazear, circa 1896

Aristides Agramonte, circa 1902

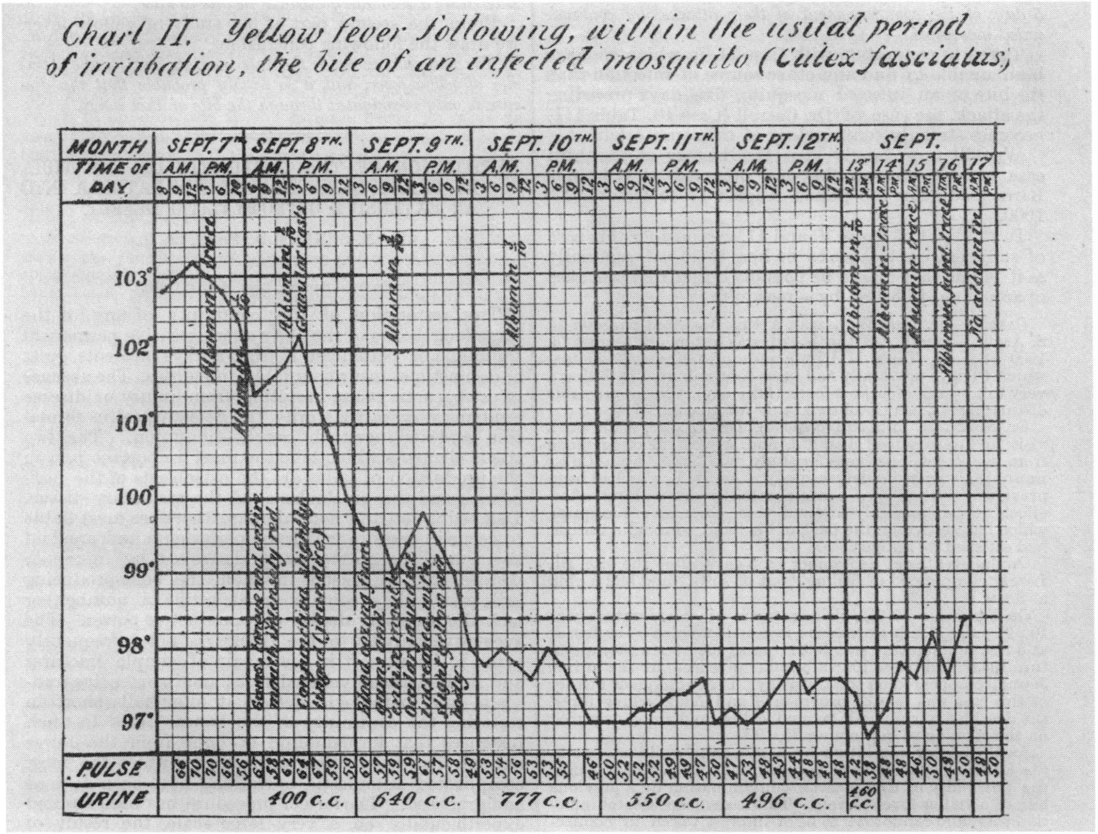

Private William Dean's fever chart, 1900

Infected bedding building (Building 1) and mosquito building (Building 2) at Camp Lazear, circa 1900; photograph taken looking toward the north

Lazear's laboratory notebook entry on the day he was infected with yellow fever, September 13, 1900

The officers and enlisted men of the Detachment Hospital Corps, Columbia Barracks, Cuba, 1900. Nine of the men pictured volunteered for the yellow fever experiments.

Post Hospital, Columbia Barracks, Cuba.

May 30 1901.

I CERTIFY that Private _John R Kissinger_ Hospital Corps,
U. S. Army, whose signature appears below, was admitted to this Hospital
on the _9_ " day of _Dec_, 190 , and was discharged on the _23_ " day
of _Dec_, 190 0. Diagnosis: Yellow Fever.

Roger Post Ames.

Captain, Assistant Surgeon, U. S. Vols.,

Attending Surgeon.

John R Kissinger

Signature of Patient.

-----oooOOOXOOOooo-----

Havana, Cuba.

May 31 1901.

We, the undersigned, members of the Yellow Fever Board of the City of

Havana, do concur in the above diagnosis.

D D Albertini M. D.

Member.

Charles Finlay M. D.

President.

Juan Guiteras M. D.

Member.

W. C. Gorgas.

Major, Surgeon, U. S. A.,

Chief Sanitary Officer,

City of Havana.

Certification of Private John Kissinger's case of yellow fever signed by Dr. Roger Post Ames
and the Yellow Fever Board of the City of Havanna and Drs. Albertini, Finlay, Guitéras,
and Gorgas, 1901

RECEIVED at WAR DEPARTMENT.   Oct, 22nd, 1901.   189

8 CO. G. KN. Government.

                Havana 27.

Surgwar,

        Washington.

            Filtrate positive in two apparatus perfect temperature results ideal three cases five in all outlook very favorable close up return ten days.

                  Carroll,

                      Contract Surgeon.

12:52 P.M.

Cable from James Carroll to Surgeon General George Sternberg reporting the discovery that the yellow fever germ was a filterable virus

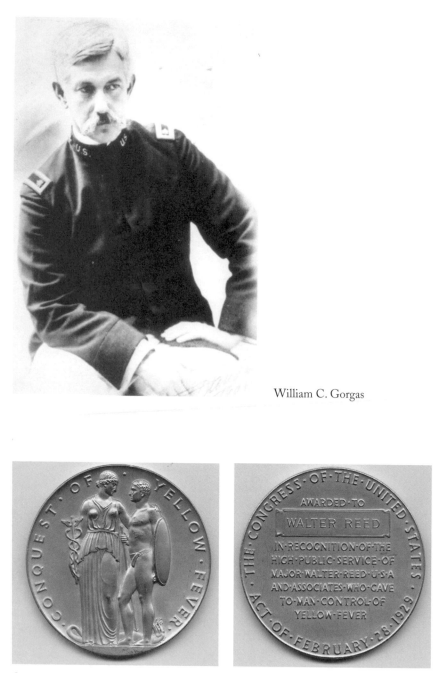

William C. Gorgas

Congressional Gold Medal awarded in 1929 to participants in the U.S. Army's yellow fever experiments (front and back)

Chapter 9

The Opportunity of a Lifetime

T HE *SEDGWICK* MOVED THROUGH THE VERRAZANO NARROWS ABOUT noon on Thursday, June 21, 1900, beginning its regular four-day run between New York and Havana. On board were Walter Reed and James Carroll en route to Cuba and their new duties on the U.S. Army Yellow Fever Board. The five-thousand-ton *Sedgwick* was the former *City of Chester*, the same ship that Reed's son, Sergeant Lawrence Reed, had taken to Cuba in January 1899. As the senior officer on board, Walter Reed had been given the best stateroom, but he shared it with his friend and colleague Carroll. The pair had worked together for the past several years, and while officially they had been preparing for their trip to Cuba for less than a month, they had in reality been preparing for it their entire lives.

In May 1898, shortly after Congress declared war on Spain, Carroll was appointed as a contract acting assistant surgeon in the U.S. Army and for the first time in almost twenty-four years in the army wore the uniform of an officer. A rather unflattering description of him was written by a physician who knew him while they were in Cuba. In a letter home, he said that Carroll is "not a very entertaining person. He is a bacteriologist pure and simple. To me bacteriology is interesting only in its relation to medicine. He is interested in germs for their own sake, and has a very narrow horizon . . . . He is very tall and thin. Wears spectacles, bald headed, has a light red mustache, projecting ears and a rather dull expression."[1]

This was Carroll's first time to serve on the prestigious Army Board and his first real assignment of substance; it was also his first time to see Cuba. Any scientist who begins research in a new field does so with interest, curiosity, and excitement, as well as hope for an important discovery and contribution to the advancement of science. If knowledge, judgment, and intuition lead you to correct decisions, you just may also make discoveries that improve or even save human life. Carroll was brimming with excitement and anticipation of the opportunity to prove himself and thus become his own man, instead of being simply Major Reed's assistant.

Reed never looked forward to a sea voyage because he had to squarely deal with his own humanity and the unworthiness of his "sea legs." He had, of course, been to Cuba before and knew he would most likely repeat the seasickness of his previous voyages. Despite the fact that the bromide he took on the first day out appeared to be working at first, this trip would be no different. His dinner came back up a half hour after he ate it, and he described the second day as "miserable." However, Saturday was a "little better" save for a few episodes of "feeding the fish." Sunday turned out to be "quite comfortable,"[2] and on Sunday morning at one point off the coast of Florida, he borrowed Carroll's opera glasses to survey the shoreline and commented on his sightings of the Palm Beach and Royal Poinciana Hotels. He spent an enjoyable evening on deck that Sunday watching the other ships at sea, including a U.S. revenue cutter with a large searchlight looking for smugglers along the Florida Keys. By nine o'clock Monday morning, Morro Castle had come into view, and he expected to be at anchor in Havana harbor by eleven.

Reed was aroused enough by the sight of the half-sunken battleship USS *Maine* in Havana harbor to write to his wife, "I never saw anything that so touched my inner nature, as the sight of those bare ribs of iron and her foremast sticking out of the water."[3] He thought that every American ship entering the harbor should dip its colors and fire its cannon in salute to the dead of the *Maine*.

While in Cuba, Reed and Carroll were quartered in the Bachelor Officers Quarters within the hospital compound at Columbia Barracks. The location was well known to Reed, as he had stayed in this same building just a few months before. One of the first things he did was head to the hospital to see his good friend Jefferson Randolph Kean, whom he had met several years before in Key West. Kean was in the early stages of yellow fever, when survival is uncertain. Reed was anxious to see his friend, but he also wanted to see his first case of acute yellow fever. At this point Reed, who had only read about yellow fever and heard others talk of its characteristic clinical signs and symptoms, was certainly not an expert on the subject, and neither was Carroll. They were both anxious to get some clinical experience with their deadly foe. Kean, in the fifth day of illness, was being cared for in one of several "huts" across a railroad cut west of the hospital compound and away from the main hospital buildings. These huts originally had been used by the Second Division Hospital of the Seventh Army

Corps for smallpox cases, but they had been abandoned and left unused until the recent yellow fever epidemic necessitated their use as isolation wards. Kean was being cared for by Roger Post Ames and his trusted corpsman, Private Gustaf E. Lambert, who had the general responsibility of running the yellow fever wards. Ames had the most experience in caring for acute cases and was becoming the army's clinical yellow fever expert. In April 1900, he had been transferred from Military Hospital No. 1 in Havana to Columbia Barracks. Reed was relieved to learn that Kean's attack of yellow fever appeared mild and his chances for recovery looked good.

Reed called a meeting of the board for his first afternoon in Cuba. The four—Reed, Carroll, Agramonte, and Lazear—met in a familiar setting, the veranda of the Bachelor Officers Quarters at Columbia Barracks. No doubt other Medical Corps officers attended, possibly even some senior ones, but Major Reed was clearly in charge. In addition to their formal written orders, he had verbal orders from Surgeon General Sternberg and presented them to the board. Agramonte later described the "almost reverential mood" in which they listened to Reed's monologue.[4] The first order of business was to search for Sanarelli's *Bacillus icteroides* in the blood of yellow fever cases and the bodies of yellow fever victims. Sternberg wanted to prove once and for all that this was not the agent of yellow fever. Reed, as the officer in charge, would direct and oversee the work. Carroll, the next senior officer, was considered second in command and would work in the bacteriology laboratory with Lazear at Columbia Barracks. Agramonte would continue his pathology work at Military Hospital No. 1 in Havana. Lazear and Agramonte were not relieved of their primary duties and would accomplish their work for the board as additional duties. In his written description of the meeting, Agramonte recorded that they began their work "like men of honor, inspired solely with a noble purpose, by binding ourselves to give out no result as the work of any one man so that whatever came from our labors might be credited to the board as a whole."[5] Fortunately for the board, the epidemic in nearby Quemados provided plenty of clinical material, and they got right to the task at hand.

Within his first week in Cuba, Reed had settled into the pattern of writing his wife and daughter first thing each morning before the mail came at 7 A.M. For the first several days, he forgot to use Cuban stamps on his letters and used U.S. stamps instead. Despite this oversight, his letters got through. As soldiers away from home had done for years before him, he wrote his letters in almost a frivolous way, dealing with many issues far from the danger of death and disease in which he had come to work. He used affectionate pet names for his wife and daughter; he signed all his letters, "Devotedly, Papa." In several, he went on at length about the joys of the shower bath that he used each morning. His enthusiasm and playful personality often shone through, such as when he used the term "exsqueeze me" for "excuse me."[6]

One early letter described his living arrangements in detail. He occupied quarters number two, the second set of rooms from the east end of the Bachelor Officers Quarters, a one-story building constructed of pine lumber that had been brought from the United States, set up four or five feet above the ground on concrete blocks. There were five sets of quarters in the building itself with a kitchen, mess hall, and bath attached. Reed's two rooms were about ten by fifteen feet each, with a partition between them from the floor to about seven and a half feet high. The partition had a door connecting the two rooms. The front room looked north to the sea and had a large outside door that ran from floor to ceiling. There were windows on either side of the door with glass sashes and heavy wooden shutters to close during the storms that blew in off the sea. He worked in the front room on a long wooden table stretching nearly across the room that he used for a writing desk and for his official papers; there was a coal oil lamp and a long shelf for books. He slept in the rear room on an iron bed with a hard cotton mattress and a mosquito bar (netting); he described it as a "good hospital bed."[7] There was a small wooden table for a washstand, shelves for underwear, and a place to hang his uniforms and other clothes. He had a couple of comfortable folding chairs and a small shelf in the corner for his shaving outfit. There was no electricity, but the Signal Corps had run a telephone line that Reed could use for local service.

A unique feature of the tropical environment he did not tell his wife about were the large tree frogs that gathered at certain times in the rafters above his quarters. The rafters that supported the corrugated iron roof were open to the room below to allow movement of air and ventilation. This openness allowed the tree frogs, which either seemed to enjoy the protection of the roof or were simply out on a nighttime adventure, to fall onto whatever was below when they lost their grip on the rafters. When the wet frogs hit the floor with a loud "splat," it was annoying; when they landed in the bed, it was more than that. Unable to prevent the frogs from climbing the rafters, Reed and the others at least somewhat protected themselves from the cold, wet bombardment by placing newspapers over the mosquito bar that covered the head of the bed. Occasionally during the night, frogs would find their way into the pail of water that the occupant had set aside for washing and shaving in the morning. This problem was finally solved when the officers covered their wash pails.

On his first Saturday afternoon in Cuba, Reed went to Havana to see his fellow physician and friend Leonard Wood, the governor general of Cuba. Reed was nine years older than Wood and had been a more senior officer in the regular army, but Wood, following his successful and well-publicized service in the Spanish-American War and afterward as military governor, was now wearing the rank of major general. They had known each other and their families for some time; well enough, in fact, for Wood to recognize Reed's son, Lawrence, in a hotel lobby in Havana. In a letter to Reed over a year before, Wood had said, "I saw your boy today as he was passing through the hotel lobby, and hailed him and had quite a talk with him. He is looking very well and the work seems to agree with him."[8] In a gesture indicative of his level of support, at the time and in times to come, Wood assigned a driver and wagon for the board members' use. The next day, Sunday, July 1, Lawrence came out to Columbia Barracks to see his father, and they had lunch and dinner together. Reed thought that Lawrence's twenty days of exams for his commission had taken "the flesh off him."[9]

During this first week, Reed was busy setting up his laboratory at Columbia Barracks and making other arrangements needed for the board's work. He found the midsummer heat in Cuba "much less trying than in Washington" and also commented on another of Havana's attractions, mosquitoes, simply saying they "are here in some numbers but not enough to bother me."[10] He does not mention yellow fever in connection with mosquitoes, at least not yet.

An article appeared in the *Washington Evening Star* about yellow fever in Havana, and Emilie Reed asked her husband about it. In response, he mentioned for the first time the presence of the yellow fever epidemic in Quemados, where a hospital corpsman and female nurse who were caring for a Mrs. Edwards in her "infected house" developed yellow fever. Reed reassured his wife that he was not going into any infected houses or seeing yellow fever patients anywhere but at the hospital. Although it probably was not very comforting, he did promise her that if he got yellow fever, "a Cablegram shall be promptly sent to you."[11] In the same July 8 letter, Reed mentioned that he expected to be home by the first or second week of August. The death of Edward O. Shakespeare in June required that Reed return to assist Victor Vaughan with completion of the Typhoid Board Report.

At the time, the newly established Liverpool School of Tropical Medicine in England was sending physicians on expeditions around the world to study diseases in the new field of tropical medicine. The school had been founded by wealthy merchants who sought to do whatever they could to protect their employees as well as their investments. The members of the yellow fever expedition, Herbert E. Durham and Walter Myers, were invited by General Sternberg to visit Reed and the army's Yellow Fever Board. Durham and Myers spent several days in Havana on their way to Brazil. On July 18, Reed entertained Durham and Myers at the beginning of a planned ten-day stay in Havana. Reed shared what information he had with them and put his laboratories at their disposal. He must have thought it important to cultivate their friendship, as he went to Havana twice to see them. While in Havana, Durham and Myers also met Major William Gorgas, Carlos Finlay, and Henry Rose Carter, learning all they could from their experiences and research on yellow fever. After their brief stay in Havana, they departed for South America to continue their expedition. In January 1901, both Durham and Myers came down with yellow fever. Durham survived, but Myers died after just four days of illness.

To ease his family's concern about his safety, Reed continued to write home with details of almost everything but his research. On one trip to Havana, he stopped to pick up a couple of suits he had ordered at a Spanish tailor and ran into Lawrence wearing a white suit and helmet. Lawrence had already ordered two suits, but his father bought him another one, probably in anticipation of his expected commissioning as an officer. In planning his return to Washington, Reed also stopped by the chief quartermaster's office to check on the next transport back to New York.

In late June and July 1900, an unusually high rate of illness and death was occurring at a military camp in Pinar del Rio about a hundred miles west of Havana. Agramonte was sent to investigate what was being diagnosed as "pernicious malaria." Shortly after his arrival on July 19, 1900, he autopsied a patient and determined he had died of yellow fever. Reed quickly came to study the cases. The medical officers at Pinar del Rio Barracks did not yield in their diagnosis of pernicious malarial fever until Reed and Agramonte autopsied another dead soldier, the commissary sergeant. At last the camp's medical officers agreed that they were dealing with yellow fever, which had by then caused eleven deaths. Reluctantly, the colonel in command of the troops agreed to move them out of the garrison into the field, and the epidemic stopped.

The conventional wisdom of the day held that yellow fever was spread by fomites. Dr. William Osler, in his authoritative *The Practice and Principles of Medicine*, said, "Unquestionably the poison [of yellow fever] may be conveyed by fomites."[12] Fomites were classified as all contaminated objects or materials from yellow fever patients (clothing, bedding, furniture, and so on). However, there were many facts that did not support this theory. Because the camp had not suspected yellow fever, none of the usual precautions were taken to protect the soldiers from fomites. Reed observed that to his surprise, of the people most exposed to the fomites, such as the nurses and other care providers, none had come down with the illness.

More baffling was the "guardhouse case" that had occurred at Pinar del Rio just a few weeks earlier. A soldier under close guard for six days, with eight other soldiers in the same cell, took sick with yellow fever and died. He had not had any contact with another yellow fever case or with any fomites. His eight other cell mates who were exposed to him and his fomites remained in perfect health, despite their close exposure to a deadly case. Reed and Agramonte puzzled that it was just as if yellow fever had flown in through the window, touched the one soldier with its deadly hand, and flown back out through the window.

On July 24, letters of reprimand from Captain Alexander N. Stark, acting chief surgeon, were sent to Pinar del Rio Barracks' four medical officers: regular army officer and acting chief surgeon Lieutenant Guy C. M. Godfrey, and contract officers, acting assistant surgeons James F. Presnell, Auguste A. Nouel, and Robert P. Cooke. Godfrey was told to remain at Pinar del Rio, as "Major Reed has written the Surgeon General a full report of your conduct of affairs and you will doubtless hear from him at length."[13] Presnell and Nouel were ordered to New York with the First Infantry. Robert P. Cooke, a recent University of Virginia graduate, was told, "[Your] lack of experience cannot be advanced as an excuse, you were warned to be observant of conditions; let this awful experience be a lesson to you and do not again run counter to advice founded on experience in such matters. While not as culpable as your associates, do not flatter yourself that authorities will hold you guiltless."[14] Cooke later redeemed himself when he volunteered for the yellow fever experiments conducted by the board.

During July, the board's actual studies began when blood cultures were taken from yellow fever victims both before and after death. Carroll and Lazear did the bacteriology work in the laboratory at Columbia Barracks. They drew a series of blood samples for culture from eighteen patients during the course of their acute illness; of these eighteen, four died. Altogether, forty-eight cultures were taken during life, and none grew *Bacillus icteroides* or any other disease-causing organism on a consistent basis. They also performed autopsies on eleven patients who had died of yellow fever, taking cultures from the blood, body organs, and body cavities. Somewhat to their surprise, not one culture grew *Bacillus icteroides*; some pathogenic bacteria were grown but not consistently. At the same time they were doing this laboratory work, Carroll was beginning to look into the idea of studying intestinal flora to determine what role, if any, it might play. Sternberg, who thought that yellow fever entered the body through the intestinal tract, no doubt influenced this line of thought. The board concluded that *Bacillus icteroides* was not the causative agent of yellow fever. The true agent, a virus, would not be found for more than twenty-five years.

It is difficult to pinpoint the exact date that the board members visited Dr. Carlos Finlay at his home in old Havana at 110 Aguacate Street. None of the participants mention it in any of their letters, but it was probably sometime in July, and it is very likely that they met with him more than once. Lazear had worked with malaria and mosquitoes in Baltimore and was the first board member truly interested in pursuing the possibility of mosquito transmission. In fact, Lazear had done his own independent investigations prior to being named to the board. On May 23, he had gone to 20 General Lee Street in Quemados, where the epidemic had begun four days before, and captured four mosquitoes in a victim's room. Over the course of several days, he killed and examined them under his microscope, looking for evidence of the yellow fever germ as he had done for malaria. This time he was unsuccessful.

Finlay was convinced that only the female *Culex fasciatus* mosquito (later called *Stegomyia fasciata* and now called *Aedes aegypti*) transmitted the disease. He must have been thrilled that the Army Board was showing interest in his theory and his work. He was enthusiastic and excited when he gave them some mosquito eggs from the very mosquito he was sure transmitted yellow fever that he kept in porcelain soap dishes. The eggs were described by Reed and Carroll in a later publication as "jet-black color and, to the naked eye, cylindrical in shape, one end of the egg being rounded and blunt, while the other is slightly pointed, the whole closely resembling a Conchita cigar. They measure about 0.65 mm long by 0.17 mm wide at the broadest part. Under low power, the surface of the eggs is seen to be marked by tolerably regular six-sided plates, each of which is further marked in the center is a little round elevation, which gives to the surface of the egg a decidedly roughened appearance."[15]

Finlay told them that the eggs, when placed in water, would become larvae in three days; then pupae would emerge after a week or more; and in a few more days, an adult mosquito would hatch. Thus it would take about ten to twelve days for these eggs to become adult mosquitoes.

The uncertainty over when the meeting with Finlay took place—many authors say the meeting took place on August 1 or even later—supports the thought that there were several such meetings and that different people remembered or documented different ones. Taking into account several facts—such as the time that it takes for an adult mosquito to develop from its egg (at least ten to twelve days), the problems Lazear had keeping them alive for the first couple of weeks, and the known date of the board's first experiments with them (August 11)—the conclusion is easily made that the first meeting with Finlay could have been no later than early July. In contrast, there is no debate that the meeting or meetings took place and that the board took mosquito eggs from Finlay.

Henry Rose Carter was assigned to Havana in 1899 as chief quarantine officer for the U.S. Marine Hospital Service, the forerunner of the Public Health Service. As Havana was thought to be the source of much of the yellow fever that plagued the United States, this was an important position. Carter was born at Clinton Plantation, Caroline County, Virginia, on August 25, 1852, and attended Aspen Hill Academy. He enrolled in the University of Virginia as an engineering student. A leg injury around the time of his graduation made him reconsider the arduous life of an engineer in favor of the more sedate one of a physician, and he enrolled in the University of Maryland School of Medicine. He joined the Marine Hospital Corps in 1879. For the next twenty years, he served along the Gulf Coast of Louisiana, where he observed the strange but uniform timing of yellow fever outbreaks on ships traveling from the Caribbean, as well as Central and South America. Among his observations was that within a day of a ship leaving port, yellow fever cases may occur on the ship but then it was two weeks before any subsequent cases would appear.

In 1898, the year before his assignment to Havana, Carter and his assistant, Dr. Harry Gant, meticulously tracked and recorded the time intervals between cases of yellow fever occurring in the two small rural communities of Orwood and Taylor in north central Mississippi. Based on their observations and analysis, Carter concluded a building or place could not be infected and that the infectious agent "leaving the patient must undergo some change in the environment before it is capable of infecting another man."[16] From his earlier observations and those at Orwood and Taylor, he thought this period was about two weeks and called this the period of "extrinsic incubation." The results of his and Gant's research were published in the *New Orleans Medical and Surgical Journal*, May 1900, the month the U.S. Army Yellow Fever Board was established.

As Carter was in Havana at this same time, he gave copies of his article to Reed and Lazear. Carter even shared with them a version of his manuscript that had not been published, in which he discussed the possibility that yellow fever, like malaria, was transmitted by an intermediate host. On the back of his manuscript, Carter wrote Lazear an undated note that discussed Finlay's theory of mosquito transmission. Carter was impressed with the theory but not by the results of Finlay's efforts to prove it. In his note to Lazear, Carter said, "I think that this is about the argument I made to you yesterday and which you can, naturally, examine better when written out. As I said; to me the a-priori argument for Dr. F's [Finlay] theory has much in its favor and to me is more than plausible, although his observations as I read them are not convincing, scarcely corroborative."[17]

In July 1900, as the board members further developed their plan for studying the etiology of yellow fever, they kept in close touch with Carter and thus benefited from his experience. Carter added a key piece of epidemiological evidence that demonstrated how extrinsic incubation could take place in an insect that would serve as the intermediate host. His observations provided a critical piece of information on the time interval needed for an infected mosquito to incubate the yellow fever virus before it was transmissible, and thus explained Finlay's failures to produce indisputable cases of yellow fever. Carter's findings were another piece of the puzzle that helped convince Walter Reed and the board to seriously consider and study mosquito transmission.

No researcher whom the board considered believable had ever been able to produce yellow fever in any experimental animals. Reed, Carroll, and Agramonte had all tried and failed; this meant that if they were to study it effectively, they had to use human subjects. In his July 24 letter to Sternberg, Reed wrote, "There is plenty of material in Havana, with every possibility for its rapid increase. . . . Personally, I feel that only can experimentation on human beings serve to clear the field for further effective work. With one or two points cleared up, we could then work to so much better advantage."[18]

Reed had been planning for an early August return to Washington to finish work on the Typhoid Board report. Edward O. Shakespeare's death on June 1, 1900, left Victor Vaughan to finish the voluminous report alone. Lawrence Altman, in his 1986 book, *Who Goes First?*, implied that Reed was possibly running away from the very real danger to himself of human experimentation. He said that no military orders were found for Reed's return to Washington, insinuating that Reed took it upon himself, without orders, to return to Washington and thus avoid the danger of experimentally contracting yellow fever. Altman is correct that no orders for this particular movement have been located, but James Carroll said that Reed traveled at will—"he was given carte blanche by General Sternberg to go and come as he pleased."[19] Reed probably knew of Shakespeare's death before he sailed for Cuba, as it had occurred three weeks earlier. Thus, he would have also known of the need to assist Vaughan in completing the typhoid report. Reed's letters home, as early as July 8, indicate that he was planning on returning in early August, although he did not specifically mention completion of the typhoid report. In the July 24 letter to General Sternberg, Reed mentioned that he would be returning about August 1 "in order to finish my other work," a clear reference to the typhoid report.[20]

Carroll described a meeting at Columbia Barracks with Reed and Lazear that took place the evening before Reed left for Washington:

Various theories and probabilities were the subject of constant consideration and discussion. . . . Carter's observations pointing to a period of incubation or development in an intermediate host . . . also the erratic manner in which the disease seemed to jump from house to house, often across a street or farther, without intercommunication between the inhabitants, in other words the transmission of the disease through the atmosphere; the numerous points of resemblance between the modes of dissemination and seasonal occurrence of yellow fever and malaria; etc. These were not new topics for they had been discussed almost daily, and a decision was promptly arrived at to put the theory to a practical test, and if that failed of result, to resort to anaerobic cultivations, particularly from the intestine. The serious nature of the work decided upon and the risk entailed upon it were fully considered, and we all agreed as the best justification we could offer for experimentation upon others, to submit to the same risk of inoculation ourselves.[21]

Carroll said the decision was made by an actual vote.

This risky approach, which would be critical to their ultimate success, had been discussed and approved by both Generals Sternberg and Wood. Reed had been writing to his wife about coming home in early August and must have felt some pressure to live up to that plan. It eased his mind and gave him confidence to know that everything was well organized and under control with the trusted Carroll in charge. He knew that Carlos Finlay had tried for many years to transmit yellow fever by the bites of mosquitoes; in over one hundred attempts, Finlay did not have convincing success. Despite the new direction of their research, Reed must have been reassured that nothing significant would happen while he was away. Regretfully, he was tragically wrong!

After having all of his belongings disinfected, Reed left Cuba for New York on August 2 on board the transport *Rawlings*, which with his sharp sense of humor he dubbed the *Rollins*. His roommate was Albert E. Truby, a Medical Corps lieutenant who was assigned to accompany troops of the First Infantry who were also on board. Truby, a graduate of the University of Pennsylvania, had been caught up in the fervor of patriotism after the sinking of the *USS Maine* and joined the army. Reed knew Truby, as he had been a member of Truby's Army Examining Board. Truby remained in the army for forty years, retiring as a brigadier general after commanding Walter Reed General Hospital. In his retirement, he wrote the only first-person book-length account of the events in Cuba, *Memoir of Walter Reed: The Yellow Fever Episode*. As a young medical officer, Truby moved in and out of the events of the yellow fever story and provided in his book invaluable insider knowledge of the events. Dr. Philip Hench, who over the course of more than twenty years pursued the story of the Yellow Fever Board, interviewed and corresponded with Truby on many occasions and found his memory, even after almost forty years, to be "embarrassingly accurate."[22]

Upon arrival in New York harbor, they dropped anchor off the quarantine station at Staten Island, whose quarantine launch came out to meet them. The quarantine officers looked over their paperwork, and apparently at the request of the surgeon general, asked only Major Reed to accompany them, allowing him to leave the ship early. The other officers on board, including a general officer of the Quartermaster Corps, unhappily had to wait until the next morning. After completing his detail with the returning troops, Truby got orders for leave and then further orders for duty with troops in the Far East. Before he could leave for San Francisco and embarkation, the army determined that his services were no longer needed in the Far East and his orders were revoked; new orders came for him to return to Cuba. When he did so in September, he became post surgeon at Columbia Barracks, where he would play a pivotal role in the further work of the Yellow Fever Board.

Reed took the train to Baltimore and on to Blue Ridge Summit, Pennsylvania, where he was reunited with his family at Keewaydin. He reported on his son Lawrence, who remained in Cuba. Lawrence finally received his officer's commission in August and was transferred to the Tenth Infantry stationed at Rowell Barracks, Cienfuegos, Cuba. Lawrence Reed never saw his father again after those few short visits in Cuba. In Washington, Reed reported to Surgeon General Sternberg and discussed the board's research with him. They had addressed the possibility of human experimentation before, and with the agreement reached with other board members just before his departure, it was to become a reality. In describing his discussions with Reed about the mosquito theory and Finlay's lack of success, Truby said, "I do not think that any member of the board had any expectation of meeting with the sudden success that resulted.... Otherwise Reed would have either delayed the mosquito work or had his trip to the United States postponed."[23] Reed returned to work on the Typhoid Board report with Victor Vaughan.

Chapter 10

"A Soldier's Chances"

BACK IN CUBA, LAZEAR HAD TAKEN STEWARDSHIP OF FINLAY'S MOS-
quito eggs and carefully hatched them. It took a while to get the technique correct, and at first, many of the mosquitoes died. Lazear, Carroll,
and others fed them on themselves to try to keep them alive. Some that
hatched were shipped to Leland O. Howard at the Department of Agriculture in Washington for proper identification. The most distinctive
markings of *Aedes aegypti* are its broad semilunar silvery stripes seen on the
lateral surface of its dark thorax and the white stripes at the base of the
tarsal joints. It has four stripes of silvery scales on the posterior thorax, and
its proboscis is a dark blackish-brown color. The mosquito's wings are clear
and translucent. Lazear took others to the Las Animas Hospital in Havana
to feed on yellow fever patients. Las Animas, a Cuban hospital taken over by
the Americans during the occupation, was where the majority of yellow fever
cases were sent for treatment. It was described in a *New York Times* article as
"beautifully situated on the edge of the city . . . almost hidden by the great
trees that surround it. An avenue of 150 yards or more, bordered by trees
whose high branches meet overhead leads to it from the main road."[1]

Lazear kept each mosquito—or "bird," as the mosquitoes became
known—in a separate test tube. At Las Animas Hospital, he would allow
them to feed on yellow fever patients in the active stage of the disease; this
became known as "loading." He would load them by taking the test tube
each was in, turning it upside down, and gently tapping the tube to encour-
age the mosquito to move upward. When the mosquito was at the top of
the inverted test tube, he would remove the cotton plug and place the open
mouth of the test tube against the patient's skin. Then he would wait for
his bird to light on the patient and fill itself with blood. Once filled, the
mosquito would instinctively become airborne and Lazear would quickly
replace the cotton plug. Notes were made as to the patient or patients each
bird fed on and what day of illness they were in at the time.

Despite Carter's evidence of an extrinsic incubation period of at least twelve days, Lazear did not immediately embrace this idea. Lazear and Alva S. Pinto, another army doctor, were bitten on August 11 by two mosquitoes that had been loaded five days before, but neither got sick. Lazear did nine distinct inoculations, two on himself, without success between August 11 and 25, 1900. Lazear was bitten on the sixteenth by a mosquito that had fed on a yellow fever patient ten days before, on the fifth day of the patient's illness. Lazear remained well beyond what was thought to be the usual incubation period of the disease. Although the one most enthusiastic for the theory, in a letter back home he acknowledged he was discouraged and about ready to give up.

At first, the mosquitoes were kept at Military Hospital No. 1 in Havana for fear of taking them to Columbia Barracks, where there were well over a thousand nonimmune soldiers. As faith in the mosquito theory waned, Lazear began taking them with him to Columbia Barracks.

On the morning of August 27, Lazear was at the Las Animas Hospital in Havana loading his mosquitoes. He stayed until about noon, but did not make the trip to the laboratory at Military Hospital No. 1, instead taking his birds with him back to Columbia Barracks. One of the mosquitoes had failed to feed at Las Animas, and Lazear was concerned that it might die. It had fed on an active case of yellow fever on the second day of illness twelve days before; according to a large laboratory notebook kept by Lazear, this patient was named Mulcahey. After lunch, Lazear and Carroll were in the laboratory attending to their work when the conversation turned to the mosquitoes and the fact that they appeared harmless. Lazear mentioned that one had failed to feed and might die.

Carroll, who did not believe in the mosquito transmission theory, volunteered to try to feed Lazear's failing bird. Carroll said later, "I acknowledge frankly that I was, in a measure, an unbeliever at the time I submitted to inoculation, for the evidence Finlay presented was far from convincing, chiefly because he had worked in a hot bed of disease." Carroll was referring to the fact that even though Finlay's experiments were done in Havana where yellow fever was almost always present, he still had not produced a single case of unmistakable yellow fever. Carroll simply as a matter of fact stated, "I was perfectly willing however, to take a soldier's chances."[2]

At two o'clock that afternoon, Lazear placed the test tube on Carroll's arm and gently persuaded his ailing bird to feed. When it finally did so, it hardly seemed possible that this small, fragile creature could hurt anyone, much less threaten human life. Lazear seemingly did not place much importance on this experiment, as later in the day when he wrote his mother thanking her for the telegram about the birth of his second child and first daughter, he mentioned a possible upcoming vacation as well as improvements on his quarters in anticipation of his family's return but not a word about his yellow fever experiments. Lazear clearly did not have much hope of success on this, his tenth attempt to transmit yellow fever.

Carroll had not been isolated before the experimental inoculation, as it was unplanned. He actually attended an autopsy done by Agramonte and took cultures of a suspected malarial death several days before he was experimentally bitten. A yellow fever victim had been autopsied in that same death room just the previous day. Carroll continued his normal duties, ignoring the "orders" of the board that sought a self-imposed quarantine during the incubation period on those who had been experimentally bitten. Two days after the bite, Carroll was seeing patients at the Las Animas Hospital in Havana but was not feeling well. He was sick when he took an ocean swim that evening at La Playa with an army buddy, Alva S. Pinto. He did a blood test for malaria on himself; it was negative. The next day his temperature was 102 degrees, and as Carroll became sicker, Lazear repeated the blood test for malaria; it was negative again! Could Carroll have yellow fever? If so, could it have been transmitted by Lazear's mosquito? At noon that same day, September 1, Carroll was taken to the Columbia Barracks yellow fever wards, the same small huts across the railroad cut where Reed and Carroll had visited Jefferson Randolph Kean on their first day in Cuba just two months before. On his second day in the hospital, his temperature was 103.6 degrees and albumin appeared in his urine. There was no longer doubt to his diagnosis. The next day he was jaundiced. His life was clearly in danger.

Carroll was treated by Roger P. Ames, the most experienced and best clinician they had to deal with yellow fever. The mainstay of Ames's treatment was bed rest, absolute quiet, and nothing to eat. If possible, the patient was carried to the hospital in his own bed. Once in the hospital he was kept quiet and at strict bed rest, never being permitted out of bed. The only specific medication was calomel given daily in divided doses, followed by magnesium sulfate. No food of any kind was permitted until the patient began to recover.

On September 2, Kean cabled the surgeon general to inform him of Carroll's condition and his deteriorating clinical course. Lazear wrote Reed about Carroll that same day. Gorgas visited Carroll and was shocked at his condition and appearance. In and out of delirium, Carroll tried to explain to Gorgas that he might have been infected by a mosquito, but Gorgas, who knew nothing of the mosquito experiments, attributed Carroll's claims to delusional babbling. Carroll's nurse heard the same story about the mosquito, and in the nursing notes, contributed it to his delirium.

Lazear, who had placed the mosquito on Carroll's arm, was terribly concerned about Carroll's health, as Carroll was seen as somewhat frail and was well past forty years of age. Everyone knew that yellow fever could be much more severe in older patients. The burden that another man, especially a coworker and peer who had a wife and five children, had developed a potentially deadly disease by his own hand must have caused Lazear considerable anguish. However, professionally he could not have helped being excited that the mosquito he placed on Carroll's arm might have caused his yellow fever. This would be impossible to prove conclusively, as Carroll had multiple contacts with potential yellow fever sources both before and after his mosquito inoculation. He could have gotten it in any of the places he had been, no one could know for sure. This lack of certainty as to the source of Carroll's infection would later both anger and frustrate Reed.

Lazear had realized that Carroll's case could not stand the test of scientific rigor and had moved quickly to produce a confirming case. He needed another volunteer whose case would be beyond question; on August 31, the day Carroll took to his bed with fever and lassitude, Lazear had found a volunteer. Except for Carroll's probable case, there had been no yellow fever on the post or in the hospital at Columbia Barracks. Private William H. Dean from Lucas, Ohio, and Troop B, Seventh Cavalry, was about to be discharged from the hospital, where he had been hospitalized for a minor condition, when Lazear asked him if he would be willing to submit to an experiment involving his mosquitoes. Dean, recently arrived in Cuba, had not been off the Columbia Barracks post in almost two months. Lazear was convinced that the mosquito he had used on Carroll had caused his yellow fever, and so he used that same bird and three others on Private Dean, who was experimentally bitten that morning.

There are several different accounts about how Dean was bitten. Agramonte provides the following in his article, "The Inside History of a Great

Medical Discovery," published in the December 1915 issue of *Scientific Monthly*:

Two members of a detachment of four medical officers of the United States Army, on the morning of August 31, 1900, were busily examining under microscopes several glass slides containing blood from a fellow officer who, since the day before, had shown symptoms of yellow fever; these men were Drs. Jesse W. Lazear and myself; our sick colleague was Dr. James Carroll, who presumably had been infected by one of our "experiment mosquitoes."

It is very difficult to describe the feelings which assailed us at that moment; a sense of exultation at our apparent success no doubt animated us; regret, because the results had evidently brought a dangerous illness upon our coworker and with it all associated a thrill of uncertainty for the reason of the yet insufficient testimony tending to prove the far-reaching truth which we then hardly dared to realize.

As the idea that Carroll's fever must have been caused by the mosquito that was applied to him four days before became fixed upon our minds, we decided to test it upon the first non-immune person who should offer himself to be bitten; this was of common occurrence and taken much as a joke among the soldiers about the military hospital. Barely fifteen minutes may have elapsed since we had come to this decision when, as Lazear stood at the door of the laboratory trying to "coax" a mosquito to pass from one test-tube into another, a soldier came walking by towards the hospital buildings; he saluted, as it is customary in the army upon meeting an officer, but, as Lazear had both hands engaged, he answered with a rather pleasant "Good morning." The man stopped upon coming abreast, curious no doubt to see the performance with the tubes, and after gazing for a minute or two at the insects he said: "You still fooling with mosquitoes, Doctor?" "Yes," returned Lazear, "will you take a bite?" "Sure I ain't scared of 'em," responded the man. When I heard this, I left the microscope and stepped to the door, where the short conversation had taken place; Lazear looked at me as though in consultation; I nodded assent, then turned to the soldier and asked him to come inside and bare his forearm. Upon a slip of paper I wrote his name while several mosquitoes took their fill; William H. Dean, American by birth, belonging to Troop B, Seventh Cavalry; he said that he had never been in the tropics before and had not left the military reservation for nearly two months. The conditions for a test case were quite ideal.

I must say we were in great trepidation at the time; and well might we have been, for Dean's was the first indubitable case of yellow fever about to be produced experimentally by the bite of purposely infected mosquitoes. Five days afterwards, when he came down with yellow fever and the diagnosis of his case was corroborated by Dr. Roger P. Ames, U.S. Army, then on duty at the hospital, we sent a cablegram to Major Walter Reed, chairman of the board, who a month before had been called to Washington upon another duty, apprising him of the fact that the theory of the transmission of yellow fever by mosquitoes, which at first was doubted so much and the transcendental importance of which we could then barely appreciate, had indeed been confirmed.[3]

It is quite probable that Agramonte's account, written after all the other principal characters were dead, is not entirely correct. In the early 1900s, there was a running discourse between Carroll and Agramonte, who were not exactly friends, as to the actual events that transpired in Cuba. Carroll said that Agramonte did not know about the mosquito experiments until after the first paper was written by Reed and that he was shocked when Reed read the paper to him just prior to his departure to present the paper at the American Public Health Association meeting in late October. If Agramonte had not known about the mosquito experiments until early October 1900, he could not have participated in Dean's case as he described. Carroll and Agramonte also disagreed on whether Agramonte was at the meeting that took place at Columbia Barracks on the eve of Reed's departure in early August to complete the typhoid report when human experimentation was discussed.

Another version of the Dean case was told by John Kissinger in the 1930s, when he said that Lazear had his mosquitoes bite Dean while he was asleep in his bed on the hospital ward. It is probable, based on Pinto's account found in Truby's book, that Dean was bitten in his bed on the ward but highly unlikely that he was asleep at the time. Despite the fact that this version was written into Sidney Howard's 1934 play, *Yellow Jack*, no one familiar with the persons and events placed any credence in this account. It is possible that Kissinger had heard this as a camp rumor.

From August 31 until September 5, Carroll's life was in real danger; his temperature never went below 102 degrees, but he had not as yet developed the black vomit that often signaled death. On September 5, Lazear was excited when Private Dean became tired and dizzy. Being careful not to revel in someone's illness, he still must have been elated when Dean developed fever and bloodshot eyes. Over the next day or so, his symptoms progressed to albumin in the urine and jaundice. He even developed bleeding from his gums, evidence of dysfunction in his clotting mechanisms and often a forerunner of black vomit. Dean was diagnosed with "well pronounced yellow fever" by Roger P. Ames, their most experienced yellow fever clinician.[4] Like all the others at Columbia Barracks, Ames had not been told that Dean had been bitten experimentally by loaded mosquitoes.

Dean, in the hospital and essentially quarantined before his experimental bite, did not leave the post after his inoculation and thus developed the first case of yellow fever transmitted by the bite of a mosquito that was irrefutable as to its origin. Although bitten by the same bird as Carroll, Dean, who was in his early twenties, had a much milder case and recovered quickly. In fact, Dean was much improved, without fever or albumin in his urine, by the time Carroll was out of danger.

On September 8, 1900, while both Carroll and Dean were still recovering, Lazear again wrote to his mother. Unfortunately only a tantalizing fragment of this letter remains. Bursting with excitement and energized with the thrill of an enormous discovery, Lazear could not help but tell her, "I rather think I am on the track of the real germ, but nothing must be said as yet, not even a hint. I have not mentioned it to a soul."[5]

Very few people actually knew what was really going on. Reed, back in Washington, had been informed of Carroll's illness, but was hundreds of miles away and essentially out of touch with daily events; Carroll, of course, was in very serious condition in the hospital fighting for his life and in no condition to provide guidance, support, or even advice; the post commander, Colonel T. A. Baldwin, was completely in the dark, as he had not been informed at all about the human experimentation. In reality, Lazear, who was not a commissioned officer but a contract surgeon and that for just six months, was proceeding on his own. He had in his hands the secret that had produced certainly one and possibly two cases of yellow fever.

Two days later on September 10 in another letter to his mother, Lazear wrote not a word about the success of his experiments, but with the casual nonchalance of a man on summer holiday told her, "I frequently go down to the ocean in the late afternoon and have a swim. The beach is good and the water very nice. There are always a number of people from the post down there at that time."[6]

Reed was very distressed by Carroll's illness and his own absence from Cuba. In early September, Reed was happy to be able to tell Carroll's wife that her husband was making improvement. Reed then wrote Carroll a letter expressing his delight that he had improved and to tell him that he had completed his part of the Typhoid Board report. On the back of the envelope of Reed's letter to Carroll, he wrote, "Did the *Mosquito* DO IT?" The answer was probably yes, but it could not be proven beyond any doubt. When published by the U.S. Government Printing Office later in 1900, the *Abstract of Report on the Origin and Spread of Typhoid Fever in U.S. Military Camps During the Spanish War of 1898* ran to 239 pages and carried the authorship of Walter Reed, Victor C. Vaughan, and Edward O. Shakespeare. Reed is generally credited with writing the forty-five-page final summary chapter that was a compendium of what was known about typhoid and what they had learned. The full report of the Typhoid Board would not be published until 1904 and filled two volumes of sixteen hundred pages total.

The Carroll and Dean cases certainly raised Lazear's level of excitement and interest in the mosquito theory. Lazear, who was raising and caring for the mosquitoes, had not disclosed any information about his "birds" to the others, as he was probably waiting for Reed's return to do so. Although no document remains to support it, Reed probably either cabled or wrote Lazear instructing him to stop human experiments until he could get back to Cuba. Evidence suggests that Lazear did not comply.

On September 13, Carroll was well enough to leave his hospital bed and return to his quarters. Several days later, Lazear was not feeling well and missed several meals at the Officers Mess but continued to work. On September 18, he was ill enough to stay in bed and did not report to work. That same evening, several of the camp doctors, including Truby, who had just returned from leave, visited him in his quarters and made the diagnosis of yellow fever. A reliable nurse was assigned to him and treatment was begun immediately. His condition worsened, and the next morning he was carried to the yellow fever wards at the Columbia Barracks hospital.

Lazear's was still another case of yellow fever originating within Columbia Barracks in less than three weeks, and of course, everyone was concerned about the possibility of an epidemic, as there had been no previous cases at Columbia Barracks even during the May–June epidemic in nearby Quemados. Lazear apparently told Carroll, who was still recovering from his own case, and William C. Gorgas that he had been bitten on the hand by a mosquito in a ward at Las Animas Hospital in Havana on the thirteenth of September. Lazear said he had visited the Havana hospital to load his experimental mosquitoes. He told them that he had not even bothered to knock the mosquito off his hand because he did not think it was the *Culex fasciatus*, the species they thought might carry yellow fever and the species he was using for his experiments. In addition, he thought he was immune because he had been bitten before and had not gotten yellow fever. Carroll, of course, knew of his own inoculation with a loaded mosquito, but Gorgas knew nothing of these experiments and did not question Lazear any further.

On September 20, Carroll wrote Reed and told him of Lazear's attack of yellow fever. It would take several days for the letter to reach Reed, and in the meantime a cable from Kean arrived on the twenty-third with the stark news, "Severe case, much albumin—high temperature."[7] Carroll's letter arrived on the twenty-fourth, and Reed immediately wrote back to Carroll relaying his anguish over Lazear's illness. Reed, as they all did, hoped that Lazear's age and constitution would pull him through. Reed's scientific mind took over as he went on to tell Carroll that neither his nor Lazear's case would prove anything. Almost scolding Carroll, Reed said, "If you, my dear Doctor, had, prior to your bite remained at Camp Columbia for ten days, then we would have *a clear case, but you didn't!* You went just where you might have contracted the disease from another source." Reed said about Lazear's case, "Unfortunately Lazear was bitten at Las Animas Hospital! *That* knocks his case out; I mean as a thoroughly scientific experiment." Reed expressed his belief in the theory of mosquito transmission but was frustrated over what he considered useless danger. He concluded, "I am only regretting that two such valuable lives have been put in jeopardy, under circumstances in which the results . . . would not be above criticism."[8]

Reed also wrote to Kean, declaring, "I have been so ashamed of myself for being here in a safe country while my associates have been coming down with yellow jack." The surgeon general had suggested that he not return, but Reed said he felt his place was in Cuba doing the board's work. Some writers have criticized Reed for saying to Kean that he would return to his old quarters at Columbia Barracks if there "is no probability of that being in an infected area—that is, on the supposition that Carroll and Lazear may have contracted the disease in some other way than by the mosquito."[9] It hardly seems appropriate to malign Reed for such caution. Carroll nearly died, and Lazear was on his deathbed and, of course unknown to Reed, would die that same evening. Reed himself stated the obvious when he said it would have been "fool-hardy in the extreme" for him to risk getting yellow fever.

Tragically, Lazear had a severe case of yellow fever that progressed rapidly to its terminal stages of delirium, convulsions, and black vomit. His delirium was so severe, he had to be restrained. Lazear had been on top of the world just two weeks before, with a new daughter and a breakthrough on the transmission of yellow fever, but after a brief and terrible illness, his world ended at 8:45 P.M. on September 25, 1900. Jesse Lazear was thirty-four years old when he died.

Kean sent a cable message via Western Union to Lazear's wife informing her of her husband's death, thinking that she had been previously told of his illness, when in fact she knew nothing about it. How shockingly horrible it must have been for Mabel Lazear when she received Kean's cryptic message: "Dr. Lazear died at 8 this evening."[10]

The post adjutant wanted to bury Lazear quietly, as the post was shaken by the mounting deaths from yellow fever. Major George S. Cartwright, the quartermaster on General Lee's staff, had died just two days before. But Albert Truby, now the Columbia Barracks post surgeon, insisted on a proper military funeral. The post commander agreed to full military honors, including the use of the post band. Truby described the funeral in his book: "Friends from the post, officers from the Department Headquarters . . . and the entire medical personnel of the hospital were present at the funeral in the afternoon of September 26. As the cemetery was but a short distance from the hospital, everyone except the nurses walked. We were able to transport the latter in ambulances. Officers, enlisted men, and nurses were all in white uniforms. Carroll, who was still sick, was unable to attend the funeral. Full military honors were accorded and it was a spontaneous demonstration of affection for our lamented friend and co-worker."[11]

Another discrepancy in Agramonte's 1915 article in *Scientific Monthly* is whether he was with Lazear when he died. Agramonte says that he was, but based on leave orders and letters written from the United States during this time, Philip Hench, who researched the issue thoroughly, believed he was not.

Lazear was buried in plot 138 in the temporary government cemetery located on the road that led between La Plaza and Quemados. In March 1901, Jesse Lazear's body was returned to his hometown, where it was reinterred in a family plot in Loudon Park Cemetery in Baltimore.

In 1902, Battery "Lazear" was named in his honor at Fort Howard, Maryland, an active U.S. Army post until 1940. In 1904, a memorial plaque was placed at the Johns Hopkins University Medical School in Baltimore, where speakers included Drs. William Welch, W. S. Halsted, and William Osler. In 1940, the Jesse W. Lazear Chemistry Hall was dedicated at his alma mater, Washington and Jefferson College in Washington, Pennsylvania.

The mystery of how such a careful scientist as Jesse Lazear could have contracted yellow fever has never been fully solved. The story Lazear told Carroll and Gorgas was repeated in the board's first published article. In a matter-of-fact fashion, it reads, "September 13 (forenoon), Dr. Lazear while on a visit to Las Animas Hospital, and while collecting blood from yellow fever patients for study, was bitten by a *Culex* mosquito (species undetermined). As Dr. Lazear had been previously bitten by a contaminated insect without aftereffects, he deliberately allowed this particular mosquito, which had settled on the back of his hand, to remain until it had satisfied its hunger."[12]

It simply does not make sense that a scientist as experienced with mosquitoes as Lazear did not recognize what species of mosquito had landed on his own hand. Lazear had actually taught the others how to differentiate the females that fed on humans from the males that did not. Lazear had worked with mosquitoes in the past, and for several weeks he had spent every day with mosquitoes, raising them from eggs and caring for them in test tubes. Entries in a laboratory notebook in the possession of the New York Academy of Medicine in Lazear's own handwriting identify the various species of mosquitoes that he had captured for study. Obviously, he would have known.

Why then did he tell such a story? After Carroll's and Dean's cases, Reed may well have told him to cease human experimentation until he returned, and Lazear did not want it known that he had gone against orders. Reed did speculate, although there was never any proof of such, that Lazear had a life insurance policy that might not have paid if he admitted to self-experimentation. Lazear's wife later said no such policy existed. Truby wrote in his book that he believed that Lazear experimented on himself. Dr. Pinto and the hospital corpsmen who worked in the laboratory with Lazear agreed. Pinto said in a statement for Truby's book, "The story that Lazear allowed a mongrel mosquito to bite him at Las Animas Hospital is fantastic. Reed discussed it with me. You [Truby] and I, as well as Ames, were certain that Lazear was hiding something regarding his infection. He already had had two cases and in his own mind was certain that the mosquito was the intermediary host."[13] In addition, if there had been a stray mosquito ripe with yellow fever loose in the Las Animas Hospital, why did none of the other nonimmunes who worked there come down with yellow fever?

There are known to be two laboratory notebooks associated with the Yellow Fever Board. A notebook in Lazear's blouse pocket when he died was secured by Truby after Lazear's death and given to Reed. It disappeared after Reed's death and has never been found. Because this was in Lazear's blouse pocket, it is thought to be of the small notebook variety that was used in the army at the time. There was an additional larger laboratory notebook that was used by Lazear and several others, including Reed, to record various experiments and other data about the work of the board. This notebook, currently in the possession of the New York Academy of Medicine, was discovered by Laura N. Wood when she was doing research for her 1943 book, *Walter Reed: Doctor in Uniform*.

The notebook in possession of the New York Academy of Medicine is $8\frac{1}{2}$ by 14 inches; the pages are lined, numbered in sequence 1 to 240, and carry the watermark, Royal Writing. The entries in the notebook are divided into several sections; some entries concern yellow fever patients who died during the Quemados epidemic in May 1900 and studies Lazear conducted on mosquitoes that he captured in the house where the epidemic started, others are about patients with malaria, and still others concern the human experimentation of the Yellow Fever Board. In his pursuit of the yellow fever story, Philip Hench obtained photostatic copies of this notebook from the New York Academy of Medicine. The entries in the laboratory notebook were not signed, so Hench had the families of Reed and

Lazear examine the notebook and authenticate the handwriting of each. Most of the entries were made by Lazear, some by Reed, and others were probably the writing of Reed's laboratory assistant, Sergeant John Neate.

The entry on page 100 is in Lazear's hand. It is dated September 13, 1900, the very day that Lazear said he was bitten by a stray mosquito in the Las Animas Hospital. It reads:

> Guinea pig No.1—red
> Sep. 13 This guinea pig bitten today by a mosquito which developed from egg laid by a mosquito which bit Tanner—8/6.
> This mosquito bit Suarez 8/30
> Hernandez 9/2
> De Long 9/7
> Fernandez 9/10

Earlier pages in the laboratory notebook document that on August 30, 1900, Suarez was in the second day of illness with yellow fever in Las Animas Hospital. This was fourteen days earlier and would mean that according to the facts as learned from Carroll's presumed case and certainly from Dean's case, this mosquito would be ripe and capable of transmitting yellow fever.

Despite the writings of Sanarelli and others, none of the board members thought there was an animal susceptible to yellow fever. Other than this one note, there is no other documentation in this laboratory notebook or elsewhere that the board did any animal experimentation in regard to the transmission of yellow fever. No one mentions it in any letters to family, friends, or superiors. Reed and Carroll had already published negative results in this area, as had Agramonte. Sternberg's position was that "there is, as far as I know, no satisfactory evidence that any of the lower animals suffer from the disease during the prevalence of an epidemic."[14] With the close contact between man and so many domestic animals, Sternberg did not see how animals, if they were susceptible, could have escaped yellow fever during the many epidemics he had observed. The board did have animals in their laboratory at Columbia Barracks, but there is no evidence they were used for yellow fever experiments. There are no later entries in this notebook in regard to animal experiments. If Lazear was truly doing them, why would he stop after just one? He was bitten on September 13, but he did not become ill for several days and could have carried out additional animal experiments. None of the corpsmen who were charged with keeping the animals were aware of any mosquito experiments with their animals. More important, why would Lazear be doing animal experiments at this time when he had already transmitted one indisputable case (Dean) and probably another (Carroll) to humans and he had other willing human volunteers?

After being unable to identify an organism as the causative agent of yellow fever, the board agreed to shift its research to study Finlay's theory of mosquito transmission and had gone to human volunteers. Lazear had been convinced that Carroll and Dean had gotten sick from the bites of his experimentally loaded and ripe mosquitoes. The "coincidence" of all this is almost too much. This is the exact day, September 13, on which Lazear said he was bitten! Although it cannot be proven, the circumstantial evidence is significant that this entry is Lazear's description of his self-experimentation in his own handwriting. A yellow fever virus that probably came from a man named Suarez killed Jesse Lazear.

Several additional observations add to the uniqueness of this entry. It would not have been unusual in this situation to use the words "guinea pig" to refer to a human being. Two of the subsequent yellow fever volunteers used the term "guinea pig" in their own unpublished memoirs of their participation in the experiments. It could be inferred from this that the term "guinea pig" was commonly used by the soldiers of the day to describe a person subjected to experimentation. Therefore it is reasonable to suggest that Lazear would have been familiar with this analogy. Another observation is that this entry in the laboratory notebook is dated "Sep. 13"—a clear departure from the other entries made by Lazear that used a number to designate the month, that is, 9/13. Lazear could have been excited and distracted by the gravity of his self-experimentation, or he could have wanted to make this entry stand out from all the others because of its significance. Lazear said he was bitten while loading mosquitoes at Las Animas Hospital. However, there are no other entries in the laboratory book on this date to support this activity, no names of yellow fever victims and day of their illness as there were on previous dates when he had loaded mosquitoes. The only other entries dated 9/13 are the results of laboratory blood work on Dean and De Long, both of whom were at Columbia Barracks.

In the 1940s, Hench had Albert Truby and Jefferson Randolph Kean study his photostatic copies of this large laboratory notebook. Their thoughts about the events recorded on each page of the notebook were written in their own handwriting on the back of each of Hench's photostatic copies. Truby, who was not actually in Cuba on September 13 but in the United States on leave, recorded on the back of page 100, "Different sections of the book were apparently used for various purposes—malaria—y.f.—etc. This was I think the beginning of his animal experiments as well as the end because he (Lazear) became ill."[15] Unfortunately, Kean made no comments on the entry on page 100.

Hench himself wrote on the back of page 100, "Note that he (Lazear) speaks of a mosquito from egg of a mosquito which bit Tanner and 4 other cases of spontaneous yf at Las Animas. I wonder if Lazear had a chance to do any other animal experiments before he took sick. Probably not. Note that this was labeled Guinea Pig #1. Why did Lazear's notes in this notebook stop so abruptly here? He was probably bitten (accidentally or experimentally) on this day (Sept 13) but presumably didn't get sick for 5 more days."

In reading Hench's handwritten comments, it seems he misinterpreted the words that Lazear had written. Hench understood the note to mean that the mosquito that bit "Guinea Pig No. 1" was descended from a mosquito that bit Tanner in early August as well as the other four patients. This is probably incorrect. The mosquito that bit "Guinea Pig No. 1" clearly descended from the "mosquito which bit Tanner," but Lazear's entry more likely suggests that "this mosquito" was the offspring of the one "which bit Tanner," and that this offspring was then loaded by biting the four other cases, as recorded, before being persuaded to bite "Guinea Pig No. 1."

It is very interesting that none of the three, Truby, Kean, or Hench, made the possible connection between this note and Lazear's self-experimentation, which they all believed he had done. Perhaps Hench's error in interpreting the note led him to not consider it any further, which might explain why it did not occur to him that Lazear could have been referring to himself as "Guinea Pig No. 1." It is most likely that Lazear is referring to himself here and that he provided the genealogy of his "loaded" mosquito to furnish documentation on how it came to be ripe with yellow fever. If the mosquito that had bitten Tanner had also bitten the other four, Lazear would probably have said that "this mosquito also bit . . . ."

In discerning the secrets of yellow fever, Reed probably studied both this notebook as well as the one found in Lazear's pocket. Unfortunately, no one knows what was in the smaller notebook, but it probably contained specific data on Lazear's mosquitoes as to whom they had bitten and when. Despite the fact that it cannot be proven, there is some very interesting circumstantial evidence that this note on page 100 is the record of Lazear's self-experimentation. It is an interesting irony that September 13, 1900, was Walter Reed's forty-ninth birthday.

The notebook in the possession of the New York Academy of Medicine has two loose pages from other notebooks within it. One is a small page about four by seven inches, lined but without a watermark. This page, written by Lazear, contains information on yellow fever patients not involved in the experiments of the board. Truby said this page is of the size that was common for the smaller laboratory notebooks in use at that time, and speculated that it came from Lazear's smaller notebook. It sheds no light on any of the current questions. The other loose page is eight by fourteen inches, not lined, numbered 291 on the front and 292 on the back, and carries a Yorkshire Ledger watermark. This page is clearly from a third laboratory notebook that has never been discussed. The page contains pulse, temperature, and other data on Private Edward Weatherwalks of New Jersey, a later volunteer for experiments of the board. This notebook contained at least 292 pages and thus was larger than the 240-page complete notebook held by the New York Academy of Medicine. With no other information than this, one can only speculate as to what may have been contained in this third notebook. It is known that vital sign data such as this on Weatherwalks were recorded on each volunteer; they may have been kept in a single notebook or pages may have been torn out, recorded, and kept individually in folders or on clipboards. This single page of data on Weatherwalks does not contain any revealing information, so how and why it came to be placed in the larger notebook is a mystery.

A memo found in the front of the laboratory notebook tells how it came to be in the possession of the New York Academy of Medicine. It reads:

In November 1931, Dr. Lowell C. Wormley, an interne [sic] at the Harlem Hospital, told Dr. Bullowa that he had Walter Reed's notebook of cases of yellow fever. Before Dr. Wormley brought the book to me, I heard, third-handed, that when he was working as a medical student one summer at the Army Medical library, he had rescued the book from an ash barrel. He told me, however, that this notebook was amongst the things at the Howard Medical School which had been sent by the Medical Department of the Army, and that he had recovered it as it was being thrown out. One of his instructors had said he might have it. I felt that the proper home for the MS. was at the Army Medical Library or the Walter Reed Medical Centre. Dr. Wormley had tried without success, he said, to communicate by telephone with the authorities at the latter place. He asked several thousand dollars, but on the advise of the Library Committee, I offered twenty-five with permission to go up to fifty. The book was in my safe for some time, then taken away by Dr. Wormley. Towards the end of April 1932, he telephoned, saying he would take what I had offered, namely, twenty-five dollars. It is the laboratory book of Dr. Walter Reed, and besides other notes, gives the urine findings of the group of men who voluntarily submitted to inoculation with yellow fever.[16]

The memo was dated May 13, 1932, and was signed by Archibald Malloch, M.D., the librarian of the New York Academy of Medicine.

Chapter 11

Putting It All Together

S EPTEMBER 1900 WAS THE WORST MONTH FOR YELLOW FEVER IN Havana in over two years: 269 cases, with 20 percent of the victims dead. Had Lazear found the key to the deadly centuries-old puzzle of yellow fever? Despite the surgeon general's desire and that of his family for Walter Reed to stay in Washington, he was determined, now more than ever, to find out. But first, he faced another dreaded sea voyage back to Cuba. This time, however, the bromide of sodium and a calm sea worked for him, and he had a pleasant voyage. Aboard the transport *Crook*, his stateroom mate was another University of Virginia graduate, Robert P. Cooke, a young army contract doctor headed back to Cuba for his new assignment at Columbia Barracks. Cooke was somewhat ambivalent about his unique opportunity of spending several days one-on-one with the well-known and well-respected Reed. This would be a special opportunity to spend time with Reed and learn firsthand about his work, but Cooke had been at Pinar del Rio in western Cuba in July, when Reed and Agramonte found that the medical staff had failed to recognize an epidemic of yellow fever and thus had not taken appropriate action to protect the remainder of the troops. All of the medical officers had received written reprimands, including Cooke. Reed, widely known for his sense of humor and practical jokes with his friends, could be extremely formal and "military" if he thought it necessary. Reed, however, warmed to Cooke, and their conversations were filled with the recent events in Cuba, the tragedy of Lazear's death, and Reed's plans for things to come. Cooke would later be one of the early volunteers to participate in the board's controlled experiments. The *Crook* stopped at Matanzas to off-load supplies for the Second Cavalry. Jefferson Randolph Kean and his boss, Colonel Valery Havard, chief surgeon, division of Cuba, who were in Matanzas on an inspection trip, met with Reed and filled him in on the details of the illnesses of Carroll, Dean, and Lazear illnesses. Following the overnight stay, Reed reached Havana on October 4, 1900.

The medical staff, eager to greet Reed, were gathered at their usual meeting place, the veranda of the Officers Quarters. Depressed as he was over Lazear's death, Reed was anxious to get on with their work and planned on having Carroll's assistance. Reed was shocked to find him still quite ill. Carroll, sick for over a month—an unusually slow recovery time for yellow fever—was still on sick report, and according to Truby he was "quite feeble, depressed and irritable."[1] Reed immediately knew that Carroll would be unable to help him, so he planned to send him back to his family in Washington to continue his recovery. It was almost another week before he was fit to travel, and in order to make sure the trip went well, Reed asked Pinto to accompany him. Agramonte was also home on leave, thus Reed was the only member of the board present to continue the work. Previously it had been speculation, but Reed was now convinced that the mosquito was the vector of yellow fever, but some pieces of the puzzle were still missing.

One of the first things he did on his return was to get his hands on Lazear's laboratory notebooks and other papers. Mindful of Henry Rose Carter's theory of extrinsic incubation, Reed intensively studied Lazear's papers. It had been twelve days from the time of loading until the mosquito bit Carroll, and sixteen days by the time the same mosquito bit Dean. This explained why some of the early volunteers had not become ill after being bitten by loaded mosquitoes, as they had been bitten before the disease had fully incubated in the mosquito. Reed came to the conclusion that the incubation period must be at least twelve days. This would also explain Carlos Finlay's lack of success in transmitting yellow fever, as he was unaware of the length of the incubation period and had all his volunteers bitten before twelve days had elapsed. Reed also asked extensive questions of the medical staff and especially his laboratory assistant, hospital steward John Neate. With Carroll too ill to work and Lazear dead, Reed knew Neate needed help in the laboratory, especially with the mosquitoes. Truby assigned another trusted corpsman, Private John H. Andrus, to assist Neate.

Reed felt that the cases of Carroll and Lazear were not solid scientific proof of mosquito transmission. Dean's case appeared to be more so, but he needed to be sure. He found out that Dean had been released from the hospital after he was bitten experimentally and returned to duty without restriction to the post. Could he have gone into town and there been exposed to yellow fever? If so, his case could also be criticized. Reed asked Truby to find Dean and ask him if he had left the post. When asked by

Truby, Dean immediately replied no, he had not. Reed seemed satisfied at first, but later said he had to see Dean himself. Truby, present on the veranda of the Officers Quarters when Reed met with Dean, recorded the meeting. Trying to put the private at ease, Reed opened the conversation casually: "My man, I am studying your case of yellow fever and I want to ask you a few questions. Before questioning you, however, I will give you this ten dollar gold piece if you will say that you were off this reservation at any time after you left the hospital until you returned sick with yellow fever." Dean immediately replied, "I'm sorry, sir, but I did not leave the post at any time during that period." Reed asked Dean to sit down and tell him all about his experience. Afterward, Reed told Truby that he thought Dean's "a most convincing case" and that based on Dean's "apparent honesty and his straightforward story," he was willing to risk his own reputation.[2]

While still in Washington, Reed had no doubt discussed the dramatic cases of Carroll, Dean, and Lazear with General Sternberg, and they had decided to make a preliminary report of the board's results. They both knew there were others, particularly the British physicians Herbert Durham and Walter Myers in South America, trying to solve the same mysteries of yellow fever, and they wanted to get their information presented to the medical community as soon as possible. Reed had been a delegate to the American Public Health Association (APHA) annual meeting in 1899 and was aware that its next annual meeting was in Indianapolis at the end of the October, less than a month away. Sternberg made the unusual request for permission to add a special presentation to the program.

In order to prepare the most complete and thorough presentation possible, Reed sent his driver to see Carlos Finlay with a request to borrow the just published article by Durham and Myers from the September 8, 1900, issue of the *British Medical Journal*. Durham and Myers had no experimental results to report from their work in South America as of yet, but commented on epidemiological observations, including those of Carlos Finlay concerning the mosquito as a possible vector. They said that Finlay's hypothesis "that the disease was spread by means of mosquitoes hardly seems so fanciful in the light of recent discoveries."[3] Reed also asked to borrow any articles or publications of Finlay's concerning yellow fever and mosquitoes; five of these he mentioned in his presentation.

Usually deliberate and methodical, Reed, working without the assistance of other board members, began a week of frenetic activity. Laboring at a field mess table in the front room of his quarters, he hand-wrote the drafts, and read them to associates asking for their input and criticisms. One of the civilian clerks in the Division Headquarters in Quemados typed the final draft. In a remarkable eight days, the more-than-five-thousand-word report was completed. Equally important, General Sternberg's request to present the paper had been approved.

General Wood gave a dinner for his staff on October 9, 1900, his for-tieth birthday. Aware of the results of the initial experiments, he prophet-ically told his guests, "I have a most important thing to tell you. We have got at the cause of yellow fever. That achievement is going to be of more importance to Cuba and to the rest of the world than anything we could possibly do here. We are going to rid Cuba of yellow fever. But we are going to do even more. We are going to make it certain that at the end of five years there will be practically no yellow fever left anywhere in the world."[4] Even though Wood's disclosure may have been somewhat premature, he was clearly eager to share the incredible news. It is interesting to note that despite his eagerness, he was careful not to reveal the facts of the discov-ery or how those facts had been obtained.

Prior to Reed's departure for Indianapolis to give the board's presenta-tion at the APHA meeting, Jefferson Randolph Kean insisted that he visit General Wood to seek additional support for their research. It would be a singular event in this grand drama of man against disease. Kean later described Reed as he presented to General Wood as "tall, slender, keen and emotional." Reed described his planned experiments and the support he needed for them "with that earnest and persuasive eloquence of which he was a master."[5] It was clear that more human volunteers would be needed to complete their work. Reed felt it was only proper to pay these brave men if they were willing to risk their lives to participate in the research. Because they planned to seek volunteers from the local immigrant population, Reed asked General Wood to seek approval from the Spanish consul. Reed wanted the consul to know that experiments would only be done on vol-unteers of legal maturity (age twenty-four in Cuba), and that they would be provided the best medical care and compensated for their participation. Wood, the physician, had already recognized the scientific validity and sig-nificance of their early work; Wood, the governor general, had a clear grasp of its potential importance to health and commerce. He eagerly offered Reed $10,000 and more, if he needed it, to finish the job. Buoyed by the general's support and rightly enthused about the results of the preliminary research, Reed left for Indianapolis and the meeting of the APHA with mixed emotions. As he departed Cuba on October 14, 1900, he could feel that a great scientific advance was close at hand, but the death of Lazear and the debilitation of Carroll hung like a dark, damp drape over what should have been the moment of a lifetime.

Kean, who had taken Reed to see Wood, was obviously emboldened by the general's reception and response. As the chief surgeon of the Department of Western Cuba, Kean issued a communication concerning the health of the command to the adjutant general of the Department that same day, October 13, 1900. The communication read:

Sir: I have the honor to invite your attention to the following facts and their bearing on the health of the Command:

The role of the mosquito in the transmission of certain diseases is now well established. The evidence is now perfect and conclusive that malaria, as well as filarial infections, are carried by this insect, and there are reasons to suspect that it may be connected with the transmission of yellow fever, also.

Every consideration of prudence, as well as comfort, demands, therefore, the protection from them of the commands at all posts. It is believed that this can be done with a very slight expenditure of time and trouble, by the enforcement by post commanders of two precautions, namely:

1. The enforcement of the use of mosquito-bars in all barracks and especially in all hospitals.
2. The destruction of the larvae of young mosquitoes, commonly known as "wiggletails" or "wigglers," by the use of petroleum on the water where they breed.

The mosquito does not fly far, and seeks shelter when the wind blows; so it is usually the case that every community breeds its own supply of mosquitoes, in water-barrels, fire-buckets, or undrained puddles, post-holes, etc. An application of one ounce of kerosene to each fifteen square feet of water once a month will destroy not only all the young, but the adults who come to lay their eggs. The water in any cistern or tank is not affected in the least for drinking or washing purposes. For pools or puddles of a somewhat permanent character, draining or filling-up is the best remedy. It is recommended that the medical officer who makes the sanitary inspections at each post be charged with the supervision of the details of these precautions.[6]

Two days later, this was passed on to the command as Circular No. 8 with the instruction from General Fitzhugh Lee: "The necessary action will be taken as therein recommended."[7] Kean's memo and General Lee's response constituted the first official military order making the connection between yellow fever and mosquitoes. Fitzhugh Lee, a graduate of West Point and major general in the Confederate army, had been the U.S. consul general in Havana before the Spanish-American War. During the war and following occupation, he commanded the Seventh Army Corps.

About October 20, Lieutenant Lawrence Reed wrote his mother and told her of the tragic deaths of Major Matt R. Peterson and his wife. Major Peterson, the chief commissary officer of the Division of Havana, contracted yellow fever and was hospitalized at Las Animas Hospital. A graduate of the United States Military Academy and former lieutenant in Lawrence's unit, the Tenth Infantry, Peterson was well known and loved. His wife was notified of his illness and traveled from Cincinnati to be by his side. As her husband's illness progressed and it became clear he would not survive, she became distraught and threw herself on him, apparently hoping to contract yellow fever herself. She prayed that God would take her with him and insisted that her husband do the same. While he was still able, he did. Major Peterson died on October 17. His wife, overcome with grief, shot and killed herself that same day. They were buried together in the military cemetery. Not that it lessened the tragedy, but there was a rumor that she had recently been diagnosed with cancer.

On his way to Indianapolis, Reed stopped in Washington to discuss his presentation and leave copies of the board's paper with the surgeon general. Sternberg told Reed that he would send the paper to a proper journal for publication.

Walter Reed read the board's paper, "Yellow Fever: A Preliminary Note," before the meeting of the APHA on October 23, 1900. The paper presented their evidence against *Bacillus icteroides* as the etiologic agent of yellow fever, in that they did not find it in any of their eighteen living cases or eleven cases studied after death. Before detailing their experiments with mosquitoes, Reed was careful to credit those whose work had preceded that of the board. He prominently thanked Carlos Finlay for his theory of the mosquito transmission of yellow fever and specifically mentioned five of his published papers. Reed also thanked Finlay for providing the board with eggs of the species *Culex fasciatus*, which they used in their experiments. He also stressed the importance they had placed on the work of Henry Rose Carter in the identification of the extrinsic incubation period. He then presented the board's preliminary data from their experiments with mosquitoes. They had eleven human volunteers bitten with mosquitoes that had been loaded from two to thirteen days previously. None of the volunteers became ill until the tenth one, James Carroll. Reed presented Carroll's case and then the cases of Dean and Lazear. Reed did not refer to Dean by name but rather as XY, because permission had not been received from his commanding officer for him to participate in the experiments. After Reed's forty-minute presentation, twice as long as scheduled, he gave the board's bold conclusions:

> The blood taken during life from the general venous circulation, on various days of the disease, in 11 cases of yellow fever, successively studied, has given negative results as regards the presence of *B icteroides*. (2) Cultures taken from the blood and organs of 11 yellow fever cadavers have also proved negative as regards the presence of this bacillus. (3) *Bacillus icteroides* (Sanarelli) stands in no causative relation to yellow fever, but, when present, should be considered as a secondary invader in this disease. From the second part of our study of yellow fever we draw the following conclusion: The mosquito serves as the intermediate host for the parasite of yellow fever, and it is highly probable that the disease is only propagated through the bite of this insect.[8]

Based on only one convincing case, Dean's, which occurred when he was not present, Reed had, professionally speaking, "stuck his neck way out," to make such a definitive concluding statement.

After the presentation, Reed wrote Sternberg, asking him to make some minor changes in the paper. Sternberg had already sent the paper to a journal, however, and it was too late to make any changes. The report was quickly published in the October 27, 1900, issue of the *Philadelphia*

Medical Journal with Reed, Carroll, Agramonte, and the late Jesse Lazear listed as authors.

The presentation did not receive much attention in the local press. The next morning, the *Indianapolis Journal* noted only that Reed had been given extra time to finish his "fascinating" presentation.[9] The evening *Indianapolis Sentinel* simply said "the article was listened to with absorbing interest."[10] In contrast, the *Washington Post* was scornful of "the mosquito hypothesis," calling it "the silliest beyond compare."[11] As expected, opposition came from several corners of the medical community, especially from the supporters of Sanarelli's *Bacillus icteroides* theory and from others invested in the fomite theory.

Reed returned to spend a few days with this family in Washington and left New York on Monday, November 5, 1900, on his now familiar shuttle to Cuba. As it was later in the fall, the weather was not as cooperative as on his previous trip and he experienced significant seasickness, "feeding the fish" on several occasions. As they sailed farther south, the seas calmed and he was able to think of other things, mentioning to his wife the presidential election of Tuesday, November 6. Clear in his political leanings, he hoped the voters were busy "burying the big mouth Bryan."[12] A few days later, Reed was happy to find out they had, as incumbent Republican William McKinley had defeated William Jennings Bryan in the national election. McKinley's vice-presidential running mate was forty-two-year-old Spanish-American War hero Theodore Roosevelt.

Chapter 12

Affirmation

REED AND STERNBERG KNEW THAT CLEAR, UNDISPUTED SCIENTIFIC proof was needed. Immediately upon his return to Cuba in early November, Reed went to see Generals Wood and Lee and briefed them on the board's plans. Reed wanted to prove the following hypotheses: first, that the mosquito is the intermediate host and thus the vehicle of transmission of yellow fever; and second, that intimate exposure to fomites does not transmit yellow fever. Additionally, Sternberg wanted the board to demonstrate that the disease could be transmitted by the injection of blood taken from yellow fever patients early in the course of their illness, as had been done for malaria. In order to conduct the required experiments, the board needed a new and isolated location that was free of yellow fever.

Reed left no detail undecided in planning the new experimental camp that was to be known as Camp Lazear. While Reed had been in Indianapolis at the American Public Health Association meeting, Agramonte had looked for a suitable location and had found one about a mile southeast of their headquarters at Columbia Barracks. Agramonte described the open, uncultivated location as "a bit of a clearing, about two acres in extent, surrounded by wild country, at sufficient distance from the highway to discourage social intercourse."[1] After looking at several other options upon his return, Reed found it the most suitable, as it was well drained with no places for water to stand and attract breeding mosquitoes and was fully exposed to the sun and wind. The location was a portion of a farm owned by Dr. Ignacio Rojas, a well-known physician and dentist who was a friend of Agramonte. The ancestral home on the property, the Finca San Jose, was over 150 years old and had come through the family of Señora Rojas's first husband. Years before, when Jesuit priests had leased it as a summer residence, some of the priests had served as volunteers for Carlos Finlay's early mosquito experiments. In 1900, the farm was being leased to Don Antonio Sosa. The location for Camp Lazear was rented for $20 a month, which Major Kean, who had been entrusted with the board's money by General Wood, paid Dr. Rojas, who gave half to Sosa. Importantly, yellow fever had never been known to be in the area.

To eliminate the danger of potential contamination of the camp with yellow fever, new tents and field equipment in original packages were obtained from the quartermaster in Havana. In addition to the initial seven army tents, two small wooden buildings were to be constructed for the experiments, which Reed personally drew the plans for. These became the distinctive features of the camp. The men of the Columbia Barracks hospital detachment built the wooden floors on which the tents were pitched, and did all the other work in establishing the camp except for erecting the two wooden buildings. These were built to Reed's design by the quartermaster with hired Cuban laborers. Camp Lazear was staffed with volunteers who were personally selected because of their military record of good conduct and their interest in the experimental work. There was one acting hospital steward, nine privates of the hospital corps, and one ambulance driver. They were strictly quarantined. The only ones allowed to leave were those known to be immune to yellow fever. If a nonimmune worker left camp, he was not allowed to return. In order to quickly identify yellow fever or any other illness, the temperature and pulse of each nonimmune was recorded three times every day. The medical officers placed in charge of the camp were Roger P. Ames and Robert P. Cooke as his assistant. Truby, post surgeon at the time, described Ames as being overweight and somewhat sloppy in his appearance, but he was their most experienced clinician in dealing with yellow fever, and what was most important, Reed wanted him. Cooke, of course, had earned Reed's respect when they shared a stateroom on their return trip to Cuba just a few weeks before.

The board planned to seek volunteers from the local Spanish immigrant population to participate in the experiments. Volunteers were to receive payment of $100 in gold to participate and another $100 if they became ill. They were also to receive the best care possible if they became sick. Agramonte spoke Spanish and was in charge of recruiting the Spanish volunteers. He described his technique:

> Our method was as follows; as soon as a load of immigrants arrived, I would go to Tiscornia, the Immigration Station across the Bay of Havana, and hire eight or ten men, as day laborers, to

work in our camp. Once brought in, they were bountifully fed, housed under tents, slept under mosquito-bars and their only work was to pick up loose stones from the grounds, during eight hours of the day, with plenty of rest between. In the meantime, as the days of observation passed, I carefully questioned them as to their antecedents, family history and the diseases which they might have suffered; those who had lived in Cuba or any other tropical country before were discarded at once and also those who were under age or had a family dependent upon them. When the selection was finally made, the matter of the experiment was put to them. Naturally, they all felt more or less that they were running the risk of getting yellow fever when they came to Cuba and so were not at all averse to allow themselves to be bitten by mosquitoes: they were paid one hundred dollars for this, and another equal sum if, as a result of the biting experiment, they developed yellow fever. Needless to say, no reference was made to any possible funeral expenses. A written consent was obtained from each one, so that our moral responsibility was to a certain extent lessened. Of course, only the healthiest specimens were experimented upon.[2]

By today's standards, this approach may seem somewhat subversive or even coercive; however, a century ago the consent portion was revolutionary. Although research on humans had been conducted for years, it was not routine to get written consent. There were no army or government regulations that covered medical research and thus no requirements of any kind. The Yellow Fever Board is regarded as the first research group to use consent forms in its research.

Prior to the U.S Army Yellow Fever Board, written informed consent was generally not sought and may have even been unknown in human clinical research of this magnitude. Carlos Finlay had conducted experiments on more than ninety individuals in over one hundred experiments without written informed consent. Sanarelli had reported five attempts to verify his claim that *Bacillus icteroides* was the agent of yellow fever by injecting cultures into patients. He did this without permission or consent. Three of his patients died. The outrage of U.S. physicians and scientists had appeared in 1898 in the *Transactions of the Association of American Physicians*, where Dr. Victor Vaughan, a member of Reed's Typhoid Board, called the experiments "ridiculous." Dr. William Osler of Johns Hopkins went even further and railed, "To deliberately inject a poison of known high degree of virulency into a human being, unless you obtain that man's sanction, is not ridiculous, it is criminal."[3]

Walter Reed discussed the plans for experimentation on humans with Generals Sternberg and Wood, as well as the need for informed consent. Truby said, "Every man who took part in the tests was required to sign a statement that he voluntarily offered himself for the yellow fever experiments and that he absolved the Government from any claims."[4] As post surgeon and thus commander of the detachment of enlisted corpsmen, he was in a position to know whether his soldiers had signed a consent form.

One of Jefferson Randolph Kean's proud possessions, which years later hung on his office wall, was the original of the bilingual informed consent contract signed by Antonio Benigno and Walter Reed. Kean described Benigno as "a jolly young Spanish peasant . . . whom Reed called Boniato, which means a sweet potato, on account of his fondness for that vegetable."[5] Benigno was the first Spanish volunteer to contract yellow fever. He recovered.

In her book, *Subjected to Science: Human Experimentation in America before the Second World War*, Susan E. Lederer said, "They [the consent forms used by the Board] marked a significant departure in the history of human experimentation."[6] The Walter Reed biographer, Dr. William Bean, made an even broader statement in an article published in the *Journal of the American Medical Association* in 1983, when he said that Walter Reed and the U.S. Army Yellow Fever Board were "in a true sense the founder of modern and ethical clinical experimentation."[7]

Reed was concerned that a severe tropical storm that had blown through in mid-November would end the mosquito season and make it difficult to raise the mosquitoes necessary to complete the work. He was pretty sure from Carroll's and Dean's cases that it took at least twelve days for a loaded mosquito to ripen. He did not know how long it would take now that the weather had cooled or if the mosquitoes would ripen at all in the cooler weather. Carroll returned from convalescent leave in mid-November. Despite still suffering from the lingering effects of yellow fever, he reported to the laboratory at Columbia Barracks.

The responsibility of human experimentation weighed heavily on Reed, but he knew it was necessary to complete the research. Although Reed did not actively seek volunteers among the soldiers, Roger Ames let it be known that volunteers were needed. A young private, John R. Kissinger, and a civilian clerk, John J. Moran, stepped forward and volunteered. They refused to accept any payment, stating that their actions were "solely in the interest of humanity and the cause of science."[8] Following their example, over the next three months there were many additional U.S. soldiers who volunteered. All these men knew what lay ahead, as many had worked in the hospitals and had seen the terrible toll of yellow fever. They had seen men die but still volunteered, some repeatedly.

Private John R. Kissinger, a native of Ohio and a member of the Hospital Corps, and John J. Moran, a former enlisted hospital steward at Columbia Barracks, became the first volunteers among the Americans to be subjected to the experiments at Camp Lazear. Howard Kelly in his book *Walter Reed and Yellow Fever* first told the story that after Kissinger and Moran volunteered, Reed touched his cap and said, "Gentlemen, I salute you."[9] Years later, when Philip Hench questioned both Kissinger and Moran about this event, they could not agree on whether they went to see Reed together or alone, but both agreed that Major Reed would not have, and did not, salute them. The Hench Collection contains a February 1905 letter from Dr. Henry Hurd of Johns Hopkins to Caroline Latimer, one of Kelly's primary assistants in writing his book. The letter told of a conversation between Hurd and Reed after he had returned from Cuba and details the events with Kissinger and Moran. According to Hurd's description of Reed's response to their offer to volunteer and accept no payment, he said, "I take my hat off to you, gentlemen."[10]

It is probably within Kelly's "literary license" to have changed the sentence to "Gentlemen, I salute you," but in the military culture that Reed, Kissinger, and Moran operated in, the term "salute" changed the meaning completely. Officers did not initiate a salute to enlisted men. This could be why Kissinger and Moran vigorously denied it had happened. When Hench asked Kelly about the story, he said he could not remember where he had heard it, but that he would not have simply made it up, so he must have heard it from someone. That someone was probably Hurd.

Regardless of the facts of the actual event, Reed would later say about Kissinger in the published accounts of the experiments that "in my opinion this exhibition of moral courage has never been surpassed in the annals of the Army of the United States."[11]

In recognition of his volunteering, Kissinger was promoted to acting hospital steward and presented a gold watch by the chief surgeon of the department. Later he was chided by the other privates of the hospital detachment for risking his life, suffering through yellow fever, and not taking the money as others were doing. He then asked for and was given the $115 balance of the $200 he was due for participating in the experiments and contracting yellow fever. Moran, a civilian who worked as a clerk at the Columbia Barracks hospital after being discharged from active duty in July 1900, maintained the high road. He received no recognition, nor did he ever ask for any compensation.

On November 17, Eugene Wasdin of the Marine Hospital Service, a supporter of the Sanarelli theory, wrote a scathing article that was published in the very same medical journal that had published the board's first article just two weeks before. In criticism of their techniques, he said:

> In regard to the first portion of it (the paper), treating of Bacillus icteroides, it is scarcely necessary to call attention to the fact that the absolute failure of these observers to isolate Bacillus icteroides from the living blood, employing as they confess a method of collecting it entirely different from that employed by us and by other observers, and discountenanced by many authors, simply proves the inutility of the method employed by them.[12]

Wasdin also went on to criticize their effort, saying their failure to find *Bacillus icteroides* was due to "a want of proper conception of the difficulties encountered and the labor demanded in isolating the organism."[13] It is interesting to note that Reed and Carroll's technique of drawing venous blood from a vein in the arm, instead of using capillary blood from the earlobe, as Wasdin had done, is still, a century later, the preferred technique for obtaining blood for culture. Because of the lack of control over Dean's movements, Wasdin also doubted the board's most convincing case of yellow fever, stating that Dean's "case is open to question."[14] Reed and Carroll were familiar with the published criticism of their work and were too busy to pay attention to it.

Camp Lazear opened on November 20, 1900. John J. Moran and several Spanish volunteers were placed in isolation. John Kissinger was not placed in isolation, as he had not left the confines of Columbia Barracks for over a month. As Camp Lazear's first volunteer, he was bitten by a loaded mosquito on the morning of the twentieth. The next day, November 21, a local Spanish newspaper severely criticized the Yellow Fever

Board, accusing it of cruelty and inhumanity in the conduct of its experiments. In regard to the Spanish immigrants, the article accused the board of "experimenting with them by injecting all sorts of poisons!" It also "called upon the Spanish consul to look after his subjects."[15] Concerned that this could endanger their work, the next day all three board members visited the Spanish consul to explain their activities. Agramonte, who spoke for the commission, recalled, "He (the consul) was surprised to hear one of us address him in his own language, having taken us all for Americans on first sight, and when I explained to him our method of procedure and showed him the signed contracts with the men, being an intelligent man himself, he had no objections to offer and told us to go ahead and not bother about any howl the papers might make."[16] With the consul's support, the criticism quickly died.

By November 30, four volunteers—Kissinger, Moran, and two Spaniards (Antonio Benigno and Becente Presedo)—had been bitten by loaded mosquitoes, some of them twice, but none had become ill. Reed found this "somewhat disturbing" but felt it was due to the cold weather.[17] He knew that Carroll's case had required twelve days of incubation in the hot weather of August and that Carter's theory of extrinsic incubation required at least twelve to sixteen days in hot weather. Reed felt it might require more time, perhaps eighteen to twenty-four days in the cooler November weather. Convinced they were on the right track, the board pressed ahead.

In addition to proving the mosquito theory, Reed wanted to disprove the fomite theory, which was almost universally accepted by the medical profession and was the basis for the quarantine restrictions that resulted in significant loss of time, money, and property. While Reed had not actively sought volunteers from the soldiers for the mosquito experiments that he now considered dangerous, he did seek volunteers for the fomite experiments that he considered disgusting but benign. He even asked contract surgeon Robert P. Cooke if he would lead the group. Testing of the fomite theory began on November 30, when three nonimmune Americans— Cooke and Privates Warren G. Jernegan and Levi E. Folk, both of the Hospital Corps—entered one of the two small wooden buildings that were constructed for the experiments. Following the army's precise but unimaginative military protocol, the building was known as Building 1, but to those at Camp Lazear, it was the "infected clothing and bedding building."

This building, designed by Reed, consisted of one room of fourteen by twenty feet. It was constructed to preclude good air circulation and the entry of mosquitoes. There were two small windows, both on the same side of the building, covered with wire screens, glass panes, and heavy wooden shutters. There was a single entrance through a small vestibule, closed by a solid wooden door and divided by a wire screen, to again deter the possible entry of mosquitoes. In the small room heated by a stove to a tropical 90-plus degrees, the three men unpacked several large boxes gathered from, among other places, Las Animas Hospital in Havana and the hospital at Columbia Barracks. These boxes contained sheets, blankets, pillowcases, and other items contaminated by "contact with cases of yellow fever and their discharge . . . purposely soiled with a liberal quantity of black vomit, urine and fecal matter."[18] They opened the boxes, shook out these items, and hung them around the room in order to thoroughly disseminate yellow fever, if it existed in these fomites. Last, they made their beds with the dirty sheets and then lay down to sleep, assuming they could. Despite the repulsiveness of their conditions, they repeated this exercise every night; during the day, they occupied a tent pitched in the immediate vicinity but bravely returned each night to the fetid and foul stench of what Reed termed a pest house. Cooke said, "We all felt like we were coming down with yellow fever every day."[19] Thus the last days of November were the beginning for Cooke, Jernegan, and Folk of a planned twenty nights spent living in the "infected clothing and bedding building."

There had been discussion about having Albert Truby become the board's fourth member, replacing Lazear, but the demands of the army for medical officers prevented it from happening. Captain Alexander N. Stark returned unexpectedly and resumed his position as post surgeon at Columbia Barracks, and Truby was reassigned to the same position at Rowell Barracks near Cienfuegos, Cuba. Normally the reassignment of a lieutenant would have drawn little interest from Reed, especially during the flurry of activity with the experimental work at Camp Lazear. However, this was different because Truby was going to the post where Reed's son, Lawrence, was assigned with the Tenth Infantry. Prior to his departure on November 30, Reed spoke with Truby at length about his new assignment, suggesting that he get right to the problems of mosquito control and thus, hopefully, control of yellow fever as well.

Despite the progress of getting Camp Lazear established, the first of December arrived without any success with the board's experiments. They were fairly certain they had zeroed in on the extrinsic incubation period, at least twelve days in warm weather and probably longer in cooler weather.

However, they had no knowledge, yet, that the female mosquito could become infected only if it bit the yellow fever victim in the first three days of illness. Unknown to them, this had kept some of their initial experiments from being successful, but that was about to change. As Philip Hench said in his description of the coming events, a grim "harvest was about to ripen with a vengeance."[20]

Private John R. Kissinger, who had been at Camp Lazear since November 20, was bitten again, for the third time, on December 5 by five different mosquitoes. Just three days later, on the afternoon of December 8, he complained of a headache before he ate his supper. Later that evening he had a chill, and by 3 A.M. on the ninth he was febrile.

Kissinger's own words excruciatingly describe the onset of this dreadful disease: "It seemed as if every bone in my body had been crushed" and "as if my head was going to burst open. I became sick to my stomach."[21] He was removed from Camp Lazear and taken to the yellow fever ward at Columbia Barracks, where he was cared for by Roger Ames and his trusted corpsman, Gustaf Lambert. Leaving nothing open for criticism, Reed planned on having each case of yellow fever from Camp Lazear examined by a board of yellow fever experts from Havana in order to verify the diagnosis. The news of Kissinger's case quickly spread through the camp. It was particularly harsh news for the three volunteers still in the infected clothing and bedding building. Concerning the news, Cooke said, "Our squad, with one accord, developed chills of our own, concluding that since it was so easy to produce a case of disease in a perfectly sanitary camp, there was small chance for us to escape."[22]

On December 9, 1900, Reed triumphantly wrote his wife:

Columbia Barracks
Quemados, Cuba
Dec 9, 1900

It is with a great deal of pleasure that I hasten to tell you that we have succeeded in producing a case of unmistakable yellow fever by the bite of a mosquito. Our first case in the experimental camp developed at 11:30 last night, commencing with a sudden chill followed by fever. He (Kissinger) had been bitten at 11:30 December 5th, and hence his attack followed just three and a half days after the bite. As he had been in our camp for 15 days before being inoculated and had had no other possible exposure, the case is as clear as the sun at noon-day, and sustains brilliantly and conclusively our conclusions. Thus, just 18 days from the time we began our experimental work we have succeeded in demonstrating this mode of propagation of the disease, so that the most doubtful and sceptical must yield. Rejoice with me, sweetheart, as, aside from the antitoxin of diphtheria and Koch's discovery of the tubercle bacillus, it will be regarded as the most important piece of work, scientifically, during the 19th century. I do not exaggerate, and I could shout for very joy that heaven has permitted me to establish this wonderful way of propagating yellow fever. It was Finlay's theory, and he deserves great credit for having suggested it, but as he did nothing to prove it, it was rejected by all, including General Sternberg. Now we have put it beyond cavil, and it's [sic] importance to Cuba and the United States cannot be estimated. Major Kean says that the discovery is worth more than the cost of the Spanish War, including lives lost and money expended. He is almost beside himself with joy and will tell General Wood when he goes to town this morning. Tomorrow afternoon we will have the Havana Board of Experts, Drs. Guiteras, Albertini, and Finlay, come out and diagnose the case. I shan't tell them how the infection was acquired until after they have satisfied themselves concerning the character of the case, then I will let them know. I suppose old Dr. Finlay will be delighted beyond bounds, as he will see his theory at last fully vindicated. 9:30 P.M. Since writing the above our patient has been doing well. His temperature, which was 102.5° at noon, has fallen to 101° and his severe headache and backache have subsided considerably. Everything points, as far as it can at this stage, to a favorable termination for which I feel so happy.[23]

Kissinger was seen by the Havana physicians Reed mentioned in this letter to his wife (Drs. Juan Guitéras, A. Diaz Albertini, and Carlos Finlay), as well as Major William C. Gorgas. As Reed had planned, they saw him without knowing of his exposure to infected mosquitoes. On their first visit, they did not make a definitive diagnosis, but by the time they returned on December 11, Kissinger had developed jaundice, and they all agreed he had yellow fever.

The distance of almost four decades would not dim the memories of his ordeal as Kissinger later described his illness for Hench in vivid, painful detail: "By the time the doctor got there I felt as though six Ford cars had run over my body. Every bone in my body ached. My spine felt twisted and my head swollen and my eyes felt as if they would pop out of my head, even the ends of my fingers felt as though they would snap off."[24] During his illness, his weight dropped by 30 pounds, from 148 to 118.

Between December 10 and 15, three additional cases among the Spanish volunteers were produced in the same manner and confirmed as yellow fever by the Havana board of experts. These volunteers were Antonio Benigno, Nicanor Fernandez, and Becente Presedo. All three recovered. Agramonte wrote about the events that followed Presedo's case:

> The first three cases (two of them Spaniards) which we produced came down with yellow fever within a very short period, from December 8 to 13; it will therefore not surprise the reader to know that when the fourth case developed on December 15, and was carried out of the camp to the hospital, it caused a veritable panic among the remaining Spaniards, who, renouncing the five hundred pesetas that each had in view, as Major Reed very aptly put it, "lost all interest in the progress of science and incontinentally severed their connection with Camp Lazear." But there was a rich source to draw from, and the unexpected stampede only retarded our work for a short time. Our artificial epidemic of yellow fever was temporarily suspended while a new batch of susceptible material was brought in, observed and selected.[25]

Despite Agramonte's statement, there was at least one of the Spanish volunteers who remained. Jose Martinez was bitten on December 17 and 24 without resultant illness.

This unplanned break in the production of experimental yellow fever at Camp Lazear gave the board an opportunity to demonstrate that the camp itself was not infected. This proved to be the situation when no new cases developed between December 15 and December 25, when another volunteer became ill. Prior to the work of the Yellow Fever Board, buildings and towns were thought to be infected and therefore dangerous. Recall the infamous incident during the Spanish-American War in 1898, when Siboney, a town on the southeast sea coast of Cuba, was burned to the ground because it was believed to be infected with yellow fever.

Years later, William Crawford Gorgas would publish *Sanitation in Panama*, which contains an amazingly cynical account of events that took place at Camp Lazear in December 1900, possibly referring to the departure of the Spanish volunteers from the camp. Published fifteen years after the events, his story is inaccurate in several areas. It is true that the first two cases occurred in August, but otherwise his dates are off. Gorgas implies the research stopped in August 1900, but Camp Lazear was not opened until November 1900. Reed was not in Cuba in late August; he was in the United States writing the report of the Typhoid Board. The amount of money paid to the volunteers was $200, not $250. The most extraordinary part of this story, which is not found in any other accounts of the events in Cuba, is the cynicism Gorgas displays toward the U.S. soldiers in the last paragraph. It is difficult to understand why Gorgas, who was the surgeon general of the U.S. Army at the time his book was published, would so demean the motives and belittle the suffering of the young American soldiers for the sake of what may have been a "rumor" floating around Havana.

His [Reed's] first nine cases bitten between August 11 and August 25 were unsuccessful. The next two, bitten on August 27 and August 31, were positive and well-marked cases of yellow fever.

Dr. Reed's work was now brought to a standstill. He found that all his Spaniards were deserting, and that he could get no more for love or money to come to the camp. The work from being much sought had become very unpopular. For some time he was unable to find any good reason for this. The story in Havana was that the American soldiers, who were doing the guard duty for the camp, had found an old lime kiln in the lower part of the grounds. In this kiln they placed a lot of bleached old bones, and here they would take the newly arrived Spaniards and darkly insinuate that these were the bones of their predecessors in Dr. Reed's camp, and that if they did not leave before they were bitten by Dr. Reed's mosquitoes, their bones would soon be bleaching in the same place. It was useless for Dr. Reed to argue and explain. This ocular evidence was too strong for any argument by word of mouth, and Dr. Reed had to give it up.

Our soldiers had seen that the disease was very mild; that the patients while they were in camp had the very best of high living and a mighty good time, and when they left, were presented with a gratification of two hundred and fifty dollars in shining gold coin. They concluded that this was too good for Gallegos, and belonged of right of birth to natural-born Americans. When the Spaniards had decamped, our men came forward and volunteered. Dr. Reed accepted them, and the work went forward.[26]

On December 12, a new box of soiled materials was added to the nasty collection at the infected clothing and bedding building, or fomite house. This particular box from the Las Animas Hospital was loaded with articles heavily soiled with bloody stools from a fatal case and had been packed and closed for several days. When the box was opened, the odor was so overwhelming that the three soldiers had to run from the house into the night air, where one vomited in an uncontrollable visceral response to what he had experienced. Agramonte wrote that "with a courage and determination worthy only of such a cause, they went back into the building and passed a more or less sleepless night, in the midst of indescribable filth and overwhelming stench."[27] On December 19, 1900, the greatly relieved Robert Cooke and Privates Jernegan and Folk completed their planned twenty-night stay. They were placed in isolation for another five days, where they all remained well. On December 21, two new soldier volunteers, Privates Edward Weatherwalks and James L. Hanberry, entered Building 1 and began their twenty-night stay.

In another letter to his wife, Reed addressed the subject of the fomite theory and its general acceptance among the medical profession. He told her, "They were simply accepting the statements of others who had nothing on which to base such statements. A little careful testing of this theory has served to knock it to smithereens. I thank God that I did not accept anybody's opinion on this subject, but determined to put it to a thorough test with human beings in order to see what would happen."[28]

A dinner to honor Carlos Finlay was arranged by Major General Leonard Wood at Delmonico's in Havana for December 22, 1900. It was attended by dozens of physicians from Havana, and Finlay's good friend Juan Guitéras was the master of ceremonies. Wood, of course, was in attendance, along with Gorgas and Kean, as well as Reed and Agramonte. Juan

Guitéras likened Finlay to Sir Patrick Manson, who had proposed that mosquitoes carried malaria, and Reed to Ronald Ross, who had proven it. Finlay was lavished with praise by many who had previously ridiculed him; to cap off the evening, he was presented with a bronze statuette. Reed, who may have been beginning to rest easy about the safety of his volunteers, thoroughly enjoyed the evening.

Carroll was probably suffering from depression about his slow recovery from yellow fever and was the only principal of the board who did not attend the Finlay dinner. His reason was that he "had no evening dress and no blue uniform to wear."[29] It is probable that he did not have one because he could not afford to buy one. He had been a contract physician and thus authorized to wear the uniform of an officer for over two years, but officer's uniforms were obviously different from the enlisted uniforms that he owned and were quite expensive. With a family of five children, he probably could not afford the luxury of such an infrequently used uniform. Carroll was also becoming resentful of Reed, his longtime friend and mentor. Reed had not suffered the ravages of yellow fever that Carroll had, and thus far, had not volunteered for any of the experiments. Intellectually, Carroll knew it would be folly for Reed to do so, but personally he could not help but think that he himself had risked so much and had received so little in return. He was forty-six years old, a physician for almost ten years, twenty-six years in the army, and just a lieutenant. Of course, Reed was a few years older and had always been an officer, but why was he getting all the credit, having taken minimal risk? And what about the others whom he had known for so long? Kean was six years younger than Carroll and wore the rank of major. Wood, also six years younger than Carroll, had been a Medical Corps captain just months ago and now wore the two stars of a major general! When would anything good happen to him? Unknown to Carroll, Reed was doing all he could to try to get him promoted. In multiple letters to the surgeon general, Reed sought a promotion for Carroll, but to no avail. Unfortunately, Carroll was developing a resentment and anger that would haunt and embitter him for the rest of his life.

In late November 1900, Jefferson Randolph Kean had been made acting chief surgeon, Division of Cuba because of the absence of Colonel Valery Havard, who was in the United States on leave. Kean took advantage of his acting position and was responsible for getting General Wood to approve an expansion, to all military units in Cuba, of his earlier order for the universal use of mosquito bars and mosquito control measures. This order, General Order No. 6, Headquarters Department of Cuba, Havana, was issued on December 21, 1900.

While the mid-December ten-day break from new experimental cases was not planned, an experiment to address the question of whether a house could become infected with yellow fever was planned in the other small wooden house constructed at Camp Lazear. Building 2, the "infected mosquito building," was on the opposite side of a small valley, about eighty yards from Building 1 and about seventy-five yards from the camp proper. The two small buildings faced each other, with Building 1 facing south and Building 2 facing north. Similar to Building 1, Building 2 was also fourteen by twenty feet in size but was divided into two areas by a wire screen partition. The only furniture in the building was three beds, one in the mosquito half and two in the "control," or nonmosquito, side. The beds and bedding had been disinfected by steam. On December 21, 1900, at noon, John J. Moran, who had earlier been bitten by loaded mosquitoes without result, entered the mosquito side of the building, where fifteen loaded mosquitoes had been freed. Moran, wearing only his nightshirt, lay down on the bed for thirty minutes, during which time he was bitten by seven mosquitoes. Later that afternoon and again the next day, he entered the room twice more and was bitten a total of fifteen times. From the mosquito-free side of the screen, Reed observed Moran being bitten. Also on the nonmosquito side of the room were two volunteers who served as controls; they, of course, were not bitten, as the mosquitoes could not get to them. They were required to sleep in the infected mosquito building for eighteen additional nights, breathing the same air as had Moran. Four days after he first entered the infected mosquito building, John Moran awoke with dizziness and headache, not such a good beginning to Christmas morning. For soldiers away from home, the holidays are always a particularly difficult time, but this would be a Christmas Moran would never forget. By early afternoon he had a fever, and later that day he was removed to the yellow fever ward at Columbia Barracks. The Havana board of experts diagnosed yellow fever. Moran later described his diet and treatment. "I was allowed cracked ice ad libitum, small sips of strained watermelon juice, tablespoonful quantities of champagne, ice pack and ice enemas, all intended to keep down the temperature and assist the kidneys in functioning."[30]

The two soldiers, whose names are unknown, were not exposed to the mosquitoes and continued to sleep in Building 2 until January 8, 1901. They remained well and in good health. On December 28, Private Warren

Jernegan, who just the week before had left the fomite house, volunteered again and entered the mosquito side of the building, where he was bitten, but by only one mosquito. He returned the next day and was bitten again, but only once this time. He remained well, probably because these surviving mosquitoes were not "ripe," as those that had bitten Moran had obviously been. With this experiment, the Yellow Fever Board had proven that houses become infected only by the presence of infected mosquitoes.

Walter Reed's last letter of the year was written on New Year's Eve. His words speak to the sense of accomplishment that enveloped the members of the board. A portion of this letter is shown below, and as did all his letters, it showed great affection for his wife and daughter.

Columbia Barracks,
Quemados, Cuba

11: 50 p.m. Dec 31, 1900 Only ten minutes of the old century remain, lovie, dear. Here I have been sitting, reading that most wonderful book,—La Roche on Yellow Fever—written in 1853. Forty-seven years later it has been permitted to me and my assistants to lift the impenetrable veil that has surrounded the causation of this most dreadful pest of humanity and to put it on a rational and scientific basis. I thank God that this has been accomplished during the latter days of the old century. May its cure be wrought in the *early* days of the new century! The prayer that has been mine for twenty or more years, that I might be permitted in some way or sometime to do something to alleviate human suffering has been answered! *12 midnight* A thousand happy New Years to my precious, thrice precious wife and daughter! Congratulations to my sweet girls on their good health on the arrival of the new century. Hark! there go the twenty-four buglers all in concert, sounding "taps" for the old year! How beautiful it floats through the midnight air and how appropriate! Goodnight my great joys, a thousand sweet dreams of father and dear brother! Kisses and love and love and kisses for my precious girls in these first minutes of the 20th century.[31]

Chapter 13

Presentation

GENERAL STERNBERG HAD MADE IT CLEAR FOR MONTHS THAT IT was his desire to conduct experiments by injecting blood taken from acute yellow fever patients into volunteers to see if the disease could be transmitted in this manner, as had been shown for malaria. Reed wrote Sternberg in mid-December 1900, informing him of the successful mosquito bite experiments and asking if he still wanted to carry out the blood injection experiments. Reed asked in such a way as to indicate that he thought them unnecessary. However, Sternberg's response was a definite affirmative; therefore, on December 26, 1900, a Spanish volunteer named Alvarez was injected beneath his skin with 2 cc of blood taken from the vein of an acutely ill yellow fever patient. Alvarez remained well, as he did later after the subsequent bite by a mosquito that had already proved to be able to convey yellow fever. Despite the screening and questioning, Alvarez obviously had already had yellow fever and may have not known it or may have withheld the information in hopes of receiving the monetary reward.

On December 30, a Spanish volunteer named Jose Martinez was bitten by four mosquitoes, seventeen days after their loading. Four days later on January 3, 1901, Martinez became ill and developed a typical case of yellow fever. Martinez had been bitten twice before by the same mosquitoes, originally on December 17 by fourteen mosquitoes and on December 24 by the remaining seven of the original fourteen. No illness developed either time. Prior to Martinez's first inoculation on December 17, the mosquitoes had been taken to the men's tents and applied there; however, on the seventeenth, Martinez went to a special room attached to the mosquito building where mosquitoes were kept in jars at summer temperatures. In this special room, the volunteers were bitten after placing their hand into a mosquito-laden jar. Martinez's third inoculation on December 30 was the charm. Apparently, Martinez was the only Spanish volunteer who had remained at Camp Lazear after the cluster of cases in mid-December sent all the others scurrying away. This case, along with other careful observations the board had made, proved that the time required for the mosquito to become "ripe" and thus able to transmit yellow fever was between eleven and fourteen days. Martinez recovered.

On January 4, 1901, Private Warren Jernegan became the only volunteer to participate in and complete the cycle of experiments when he was injected beneath his skin with 2 cc of blood taken from Jose Martinez on the second day of his illness. Four days later, Jernegan became ill and suffered a moderate case of yellow fever from which he recovered. Jernegan was the only volunteer to participate in all three phases of the board's experiments. He had been in the first group of volunteers to sleep in the infected bedding and clothing house, and he had been bitten by a loaded mosquito in the mosquito house on December 28 and 29 but did not become ill. His illness following the injection proved he was susceptible and had not had yellow fever before.

On January 8, Private William Olsen was injected with 1.5 cc of blood taken from Jernegan, who was in the first day of his illness. Three days later, Olsen became ill and suffered a mild attack of yellow fever. On January 22, Private Wallace Forbes was injected with 0.5 cc of blood taken from a fatal case of yellow fever that was not related to the Camp Lazear experiments. Two days later, Forbes became ill and suffered a moderately severe case of yellow fever. Forbes was the third case produced by blood injection, and Reed needed one more to complete the planned four cases. When the volunteer who was lined up for the last injection experiment backed out, Reed said that he would take the injection himself.

At this point in the experiments, it was almost 100 percent certain that Reed would develop yellow fever from the injection. Private John H. Andrus of the Hospital Corps had been assigned as an assistant in the laboratory after Lazear's death, and on January 24 he overheard the all-day argument between Reed and Carroll as to the wisdom of Reed taking the injection. Reed's age and the fact that he was run-down by a recent illness increased the danger to him if he developed yellow fever. The two physicians made no attempt to hide their discussions from Andrus, who later said, "They paid no more attention to me than to any other article of furniture."[1] During the heated discussion, Andrus thought of the yellow fever patients he had nursed, seeing two men die and others become critically ill. Because of what he had seen, Andrus "was afraid to do what seemed the obvious thing."[2] Despite Carroll's vigorous objection and the fact that Reed had said just a few weeks before that it would be folly for him to risk yellow fever, Reed showed up the next morning, January 25, 1901, determined to be injected. After what must have been a difficult and sleepless night of considering the consequences, incredibly, the twenty-one-year-old Andrus stepped forward and volunteered. That same day he received an injection of 1 cc of Forbes's blood and three days later developed a severe case of yellow fever. During his illness, Reed, probably feeling somewhat guilty over Andrus's selfless decision, wrote the surgeon general expressing his concern about Andrus.

> He seems to have acquired a very serious infection, his temperature running along the 104° line now for three days. Albumen appeared at the end of eighteen hours, but it is not excessive. Should he die, I shall regret that I ever undertook this work. The responsibility for the life of a human being weighs upon me very heavily just at present, and I am dreadfully melancholic. Everything is being done for him that we know to do.[3]

Reed knew Andrus better than many of the other volunteers, as he worked in Reed's laboratory. Andrus did recover, but his recovery was complicated and significantly delayed by a large, painful sacral boil.

In an additional attempt to be thorough and to place their results above criticism, the board took a portion of the blood that was drawn from acute yellow fever patients for injection into nonimmune volunteers and injected it into other volunteers who had already had yellow fever. This was to further prove that the illness produced in the injected volunteers was yellow fever and not some other acute infectious disease. Private John Kissinger and John Moran, as well as the Spaniards Nicanor Fernandez and Becente Presedo, received an injection of 1 cc of this blood without any ill effects. Of course, specific viral illnesses so well known today were completely unknown to them, and the risk of blood injection for any number of other illnesses was not appreciated. In order to further pursue their efforts to identify the organism of yellow fever, at the time that they drew blood for injection into volunteers they took additional blood for culture. The results of the cultures were negative for *Bacillus icteroides* or any other disease-causing bacterium.

On January 11, two more volunteers, Privates James B. Hildebrand and Thomas England, entered the infected clothing and bedding building as the last group to endure the twenty-night stay. Regardless of the fact that by this time everyone was fairly certain that the fomites were harmless as far as yellow fever was concerned, no one could have looked forward to those three weeks. Additional articles of clothing and bedding were added to the pestilent collection as they became available from new yellow fever patients. The volunteers even slept in the same nightclothes worn and contaminated by yellow fever patients, some of whom had died. Again, the two volunteers were isolated for five days following their release from the fomite house; they remained well.

Another question the board sought to answer was how long a mosquito could remain infectious after feeding on a patient with yellow fever. Several mosquitoes that had fed on an acute yellow fever patient on the third day of illness were kept alive on sugar and water. On January 19, 1901, thirty-nine days later, they bit Private Levi Folk, a repeat volunteer who had previously spent three anxious weeks in the infected clothing and bedding building. On the fourth day following the bites, he became moderately ill with yellow fever. On January 25, Private Edward Weatherwalks, also a veteran of the infected clothing and bedding building, was bitten by twelve mosquitoes but did not become ill. For Weatherwalks to escape yellow fever, he must have been immune from a prior unrecognized illness. On January 31, 1901, Private Clyde L. West of the Eighth Infantry was bitten by two mosquitoes that had previously bitten Levi Folk, now fifty-one days after their loading. West suffered a mild case of yellow fever. Another volunteer, James L. Hanberry, was bitten on February 6, 1901, the fifty-seventh day, by these same mosquitoes and became so ill he almost died. Hanberry, of the Hospital Corps, was also a repeat volunteer who had participated in the second iteration of experiments in the fomite house. The person who had volunteered to be bitten on the sixty-second day failed to follow through on his commitment, and the remaining mosquitoes died on the sixty-ninth and seventy-first days after being loaded. This experiment showed, as Reed stated in a later presentation, "the duration of life in the case of these mosquitoes will readily explain how the poison of yellow fever can remain even in a depopulated area for a period of two and a half months, so that, as is well known, those who enter the infected area, even at the expiration of this period, are liable to acquire the disease."[4]

Hospital Corps Private Charles G. Sonntag, who volunteered and was bitten on February 7, 1901, developed yellow fever three days later and recovered after a mild case. His was the sixteenth and last case of yellow fever to be produced at Camp Lazear. Added to the cases of Carroll and Dean, the board had produced eighteen cases of yellow fever.

Just as with their preliminary results, Reed wanted to get their unprecedented findings presented and published as soon as possible. He had asked the surgeon general for permission to present their work before the Pan-American Medical Congress in Havana in early February 1901. He was made an official delegate to the congress for that purpose. The board was carefully preparing their extraordinary data for presentation and publication while they continued their research. Reed was also preparing to return home, as he felt his research in Cuba was essentially done and he wanted to get back to his laboratory in Washington, where he hoped to isolate the agent that caused yellow fever. So far, the board had been unable to find the actual germ. They were positive that the organism was not a bacterium, as they had not cultured it or seen it under their microscopes after repeated attempts. Reed was very interested in finding the "parasite" that caused yellow fever, hoping to be able to identify the actual agent, as had been done with malaria. One of the reasons for wanting to find the organism was to use it, if possible, to prepare a vaccine in hopes of preventing this awful disease.

Reed presented the second paper, "The Etiology of Yellow Fever—An Additional Note," with a tribute to Jesse W. Lazear on February 6, 1901, at the Pan-American Medical Congress in Havana. He reported five cases of yellow fever produced by mosquito bites, the negative results of the fomite experiments in the "infected clothing and bedding building," and the results of the "mosquito building" experiment at Camp Lazear. The paper ended with eleven conclusions about yellow fever. These conclusions have stood the test of a century of time and have never been disproved or even modified in any significant way. The conclusions were:

1. The mosquito—*C. fasciatus*—serves as the intermediate host for the parasite of yellow fever. [The name of this mosquito has been changed twice since 1901 to *Stegomyia* and now *Aedes aegypti*. For the sake of uniformity, the name *Aedes aegypti* will be used throughout the remainder of the text except for direct quotations from other documents.]

2. Yellow fever is transmitted to the nonimmune individual by means of the bite of the mosquito that has previously fed on the blood of those sick with this disease.

3. An interval of about twelve days or more after contamination appears to be necessary before the mosquito is capable of conveying the infection.

4. The bite of the mosquito at an earlier period after contamination does not appear to confer any immunity against a subsequent attack.

5. Yellow fever can also be experimentally produced by the subcutaneous injection of blood taken from the general circulation during the first and second days of this disease.

6. An attack of yellow fever, produced by the bite of the mosquito, confers immunity against the subsequent injection of the blood of an individual suffering from the nonexperimental form of this disease.

7. The period of incubation in thirteen cases of experimental yellow fever has varied from forty-one hours to five days and seventeen hours.

8. Yellow fever is not conveyed by fomites, and hence disinfection of articles of clothing, bedding, or merchandise supposedly contaminated by contact with those sick with this disease is unnecessary.

9. A house may be said to be infected with yellow fever only when there are present within its walls contaminated mosquitoes capable of conveying the parasite of this disease.

10. The spread of yellow fever can be most effectually controlled by measures directed to the destruction of mosquitoes and the protection of the sick against the bites of these insects.

11. While the mode of propagation of yellow fever has now been definitely determined, the specific cause of this disease remains to be discovered.[5]

After completing the presentation, Reed wrote the following in a letter to his wife:

> To-day the paper was read and met with a most favourable reception. The attention during the reading was all that I could have asked for and the applause at its conclusion long and hearty. A resolution expressive of the high appreciation in which our work was held, together with the thanks of the Congress, was unanimously adopted. I received dozens of the warmest kind of handshakes from Cuban, Spanish, Mexican, South American and North American physicians, men whom I had not even met. The hall was

crowded and the doors even packed with listeners. It was indeed a signal triumph for our work.[6]

Again the paper was quickly published, this time in the *Journal of the American Medical Association*, February 16, 1901. The accompanying editorial said, "The results of the experiments support the mosquito theory of yellow fever. . . . No one will doubt the far reaching importance of this demonstration!"[7]

The initial clinical work of the U.S. Army Yellow Fever Board was thus concluded in February 1901. Walter Reed sailed home on the *Morro Castle* on February 9; also on board were John Kissinger and John Moran, two of the board's early volunteers at Camp Lazear. James Carroll followed Reed to Washington, D.C., later that month. Aristides Agramonte remained in Havana. Walter Reed resumed his duties as the curator of the Army Medical Museum and professor of bacteriology and clinical microscopy at the Army Medical School. He also taught pathology and bacteriology at Columbian University (now George Washington University). He was, in addition, required to participate in what could only be called the most routine of duties, serving on the Army Examining Board to determine the fitness of applicants to serve on active duty with the Medical Corps. Carroll also returned to his former duties at these same institutions. The two men collaborated in the preparation of their completed research for future presentation and publication.

The army's campaign against the now-known-to-be-deadly mosquito had actually begun in October 1900 with Jefferson Randolph Kean's directive to the Department of Western Cuba to take personal precautions against mosquitoes and to systematically take action against any standing water, their hatching grounds. This order was reenforced in December by General Order No. 6 when it was expanded to all army facilities in Cuba. But, as of yet, there had been no actions taken in the city of Havana itself. Major William C. Gorgas, the chief sanitation officer in Havana, was not convinced that the campaign against mosquitoes was going to be successful in controlling yellow fever. While he believed in the validity of the commission's experiments, he felt that the disease was also transmitted by other means and that killing all the mosquitoes, if that was even possible, was not all that would be needed. Unlike some others, most notably the surgeon general, who were jumping on the "I knew it all along" mosquito bandwagon, he later readily admitted his skepticism: "I myself had seen the work and was convinced that the mosquito could convey yellow fever but I was hardly prepared to believe that it was the only way or even the ordinary way of conveying the disease." He continued, "I had very little hope of accomplishing much. It seemed to me that even if the mosquito did convey yellow fever, he could not be gotten rid of but as he evidently could carry the disease, it was our duty to take precautions in that direction."[8]

Winter was not yellow fever season, and there were only seven yellow fever deaths in Havana in January 1901 and five in February. Gorgas began his work against the mosquito in February with his "small army of inspectors" dispatched throughout Havana.[9] Carlos Finlay had proposed several years before that mosquito control would also control yellow fever, but as no one believed his evidence about mosquito transmission of yellow fever, no one tried his techniques. Gorgas devised a three-pronged attack against *Aedes*. If mosquitoes could not feed on acutely ill yellow fever patients, then they could not become contaminated with the germ and could not spread the disease, so all fever cases, no matter the cause, were carefully screened to be kept away from mosquitoes for several days until the source of the fever could be determined. The second approach, killing the adult mosquitoes, required fumigation of buildings that contained them with either sulfur, formaldehyde, or insect powder. Each method had some drawbacks; sulphur was the most effective insecticide, but its smell was noxious; formaldehyde required the rooms or buildings to be closed and sealed for two or three hours; and insect powder (pyrethrum) would incapacitate but not kill the mosquitoes, requiring them to be destroyed and removed. Not completely converted to the mosquito vector theory, Gorgas still continued the routine disinfection of buildings, furniture, clothing, and other items until August 1901. Third, and later determined to be the most important, was attacking the mosquitoes' breeding grounds, any standing fresh water, especially that in and around houses where the domestic *Aedes* enjoyed living.

Only a small portion of Havana had piped water; thus the majority of dwellings and businesses used rainwater that was collected and stored before use. The collected rainwater was stored in cisterns, barrels, and containers of all shapes and sizes; most were uncovered, and thus openly inviting to *Aedes*. It had been known for years that putting a thin film of oil on standing water would suffocate any mosquito larvae present. The film of oil created enough surface tension to prevent the larvae from pushing their breathing apparatus through the surface of the water and breathing, but until now there was no particular need or reason for anyone to take the trouble to employ this technique. Gorgas had his "mosquito brigades" attack and eliminate standing water, as well as oil and/or cover any standing water that could not be eliminated, denying the female *Aedes* its breeding places and dramatically decreasing its numbers.[10]

The results were immediate, with one death from yellow fever in March and none in April, May, or June. Could this really be true? There had been over three hundred deaths from yellow fever in Havana just the year before. Although it was impossible to know for sure, there had probably not been three straight months without a yellow fever death in Havana in almost 150 years! Gorgas "pushed in every direction" as he conducted one of the U.S. Army's most successful "wars" ever, the war against the mosquito.[11] The yellow fever scourge was essentially stopped in its deadly tracks. From September 1901 until July 1902, there was not a single case in Havana. Yellow fever had been constantly present in Havana for 150 years and was nearly wiped out in less than 150 days. The world was astounded by the results.

A fourth approach to try to control yellow fever was an ill-fated attempt at immunization. With the advice and consent of Gorgas and Leonard Wood, Dr. Juan Guitéras, a Cuban physician and yellow fever expert, began a series of experiments to try to immunize against yellow fever by producing mild cases. Guitéras was a professor of pathology and tropical medicine at the University of Havana and a member of the Yellow Fever Board of Havana that had been called upon to document the cases of yellow fever produced by the U. S. Army Board. Because the board had been so successful in producing relatively mild cases of yellow fever without any deaths, he wanted to conduct experiments by following their techniques that would "propagate the disease in a controllable form, and securing, among the recently arrived immigrants, immunization, with the minimum amount of danger to themselves and to the community."[12] He had been impressed that almost all yellow fever cases produced at Camp Lazear had been relatively mild, and he wanted to see if intentionally causing a mild case of yellow fever could be used as an "immunization" against the disease. Beginning in early 1901, Guitéras conducted a series of experiments at the Inoculation Station at Las Animas Hospital in Havana. Between February and August

1901, he made forty-two separate attempts to produce yellow fever in volunteers by the bites of loaded mosquitoes. Although he followed the techniques of the army board, he had difficulty producing cases. Tragically, the cases he did produce were much more severe, even deadly. He produced eight cases in his volunteers, three of whom—Curro, Campa, and an American nurse, Clara Maass—died. In Guitéras's report in the November 23, 1901, issue of *American Medicine*, he wrote that all three of the deaths occurred in volunteers who were bitten by mosquitoes that carried the yellow fever germ from a patient named Alvarez. Modern research has shown that different strains of the yellow fever virus possess different degrees of virulence; clearly the Alvarez strain was deadly. Guitéras sadly concluded his report with the advice that "whenever a group of mosquitoes infected from 1 case should show a very decided virulence, their use should be abandoned."[13]

The only female and American among Guitéras's volunteers had been the twenty-five-year-old nurse from New Jersey, Clara Maass. She had volunteered to serve during the Spanish-American War in 1898 and had done so at stateside camps and in Cuba. She worked as a contract nurse, as female nurses were not part of active duty military at that time. Later she volunteered again and served in the Philippines but returned home because of illness. After she recovered, she wrote Major Gorgas and ask if he needed her help. Following his positive response, she returned to Cuba to work in the Las Animas Hospital. She volunteered for the Guitéras mosquito experiments and was bitten numerous times during March, May, and June 1901 without results. She was bitten a last time on August 14, 1901. She became ill on the eighteenth, and even with the best care available, she died on the twenty-fourth. Her death and the two others sent shock waves through the army that reverberated all the way back to Washington and shortly thereafter contributed to the cessation of human experimentation.

All of those involved in the work of the Yellow Fever Board were very interested in continuing the effort to isolate the agent of yellow fever. Dr. William H. Welch, the distinguished professor and dean from Johns Hopkins who had instructed Reed and Carroll during their earlier studies at Hopkins, had followed the work of the board closely and encouraged them to pursue a line of research similar to that of Friedrich Löeffler and Paul Frosch in Germany. They had demonstrated that the agent of hoof and mouth disease in cattle was ultramicroscopic and passed through the smallest known filter. Despite the fact that this information was well known—Sternberg had mentioned it in his Address of the President at the American Medical Association meeting in 1898—this technique had not yet been attempted by the board. Carroll was eager to continue their research and sought permission to return to Cuba to conduct studies to determine if the yellow fever organism was possibly similar.

James Carroll was finally granted permission to return to Cuba, and he arrived in Havana in August 1901, just a week before Clara Maass died. Despite the three tragic deaths in the Guitéras experiments, Carroll was determined to press on. Camp Lazear had been closed in March 1901, so he worked at Las Animas Hospital. Because of the high level of anxiety resulting from these recent deaths, it was not practical for Carroll to use yellow fever cases from Havana, so he borrowed some loaded mosquitoes from Juan Guitéras and produced his own new cases. He knew from their earlier experiments that yellow fever could be transmitted by the injection of whole blood. He wanted to take the next step and determine if the agent of yellow fever was filterable.

In August, September, and October 1901, he produced six new cases of yellow fever. A Spaniard at first identified only by his initials, P.R.C., was bitten by four mosquitoes on September 16, 1901, and became ill three days later with a severe case. Two experienced physicians at Las Animas Hospital thought he was going to die, but fortunately he did not. J.M.A., another Spaniard, was bitten on October 9 by eight mosquitoes and developed a mild case. These volunteers were later identified as Pablo Ruiz Castillo and Jacinto Mendez Alvarez.

At this point, Carroll's experiments took on the decidedly different flavor of bench research, something with which he was very familiar and accomplished. Unknown to Carroll at the time and essentially unappreciated since, October 15, 1901, was a remarkable day in the history of medical research. In one day, he completed an extraordinary and unprecedented set of medical experiments. On October 15, blood was drawn from Jacinto Alvarez at the beginning of his third day of illness. A portion of it was allowed to stand and clot, and was then injected under the skin of Manuel G. Moran. Five days later, Moran would develop a mild case of yellow fever. Carroll then heated to 55 degrees centigrade for ten minutes some of the same blood drawn from Alvarez and injected it that same day under the skin of three different Spanish volunteers (A.C., B.F.M., and S.O.), who would be closely observed and would remain perfectly well for the next ten days. This, of course, would clearly demonstrate that the specific agent of yellow fever was destroyed or at least inactivated by heating to 55 degrees C.

Also on October 15, Paul Hamann, an American soldier, was injected with serum filtrate that had been passed through a new Berkefeld filter whose pores ordinarily served to prevent the passage of all known bacteria. Four days later, he would develop yellow fever. Albert Wall Covington, another soldier, was injected with serum filtrate and would become ill with yellow fever four days later. John R. Bullard, a civilian and a distant relative of Jefferson Randolph Kean's wife, was given a similar injection. Four days later, he would have a slight elevation in his temperature and pulse, accompanied by a headache and pain between his shoulders that would resolve in just a few hours. Not an obvious case of yellow fever.

One week later, Bullard was injected again with filtered serum, this time from blood drawn from Paul Hamann, and developed the symptoms of yellow fever just twenty-four hours later. Reed and Carroll were somewhat at a loss to explain Bullard's case. If his yellow fever was from the first injection, the incubation period was nine days, three days longer than any of their other cases. If it was from the second, the incubation period was one day, less than half as long as any of their other cases. They were inclined to believe that Bullard's case was from the second injection, but they were unsure. They were sure that Carroll had proven that the agent of yellow fever was a filterable agent and not a toxin in the blood of yellow fever patients. Carroll's research almost certainly demonstrated the first cases of experimental transmission of a viral disease from one human to another.

Carroll was essentially finished with the planned experiments, and shortly afterward, he received orders from the War Department forbidding him from doing further human research on American soldiers, officially ending the work of the board. The order to cease the experiments was partially due to the public outcry over the death of Clara Maass, as well as the fact that the campaign against mosquitoes in Havana had practically eliminated the disease and thus its danger to the occupying U.S. troops. The month before the mosquito control program had begun in Havana, January 1901, there had been seven deaths from yellow fever. In February there had been five, but in the following seven months combined, there had been only six.

Altogether, the U.S. Army Board had produced twenty-two cases of yellow fever, sixteen by the bites of infected mosquitoes and six by the injection of blood taken from acutely ill yellow fever patients. Neither the brilliance of their thoroughness nor the genius of their experimental design could have bequeathed the board the extraordinary luck they had, for not a single one of their "official" volunteers had died. Lazear, of course, was almost certainly an "unofficial volunteer," but this could not be definitively proven then or even today.

Shortly after James Carroll had returned to Cuba to complete the board's experiments, another fateful event took place that would have significant impact on the history of yellow fever. On September 6, 1901, President William McKinley was shot while in Buffalo, New York. He died eight days later. Theodore Roosevelt, following his highly publicized successes in the Spanish-American War, had vaulted into the nomination for vice president alongside McKinley in the general election of 1900. At age forty-two, he was sworn in as the twenty-sixth and youngest president of the United States. While in office, Roosevelt made several enormous decisions in regard to building the Panama Canal and the control of yellow fever, without which the canal would not have been completed.

Indeed, the genius of the Army Board was the conduct of its experiments with precise, accurate, and meticulous attention to detail. In addition, the board members made extraordinarily good decisions based on a thorough evaluation and use of the available knowledge. Overarching all of this, they were also remarkably lucky in that none of their volunteers died, which could have slowed or even stopped their work. They obviously had little, if any, control over their patients' survival; even today, with all of the sophisticated equipment, test, and therapies available, the survival rate for yellow fever is essentially unchanged from a century ago. The unfortunate Juan Guitéras and his volunteers had three deaths among eight cases produced. Using the same basic therapeutic techniques as Guitéras, the Army Board had none in twenty-two cases.

In light of the current knowledge of yellow fever, a discussion of some of the board's experiments is in order. Over the years, there has been little interest in their fomite experiments. As mentioned before, the prevailing knowledge at that time was that yellow fever was conveyed by fomites;

however, there was plenty of evidence that contradicted its contagiousness. The experiments conducted by the board were designed to prove that fomites were harmless. In the board's description of their methods from the second publication, there is a brief statement that has not received much attention: "These boxes [of linens and clothing contaminated by yellow fever patients] which had been tightly closed and locked for a period of two weeks."[14] Another descriptive statement follows:

> December 12, a fourth box of clothing and bedding was received from Las Animas Hospital. These articles had been used on the beds of yellow fever patients, but in addition had been purposely soiled with the bloody stool of a fatal case of this disease. As this box had been packed for a number of days, when opened and unpacked by Dr. Cooke and his assistants, on December 12, the odor was so offensive as to compel them to retreat from the house. They pluckily returned, however, within a short time and spent the night as usual.[15]

How would those two weeks or even a lesser "number of days" have affected the viability of the yellow fever virus? We know today that the yellow fever virus is not a hardy or resilient virus outside a living host, and it is unlikely that the virus would have remained viable longer than twenty-four hours even in the blood, urine, black vomit, or other body fluids in these fomites. Therefore, placing these objects in boxes for several weeks or even several days would have inactivated any virus that was present and would have rendered the contents harmless as far as transmitting yellow fever. In all probability, the first and second groups were exposed to fomites that did not contain any viable viruses. It is difficult to know for sure the status of the third group of volunteers as far as potential exposure to the live virus, as the descriptions provided are not as detailed.

A somewhat hardier virus—smallpox, for example—can remain viable for a period of time in fomites. There are several infamous examples of British soldiers engaged against Indians in western Pennsylvania in 1763 taking advantage of this by giving, or leaving for the Indians to find, blankets purposely contaminated with smallpox; because of the viability of the smallpox virus, these blankets could have been the cause of an epidemic that broke out among the Indians shortly thereafter. If yellow fever was a hardier virus, it is possible it could have been transmitted by fresher fomites. It seems that the Army Board, without any knowledge of viruses or their viability outside their living host, guessed correctly as to the contagiousness of yellow fever.

Although it is probably a rare event, we also now know that yellow fever can be transmitted by aerosol, at least in the laboratory setting. Laboratory monkeys have contracted yellow fever by being in the same facility as other monkeys sick with yellow fever, without any blood, mosquito, or direct contact of any kind. If an event of aerosol transmission had occurred during the board's experiments, it would certainly have confused and confounded them, possibly leading them astray in false directions or to incorrect conclusions.

It has become evident that primates susceptible to yellow fever are not its reservoir of maintenance in nature. Yellow fever is maintained through vertical transmission of the virus from a female *Aedes* to its offspring. Once the yellow fever virus is ingested into the female *Aedes*, through a complicated series of processes that take place in the cells of the mosquito, the virus takes about seven to seventeen days to make its way to the mosquito's salivary glands, depending on the species of mosquito and the temperature of the environment. Once in the salivary glands, it can be passed on to another primate victim the next time the mosquito takes a blood meal. The length of Carter's proposed extrinsic incubation period was thought by the Army Board to be ten to twelve days at a minimum. During the intervening years, it has been shown that it can be as short as seven days in some species of mosquitoes. This period of extrinsic incubation was not recognized by Carlos Finlay but was demonstrated and proven by the Army Board.

As the virus invades the mosquito's body, it permeates the cytoplasm of every cell, reproduces itself within the mosquito to include the genital tract, and enters her eggs at the time of fertilization. The virus resides in the cytoplasm of the egg and can remain viable for several months when the egg is dormant during the dry season. As the egg hatches, the virus is transmitted to the next generation. Vertical transmission is not efficient with less than 1 percent of the offspring infected. Female mosquitoes, whose life span may be no more than a couple of months, may take a blood meal every three to six days. Gordon Harrison says in *Mosquitoes, Malaria and Man* that it is known that, on average, a female mosquito will lay about two hundred eggs in each of the eight to ten clutches she produces in her short life. Assuming half are female, the progeny from five generations produced during the course of one summer could be twenty million. Only a small percentage will be infected, but it is easy to see how yellow fever can exist in nature in *Aedes*. Male offspring will also carry the virus but are not infective to humans, as they do not bite. It is truly amazing that yellow fever can easily kill a human being, but it peacefully coexists within a tiny mosquito. The complexity of metabolic activity in humans is probably what makes us susceptible to yellow fever, while the simplicity of the mosquito protects them.

Neither Finlay nor the Army Board could prove that vertical transmission took place and thus believed that it did not. If any of the mosquito eggs that they worked with had been infected through vertical transmission, the hatchling mosquitoes would also have been infective. This could have obscured their results, but it would not have affected the Army Board's proof of mosquito transmission. If Finlay had worked with vertically infected mosquito eggs, his hatchling mosquitoes would have transmitted yellow fever to his volunteers, as there would have been no need to wait out the extrinsic incubation period.

Chapter 14

Recognition

AFTER HIS RETURN FROM CUBA IN FEBRUARY 1901, WALTER REED resumed his duties as the curator of the Army Medical Museum (now the National Museum of Health and Medicine) and professor at the Army Medical School. He had a lot of catching up to do after his seven-month absence. In late February, he responded to a congratulatory letter from Dr. Henry Rose Carter with one of his own back to Dr. Carter, thanking him for his contributions to their success. Reed wrote: "Please accept my sincere thanks for the sentiments expressed in your kind letter of Feb. 21st. I value highly your opinion of our work. Since I know of no one more competent to pass judgment on all that pertains to the subject of yellow fever. You must not forget that your work in Mississippi did more to impress me with the importance of an intermediate host than everything else put together."[1]

In addition to his routine work, he had to prepare the remainder of the board's research for presentation and publication. In demand as a speaker, between his return in February and the end of the year, Reed spoke at meetings in Baltimore, Buffalo, Chicago, and twice in Washington, D.C. In April when he also spoke at the Baltimore meeting, Dean William Welch of Johns Hopkins said that the board's discoveries were second in importance only to the use of anesthesia in assessing American contributions to medicine.

Reed was interested in continuing his research but had little time. He had been grilled following one of his presentations about his inability to find the causative organism. His friend, Jefferson Randolph Kean, mused in a letter from Cuba, "It must be almost molecular in its smallness, and far beyond the reach of the microscope."[2] How right he was, as the organism would not be physically seen until after the invention of the electron microscope several decades later. In addressing the possibility of "serum therapy" for prevention, Kean told Reed that "if you waste your winter teaching . . . some other fellow may get on to it."[3] Reed was concerned that his boss, General Sternberg, was apparently taking credit for the work of the Army

Board. Sternberg published several articles in which Reed thought he embellished his role in the events that had taken place in Cuba. Sternberg had actually discouraged them from experimenting with mosquitoes, and Reed knew that to be the case. As Sternberg was the surgeon general, there was not much Reed could do.

Two more papers were published under the names of the members of the U.S. Army Yellow Fever Board. "Experimental Yellow Fever" appeared in *American Medicine* on July 6, 1901, and "The Etiology of Yellow Fever— A Supplemental Note" was published in *American Medicine* on February 22, 1902. These papers reported the remaining cases of yellow fever produced during the board's experiments. Jesse Lazear was not included as an author on the last three publications of the board, as the research reported in them was begun after his death.

Several of Reed's friends, most notably Kean, conducted an active campaign for him to replace George Miller Sternberg, who was scheduled to retire as surgeon general. Walter Reed was probably at least mildly disappointed when he was not chosen as U.S. Army surgeon general in June 1902 when his mentor retired after ten years in office. In a largely ceremonial selection, Colonel William H. Forwood was named to succeed Sternberg; Forwood had a mandatory retirement in just four months. Apparently, Reed was never seriously considered, as his name was not even on the list of potential candidates to replace Forwood. However, the possibility of a later selection still existed for him. After all, Reed's military record and scientific accomplishments spoke for themselves, and he had political contacts. His friend Major General Leonard Wood had just completed an extraordinary and successful assignment as governor general of Cuba, aided in no small part by the discoveries of the Army Yellow Fever Board led by Reed. Wood's good friend and wartime buddy, Theodore Roosevelt, now occupied the White House after the assassination of President McKinley. Wood surely was slated to receive an important post for his next assignment. Although Reed did not openly seek advancement, it could not hurt his immediate or future chances to have such a highly placed friend as Leonard Wood.

In early 1902, the fifty-year-old Reed was in the prime of his professional and personal life. The great discoveries of the Army Yellow Fever Board were being applied with astounding success in Cuba. Havana was essentially free of yellow fever for the first time in centuries. Reed's lifelong dream to "be permitted in some way or sometime to do something to alleviate human suffering" was coming true in resounding fashion.[4] Despite his not being selected surgeon general, national recognition had come in the form of two honorary degrees. The University of Michigan had granted an L.L.D., honoring him as "Walter Reed, most eminent physician, famous for his investigations of the causes of diseases."[5] Harvard University bestowed an M.A. presented by its president, Charles Eliot, with the citation reading, "Walter Reed, graduate of the University of Virginia, the army surgeon who planned and directed in Cuba the experiments which have given man control over that fearful scourge yellow fever."[6]

Although Walter Reed was a modest southern gentleman, it must have given him great satisfaction to have conducted such scientifically sound and practical research. And while there is no record of it, it must have entered his mind that he might be considered for the newly established Nobel Prize in Physiology or Medicine. The 1902 prize was to be awarded to Dr. Ronald Ross for his work showing that mosquitoes transmitted malaria. How could the work of Reed and his associates not receive similar recognition for the science of their work, as well as its extraordinary practical application in controlling the disease?

The secretary of war had stated in his annual report that Reed would, by law, become a lieutenant colonel within a few months. Unknown to Reed, the secretary also said that he would ask the president to authorize Reed's appointment to assistant surgeon general with the rank of colonel. In addition to his position as the curator of the Army Medical Museum, he was named as the librarian of the Surgeon General's Library, a position he had wanted for several years. In late summer, he was made the chairman of general pathology at Columbian University Medical School, where he taught night classes.

His best army friend from Cuba and even before, Jefferson Randolph Kean, had been reassigned to Washington and had moved into the same apartment house where Walter and Emilie Reed lived, at 1603 Nineteenth Street NW. Their son, Lawrence, was still on active duty and posted to the Philippine Islands. Their daughter, Blossom, still living at home, had just celebrated her nineteenth birthday and was the joy of Reed's life. Keewaydin, their mountaintop home in the Catoctin Mountains near Blue Ridge Summit, Pennsylvania, was a special retreat from the pressures of his many responsibilities and growing fame.

In the fall of 1902, his life was extraordinarily full and busy, and the future seemed limitless. There was one thing, however; Reed, now fifty-one, was not feeling all that well. He had a chronic pain in his abdomen that he just could not shake. After work on Wednesday, November 12, 1902, Reed was unable to teach his usual evening class at the Columbian University Medical School. He stayed in bed until noon on Thursday and then made an unsuccessful attempt to go back to work. On Friday, Major William C. Borden, another close friend and commander of the Army Hospital at Washington Barracks, sent him home from work early. They had agreed that his abdomen was sensitive in the proper spot, indicating that he probably had appendicitis. They discussed the possibility of Borden operating the following week.

Reed rested on Saturday, and by Sunday he was feeling better. Sunday morning, he wanted his usual breakfast of waffles; his wife knew better. Later he sat up in bed, read the paper, and talked about improvements he was planning for Keewaydin. He received friends that afternoon. His temperature went up Sunday night, and his physician friends, Borden and Kean, knew he needed surgery.

The next day, Monday, November 17, Reed was taken to the Army Hospital at Washington Barracks (now Fort Lesley J. McNair). He refused the stretcher and walked into the hospital; he did not walk out. Major Borden, the commander of the hospital, as well as the chief surgeon, operated. Many leaders of the Army Medical Department were present during the operation, including the new surgeon general, Robert M. O'Reilly. Borden had to extend the original incision and was dismayed at what he found. The appendix was grossly enlarged and partly filled with pus; it had perforated at one point. Borden later said the symptoms "in no way indicated the gravity of the . . . trouble."[7] Reed reacted adversely to the anesthesia and was nauseated for eighteen hours after the operation. There was hope for several days that he might recover, but peritonitis developed; without antibiotics, which were yet to be discovered, it was futile.

Walter Reed died in the early morning hours of Sunday, November 23, 1902. No autopsy was done, but the specimen of his appendix was maintained in the Army Medical Museum until 1926, when it was thrown away. No tissue slides were ever made. Dr. William Bean, one of Reed's biographers, speculated that he had an amoebic infection of his cecum, picked up while he was in Cuba. Others have offered various theories as to the etiology of his chronic lower abdominal pain and ultimate enlargement and inflammation of his appendix; obviously none could ever be proven.

November 25, 1902, two days before Thanksgiving Day, was a dark and rainy Tuesday in Washington, D.C. Walter Reed's funeral was at St.

Thomas's Church near Dupont Circle. Pallbearers were active duty friends from the Army Medical Department, Colonel Calvin DeWitt, Majors Louis A. LaGarde, William B. Davis, Walter D. McCaw, Jefferson Randolph Kean, and William B. Bannister. Others in attendance at the Episcopal service were Secretary of War Elihu Root and a who's who of American medicine: Drs. William Welch and William Osler of Johns Hopkins and Simon Flexner, newly selected to head the new Rockefeller Institute, represented the profession. It was striking that Emilie, his wife of twenty-six years, did not attend. In a letter to a family member, she said, "My heart was acting so badly that my Doctor did not deem it advisable for me to have additional shocks";[8] she had taken to her bed while her husband was in the hospital and was unable to visit him or attend his funeral.

After the service, the flower-covered casket was transported on a horse-drawn caisson, as senior officers and leaders are to this day, to the grave site on top of a small, south-facing hill in Arlington National Cemetery. Jefferson Randolph Kean had selected the grave site, as well as the inscription placed on Reed's marker. Taken from the honorary degree he had received from Harvard just months before, it read: "He gave to man control of that dreadful scourge yellow fever." Walter Reed was buried in section three of Arlington National Cemetery, unofficially known as the "hospital section" because many Army Medical Department officers are buried there.

Following his death, the Walter Reed Memorial Association was formed to provide his widow and daughter an annuity, as his army pension was limited; and in addition "to then devote the principal to the erection of a suitable memorial in the City of Washington" to Major Walter Reed.[9] Many Americans, great and small, contributed to the Walter Reed Memorial Association. The great included business giants John D. Rockefeller, John Pierpoint Morgan, and Alexander Graham Bell. Over the years, income was provided to Reed's widow, Emilie, and after her death to their daughter, Blossom. Emilie lived forty-eight years after her husband died; she was ninety-four when she died in 1950. Blossom had lived with her mother in Blue Ridge Summit, Pennsylvania, where she operated a summer resort, The Blossom Inn, for several years in the 1930s. The inn hosted guests from every state in the union, many foreign visitors, and Washington dignitaries, including members of the Cabinet, Supreme Court, Ambassador Corps, and former First Lady Mrs. Woodrow Wilson. Blossom apparently married briefly but had no children. She died in 1964. The Reeds' son, Lawrence, who never saw his father again after their few brief meetings in Cuba during the summer of 1900, remained in the army for over forty years and retired as a major general. He had two daughters. Lawrence Reed, who served as the inspector general of the army from 1935 to 1939, died at Walter Reed Army Medical Center in 1956. Emilie Reed, Lawrence, and Blossom are buried with Walter Reed in Arlington National Cemetery. Lawrence's grandchildren and great-grandchildren survive, but there are no direct descendants with the Reed surname.

Major William Cline Borden, Reed's colleague and surgeon, spent the six years after Reed's death jumping through hoops and over hurdles and other obstacles in the way of his building a new army general hospital within the District of Columbia and naming it for his friend. It was Borden's dream to combine the Army Medical School, the Army Medical Museum, the Surgeon General's Library, and a new hospital facility on a single campus.

Borden had blueprints and estimates done and personally took his plans to the secretary of war, who approved them but without funding. Borden was on his own as to getting the money. But he was undeterred, spending several years in the halls of Congress trying to get his "dream" funded. On one visit, he spoke to the doorkeeper of the Senate chamber, asking the Civil War veteran about his health. The doorkeeper knew an opportunity when he saw it, telling Borden that he had difficulty sleeping because of pain in the stump of his amputated arm. Borden also saw an opportunity and offered to treat him. After a successful operation, as the Senate doorkeeper was leaving the hospital, he stopped by Borden's office and closed the door. He wanted to return Borden's favor, so he told him that he had noticed that anytime anyone wanted congressional funding for a real estate project in the District of Columbia, they were usually successful if they spoke to a certain colonel. Borden spoke to this colonel, who took him to the chairman of the House Appropriations Committee, who liked the idea and placed it in the appropriation bill, seeking $500,000 for start-up costs. The funding did not get through the House committee, but it was sent to the Senate, where it did pass, and then to a joint conference, where with the colonel's help it passed, but only at the $300,000 level. It became law in March 1905.

Borden wanted to locate the new facility away from the Washington Barracks site at the confluence of the Potomac and Anacostia rivers. After looking over options, forty-three acres of land were purchased in May 1906 in the northwest part of the District of Columbia between what is now Georgia Avenue NW and 16th Street NW. An additional appropriation of $200,000 was passed to build the hospital that was to be named, according to War

Department General Order 172, dated October 18, 1905, Walter Reed United States Army General Hospital. Construction on the eighty-bed hospital was completed in 1908, but the first patients were not transferred from Washington Barracks until May 1, 1909. When Borden had first made his ideas about a new hospital public, many thought that he was dreaming, and for years after its completion many referred to the facility as "Borden's dream."

Growth of the hospital, in size and stature, was rapid and dramatic, especially during and after World War I. Phase two of Borden's dream was completed when the Army Medical School moved to the campus in 1923. The Army Medical School moved from its downtown Washington, D.C., location on Seventh Street NW to its new building on the campus that then became known as the Army Medical Center and Walter Reed General Hospital. Through the years, additional buildings were built and more property acquired. World War II, of course, brought a tremendous increase in workload, and the Forest Glen Annex in Maryland was purchased and converted into a patient care and convalescence facility.

In 1951, on the one hundredth anniversary of the birth of Major Walter Reed, the name of the installation was changed to Walter Reed Army Medical Center. In 1953, the successor of the Army Medical School, the Army Medical Department Research and Graduate School, became the Walter Reed Army Institute of Research. A new Armed Forces Institute of Pathology building was built on the Walter Reed Army Medical Center campus and dedicated in 1955. The Army Medical Museum and the Surgeon General's Library remained at the downtown 7th and B Street location for many years. It was not until the early 1950s that the library became the National Library of Medicine and was placed under the Public Health Service. The National Museum of Health and Medicine, successor to the Army Medical Museum where Major Walter Reed had been the curator, moved to the Walter Reed Army Medical Center campus in 1971.

In 1972, after more than five years of planning, ground-breaking ceremonies were held for a new Walter Reed Army Medical Center hospital facility. On September 26, 1977, the new facility was dedicated. In 1994, the building was rededicated and named the Heaton Pavilion in honor of Lieutenant General Leonard Heaton, a former commander of the Walter Reed Army Medical Center (1952–1959) and U.S. Army surgeon general (1959–1969).

Following the death of Walter Reed's daughter, Blossom, in 1964, the Walter Reed Memorial Association completed its last duty by commissioning Mr. Felix de Weldon to complete the Walter Reed Memorial on the campus of the Walter Reed Army Medical Center. Mr. de Weldon, a famous sculptor of presidents and kings, had spent nine years completing the enormous Marine Corps (Iwo Jima) War Memorial in Arlington, Virginia. He had begun the project while serving in the navy in 1945 and completed it in time for the dedication in 1954. In his career, de Weldon sculpted over two thousand public monuments. On November 21, 1966, the culmination of over sixty years of effort came to a close, as the memorial was unveiled. Special guests at the event were Walter Reed's granddaughter, Daisy Reed Royce; general of the army and former president, Dwight D. Eisenhower; and Mrs. Eisenhower.

The building where Walter Reed died remains in use by the U.S. Army at Fort Lesley J. McNair in Washington, D.C. In November 2002, a plaque was placed by the Walter Reed Society near the entrance of Building 54, commemorating the centennial anniversary of Reed's death.

Despite these efforts of the Walter Reed Memorial Association, it is the Walter Reed Army Medical Center that has become an internationally known living monument to its namesake, much more so than any built from granite, marble, or bronze. It has a long, rich tradition of patient care, research, and medical education that is out of view of the general public except in time of war. Wounded or injured soldiers returning home from war, hostility, or foreign service have come to expect the highest level of care and concern delivered by the men and women serving in the great tradition and values of the United States Army.

In the years following Reed's death, an unsightly debate arose over the significance of the contributions made by the principal characters to the discoveries made in Cuba. Feelings ran along political and nationalistic lines. If you saw the U.S. intervention in Cuba after the sinking of the USS *Maine* as an armed invasion by unwanted, unneeded, and arrogant bullies, your inclination was to give Dr. Carlos Finlay credit for the discovery that mosquitoes transmit yellow fever. If you saw America's participation in the conflict as an unselfish act of aid and assistance to a beleaguered and repressed neighbor, your inclination was to give the U.S. Army Board credit for providing the proof where Finlay had fallen short.

Americans who wanted to preserve the memory of Reed, and as some said, take all the credit for themselves, tended to downplay the contributions of Carlos Finlay, whose theory Reed and the Army Board proved. Cubans, who may have felt intimidated and overlooked by what they saw as American arrogance, defended Finlay and said that Reed had merely validated Finlay's previous discoveries. Each side claimed for their man "the conquest of yellow fever." This debate mirrored a similar one that was taking place between the British and the Italians over the priority of Ronald Ross and Giovanni Grassi and the discovery that mosquitoes transmitted malaria. Ross had first shown that mosquitoes transmitted avian malaria and Grassi had shortly thereafter demonstrated that they could also transmit human malaria. In both situations, the unseemly bickering and at times outright hostility continued to various degrees for almost fifty years, until all of the participants and onlookers had died.

If Walter Reed had lived longer, it is unlikely that these events would have occurred. He certainly appeared willing to give Finlay his due, at least publicly. In Reed's presentations of their results, Finlay was given credit for his theory of mosquito transmission and for providing *Aedes* eggs to the board. Unassuming and reserved, Finlay himself never made much of an issue of it, but his supporters did.

Curiously, the debate continues even today. At the request of the Cuban president Fidel Castro and with his support, José López Sánchez wrote an interesting biography of Carlos Finlay published by Editorial José Martí in 1985. Not surprisingly, it pumps pure oxygen onto the embers of the controversy by ardently taking the Cuban view of events. One of the critical scientific issues is whether Finlay produced yellow fever in any of his more than one hundred volunteers. His supporters insist that he did, in that several of his patients developed fever and albumin in their urine, signs of yellow fever. Because his volunteers were not quarantined before their bites by loaded mosquitoes, one cannot be sure if they truly acquired their illness from Finlay's mosquitoes or if their illness was even yellow fever. More important, Finlay was not aware of the extrinsic incubation period and did not wait long enough between loading his mosquitoes and having them bite his volunteers. Those who believe in the validity of the extrinsic incubation period, initially proposed by Henry Rose Carter and demonstrated by the U.S. Army Board along with several others who later verified their results, insist that Finlay's volunteers could not have contracted yellow fever from the bites of his mosquitoes. If the illness they had was indeed yellow fever, it could have been acquired from a wild mosquito, as they were not quarantined, as were the volunteers of the Army Board. Supporters of Finlay also say that he was more considerate of his volunteers by not wanting to produce severe cases of yellow fever. Those who say he was aware of the extrinsic incubation period point out that he believed a case would be milder and produce immunity if the mosquito bit earlier in the incubation period, so he had his mosquitoes incubate only a few days instead of the ten to twelve days the Army Board said was necessary.

Finlay's own results and those of the Army Board dispute these theories. Several of Finlay's volunteers who were bitten early in the incubation period later developed yellow fever, demonstrating that their experimental bites did not produce immunity. Three army volunteers were bitten after thirty-nine, fifty-one, and fifty-seven days of incubation. The first two had mild cases, but the third had a severe case. Finlay also believed that limiting the number of bites would produce a milder case. James Carroll's case refuted this, as only one mosquito that had incubated the virus for twelve days bit him; he almost died. John Moran was bitten by at least fifteen mosquitoes; his case was mild. Carroll was convinced that the constitution and immunologic makeup of the victim determined the severity of the case. Private William Dean, bitten by the same mosquito that almost killed Carroll, had a mild case. Guitéras tragically showed that the virulence of the particular strain of yellow fever virus was also a "factor," when three of his volunteers bitten by mosquitoes carrying the Alvarez strain died.

It seems the debate will continue as long as there are political differences between the two countries. Reed clearly learned much from Finlay, both positive and negative. Reed's genius was in the thoroughness, quality, conduct, sophistication, scope, and control of his experiments. Reed had the power and money of the United States government behind him; Finlay essentially worked alone with his own resources. Both made major and critical contributions, as did Gorgas and many others, to the conquest of yellow fever. Henry Carter's observations on yellow fever had pointed the board in the direction of a possible insect vector and a period of extrinsic incubation. Carter, who knew all the principal characters, as he was in Cuba the entire time, placed the events in their proper historical perspective when he said, "Few scientific discoveries—medical or otherwise—are in their entirety the work of any one man. He who puts the capstone on the completed structure gets—as he should—the credit for it, but the foundation and walls may—and generally have been—built by many hands."[10]

Chapter 15

Historic Application

B EFORE HIS ASSIGNMENT IN HAVANA WAS EVEN OVER, MAJOR William Crawford Gorgas, as army officers had routinely done for decades before him and still do today, began looking for his next assignment. The four-year U.S. occupation of Cuba was coming to an end, and Gorgas's sanitation campaign in Havana had been successful beyond anyone's wildest imagination. Even without his triumph over yellow fever, Gorgas would have been considered a very successful sanitation chief in Havana. The death rate in the native population in Havana had declined from ninety-one per thousand when he arrived in late 1898 to thirty-four in 1899, the first full year of the U.S. occupation, to twenty-four in 1900, and twenty-two in 1901. The decrease in deaths from disease in the American troops was even more dramatic: in 1898, sixty-eight per thousand died of disease; in 1902, the number was down to seven per thousand.

In 1902, Gorgas wrote Surgeon General Sternberg and suggested that the mosquito and disease control techniques used so successfully in Havana might be applied in Panama to support the construction of the Panama Canal. In June 1902, Congress, with the support of the new president, Theodore Roosevelt, had voted in favor of Panama over Nicaragua for the site of America's efforts to bridge the Atlantic and Pacific oceans. Congress also approved the purchase of the French concession that remained after that country's ill-fated attempt to build the canal. Everyone who was aware of world events knew that the French had literally died trying to complete the canal. The romantic dream of a canal connecting the two great oceans of the Western Hemisphere had all the ingredients of high adventure, high accomplishment, and high reward. Gorgas wanted to be part of it.

Ferdinand de Lesseps, the extraordinary French engineer who over ten years (1859–1869) had built the Suez Canal, had gone to Panama in 1880 to repeat his extraordinary feat and build the long-anticipated and dreamed-of Panama Canal. De Lesseps, known as the "Great Frenchman," was seventy-four when he began the doomed construction project in Panama. Nine years later, he halted his disastrous efforts, bankrupt and broken. He was beaten not by the enormity of the construction project itself but by disease, primarily yellow fever and malaria, that had killed and disabled thousands of his workers. He no longer had the will or the money to continue.

In the fall of 1902, Gorgas was relieved of his duty in Cuba, and he returned to the United States to prepare for his anticipated new assignment to Panama. He was sent to Egypt to attend the first Egyptian Medical Congress and to learn as much as he could about the sanitary problems that existed during the construction of the Suez Canal. Despite it being an interesting trip, he did not learn much that would be useful to him. About the only similarity between the two areas was the sweltering heat. Even that similarity was different; Panama was wet hot and the Suez was dry hot. Toward the end of 1902, Major Gorgas was promoted to colonel and assistant surgeon general, a promotion and grade intended for Walter Reed but negated by his untimely death in November.

Before the United States could begin the project, there was one small detail of permission to operate on foreign soil; at the time, Panama was a department of Colombia. In January 1903, Congress offered Colombia a treaty giving the United States control of a strip of land six miles wide extending approximately fifty miles across the isthmus. In August 1903, the Colombian senate refused to sign the agreement. The people of Panama, seeing the canal project as a great boon to their economy, renewed their attempts for independence and revolted against Colombia in November. After Colombian troops landed at Colon on the Caribbean side of the isthmus, the United States invoked an 1846 treaty that allowed it to intervene if transit across the isthmus on the American-owned railroad was threatened. When the United States Marines landed at Colon supported by a U.S. gunboat, Colombia withdrew. The revolution was essentially bloodless, as only one man was killed. Panama declared its independence, and despite some criticism of Roosevelt's heavy-handed role in foreign affairs, the United States recognized the Republic of Panama and signed a treaty to obtain the strip of land that became known as the Canal Zone. Almost twenty years later, the U.S. Congress paid Colombia $25 million dollars in reparations for its loss of Panama.

After the political changes in Panama and the signing of the treaty, the Isthmian Canal Commission was organized in January 1904 with seven members. Roosevelt was strongly urged by the American Medical Association and many others to put a physician on the commission. Everyone who was knowledgeable about the failed French effort years before knew that disease was the real enemy, but the president refused. This refusal turned out to be a blessing in disguise.

In April 1904, Gorgas received his orders as the chief sanitary officer of the Panama Canal Zone with additional duty as the sanitary adviser to the Canal Commission. When he arrived in Panama in June 1904, he began some tumultuous and difficult early years; his stay in Panama would ultimately last ten years. Gorgas knew immediately that he had to get control over yellow fever or the project would suffer the same dreadful fate as had the French attempt. Exact figures are not available, but the best estimates are that the French lost about one-third of their workers to yellow fever every year. He estimated that if the Americans suffered the same percentage of deaths as the French had, there would be thirty-five hundred dead each year.

The first place to start was, of course, where *Aedes aegypti* lived. This was in the towns at each end of the railroad, whose general path the canal was to follow. On the northern, Caribbean, end was Colon; on the southern, Pacific, end was Panama (now Panama City). In Havana, Gorgas had fumigated only the houses where yellow fever cases occurred; however, the city of Panama was only about one-tenth the size of Havana, and he planned on fumigating every house. He completed the work in about a month, but cases of yellow fever still occurred, so he fumigated again, and then once again.

As the number of nonimmune Americans increased in the winter of 1904 and spring of 1905, so did the cases of yellow fever. The first Canal Commission, possibly concerned about its own safety, made a disastrous mistake when it decided to remain in the United States and attempted to build the waterway from afar. The members of the commission looked on Gorgas's attempts to control yellow fever by killing mosquitoes as "wild and visionary."[1] The term "visionary," as used at that time, would be called "hallucinatory" today. Therefore, he got little support.

In January 1905, the entire first commission was fired and replaced. If Gorgas had been on the commission, he, too, would have been fired. A couple of months after several high-ranking officials had died of yellow fever in April 1905, the new governor of the Canal Zone and the chief engineer of the commission recommended to President Roosevelt that Gorgas be fired. Roosevelt's secretary of war, William Howard Taft, agreed. Gorgas received the enthusiastic support of the American Medical Association and that of William Welch, the same William Welch who was the dean of the Johns Hopkins Medical School, as well as the friend and mentor of Reed, Carroll, and Lazear. Welch was very familiar with their work in Cuba and the dramatic results of Gorgas's work in Havana. Welch gave a forceful recommendation to keep Gorgas. Roosevelt, however, was politically concerned about going against the recommendation of his new commission and his secretary of war. Having been in Cuba for the Spanish-American War and president during Gorgas's great successes in Havana, he was convinced of the mosquito transmission of yellow fever and Gorgas's ability to control the disease. Despite all this, Roosevelt still struggled with the decision. He called on his longtime New York City friend, Dr. Alexander Lambert. The president had heard that Gorgas was not cleaning up the filth and awful odors in either Colon or Panama. Lambert, whose uncle had worked with the French, knew yellow fever and went over some of its history. Finally, he told Roosevelt, "You must choose between the old method and the new; you must choose between failure with mosquitoes and success without them."[2] Roosevelt, a very young forty-six-year-old, was an extremely progressive and farsighted president. He refused to yield to the pressure to fire Gorgas; instead, he reiterated his support for him, called the head of the commission to his office, and directed in no uncertain terms that Gorgas receive all the support and assistance he requested.

Gorgas knew that, in addition to killing mosquitoes on the wing by fumigation, he also had to kill them while in the larval or wiggler stage. This, of course, meant getting rid of all standing fresh water in the cities of Colon and Panama. He divided the cities into districts, as he had done in Havana, and hired inspectors to visit every house, business, church, and building to ensure that all standing water was eliminated. As in Havana, ordinances were passed to allow a fine for those found not to have covered or oiled their containers of fresh water. At first, the locals were amused with the Yankees, but later they became resentful and more difficult to work with; however, as the success of the program grew, the locals again became more cooperative, possibly out of a sense of civil pride or possibly just out of resignation to Gorgas's methods. Any standing water anywhere could serve as a breeding place for the domestic *Aedes*. To keep the ever-present ants out of their beds, the Americans would place the legs of their beds in a small plate or pan of water. These, too, became breeding grounds for mosquitoes, and the water had to be either oiled or removed. Water in gutters, vases of fresh-cut flowers, and even holy water receptacles at churches also had to be covered, treated, or removed. Once the mosquito's standard breeding places had been eliminated, some clever soul decided that they should make traps by making the female *Aedes* an offer she could not refuse. Pans of clean water were placed in open locations, well lighted by the sun, a perfect situation for the gravid *Aedes*. Every few days the dishes, loaded with larvae, were emptied—just another low-tech but effective weapon in Gorgas's arsenal. Gorgas would learn that of his multipronged assault on *Aedes*, attacking the mosquito's breeding places was the most efficient way to control its numbers.

Gorgas's effort and outlook were greatly enhanced when a new chief engineer, John F. Stevens, arrived in 1905. The fact that Stevens fully supported Gorgas and his ideas concerning the prevention of yellow fever gave an enormous boost to the morale and energy of the sanitation workers. In the fall of 1905, the chairman of the commission recommended that Gorgas report directly to him instead of going by the initial arrangement under which Gorgas reported through the governor to the commission. This greatly simplified Gorgas's administrative work, adding to his anticipation of success, as it was that same fall that the incidence of yellow fever significantly dropped off and everyone began to breathe easier. The last case of yellow fever occurred in May 1906 in Colon; from then until the canal was opened in 1914, there were no more cases of yellow fever in the Canal Zone.

If Gorgas had been replaced, the man slated for the job was a physician who did not believe in the mosquito transmission of yellow fever; he believed that yellow fever was a filth disease and had plans for abandoning the mosquito work and concentrating on cleaning up the filth of Colon and Panama. His efforts, of course, would have done nothing to control yellow fever and the certain deaths that would have accompanied its continued occurrence. His approach could have led to multitudes of additional deaths, as well as the possibility that the American public and government would have called for abandoning the entire project.

In November 1906, Roosevelt came to the Canal Zone on an official visit, the first such trip outside the United States by an incumbent president.

Roosevelt's advisers clearly felt it was safe for the president to journey to Panama, both politically and physically, as there had been no new cases of yellow fever for six months. He was, in his characteristic way, literally all over the place; talking to as many workers as he could about their jobs; inspecting and trying out every machine or piece of equipment, large or small; and learning as much as he could about all aspects of the work and Panama itself. Gorgas spent a good deal of time with the president, and after he returned to Washington, Roosevelt elevated Gorgas to membership on the commission, an enormous vote of confidence.

Malaria, as much as yellow fever, threatened the success of the canal project. But malaria was as likely to live in the jungles as in the cities and towns of Panama. For those who have never seen a tropical jungle, it is hard to imagine the conditions under which the Americans confronted malaria. Marie Gorgas, who was in Panama with her husband, described these conditions in her book about her husband's life written after his death. She brought to life the malaria-infested jungle that lay between Colon and Panama with these words:

> an apparently hopeless tangle of tropical vegetation, swamps whose bottoms the engineers had not discovered, black muddy soils, quicksands, interspersed now and then by a tall volcanic mountain or crossed by rivers that, at flood tide, sometimes rose twenty feet and more in a single night. This vegetation was an impenetrable mass of palm trees, banana plants, mangroves, creepers of all kinds, bamboo, cotton woods, and the whole was a never ending panorama of animal life. Chattering monkeys, shrill parrots, and parakeets, birds of the most variegated plumage filled the trees; wild turkeys, wild boars, and wild hogs swarmed the tall grass, and poisonous snakes, great lizards, tarantulas, and all manner of reptile and insect life covered the oozy ground. This terrible place was not lacking in beauty; all kinds of tropical flowers bloomed eternally, and its orchids had led more than one venturesome collector to his doom. The intense thunder and lightning storms that frequently illuminated the darkness, the showers of rain that constantly swept down upon it—huge masses of water that for the time obliterated the landscape—also had their own element of grandeur. But the general impression was one of dank terror.[3]

Not being a city dweller like the *Aedes* mosquito of yellow fever, the *Anopheles* mosquito that transmitted malaria was much harder to reach. Malaria remained a danger even after yellow fever no longer was. Gorgas attacked the home of *Anopheles* as vigorously as he had the *Aedes* mosquito. In order to remove the breeding places of *Anopheles*, he required that all vegetation be removed for two hundred yards around any building, road, stream, or structure in the Canal Zone. Streams and pools of water were sprayed with kerosene to kill the larvae. Crude oil soon replaced kerosene because it was much cheaper. Vegetation was sprayed with a solution made of carbolic acid and rosin that was called larvacide.

Gorgas knew he had engaged a different enemy in malaria. A victim of malaria is not as likely to die as a victim of yellow fever, but malaria causes chronic recurring illness with episodes of the plasmodium parasite circulating in the victim's bloodstream. Unlike with yellow fever, where the virus is cleared from the bloodstream, never to return, if a malaria victim is bitten by an *Anopheles* mosquito during a victim's relapse, the mosquito is then loaded with malaria. In a location where a significant portion of the populace had had malaria, they served as an almost unending source of agent for mosquitoes to acquire and transmit the disease. Given these circumstances, it was not possible for Gorgas to wipe out malaria as he had yellow fever. His efforts did pay off, however, as over the period of about one year, there was a dramatic drop in cases from eight hundred per thousand admissions to eighty cases of malaria per thousand admissions to the Canal Zone hospitals.

Following the resignation of Mr. Stevens as chief engineer in 1908, the president and the secretary of war, in a paradigm shift from the makeup of previous Canal Commissions, named career military men to serve on the new commission, telling them they had to stay until the job was finished. The most important new member was, of course, the chairman and chief engineer, Lieutenant Colonel George Washington Goethals. Gorgas was retained as a member of the commission. Fortunately, the problem of yellow fever was under complete control and that of malaria was under good control. Gorgas was honored in 1908 with his election as president of the American Medical Association, a distinctly unusual honor for someone who, at the time, did not even live in the United States. Following completion of the canal, Gorgas was elevated to surgeon general of the U.S. Army, a position he held until his retirement in 1918.

While Gorgas had been fighting yellow fever and malaria, as well as administrative incompetence in Panama, yellow fever had been busy elsewhere. It was probably May 1905 when yellow jack assaulted New Orleans. It had been there many times before, but after centuries of wreaking havoc and death, this would be yellow fever's swan song in North America. The epidemic began in the French Quarter near the Mississippi River where an Italian immigrant community lived; many were employed unloading banana boats from Central America. It took two long months for the "suspicious" deaths to be recognized as an emerging epidemic and then ten more days until the epidemic was officially declared.

Two factors contributed to the tragedy that followed: the delayed recognition that yellow fever was truly present, and the fact that many, if not most, homes in New Orleans got their water from wooden cisterns. These open storage tanks bred not only *Aedes* mosquitoes but also disaster.

Dr. Joseph H. White of the U.S. Public Health and Marine Hospital Service was brought in to assist local authorities wage their campaign on *Aedes*. They used the now tried-and-true methods of Gorgas and attacked the mosquito in all its familiar places, but the efforts were initially voluntary. The public acceptance of the mosquito transmission of yellow fever lagged behind the proven scientific facts, and education of the citizenry was one of the main fronts in New Orleans's attack on the now well-established epidemic. Jo Ann Carrigan points out in her writings that before radio and television, newspapers were the only quick source of public information (*The Saffron Scourge: A History of Yellow Fever in Louisiana 1796–1905*, University of Louisiana Press, 1994). Therefore, the large immigrant population without English-language skills was almost impossible to reach rapidly. These difficulties were compounded by the fact that many of the native English-speaking and -reading citizens had not yet accepted that mosquitoes could kill. Voluntary participation went only so far, and as had occurred in Havana and Panama, city ordinances were passed requiring property owners to cover their cisterns with wire screening. Distinctly unlike Cuba and Panama, where American authorities were anxious not to offend the locals and wrote citations but truly fined very few, there were no such concerns in New Orleans. Several prominent citizens were fined and some even jailed. However brief their jail time, the message was loud and clear: this was serious business.

On August 4, the mayor, through the governor, asked for federal intervention. President Roosevelt ordered Walter Wyman, the surgeon general of the U.S. Public Health and Marine Hospital Service, to take charge. Dr. Joseph White, already in New Orleans on behalf of the federal government, assumed control of the situation quickly, establishing an elaborate network of supervisors and workers that rapidly grew to over thirteen hundred. They employed all the Gorgas techniques—fumigation, screening of fever cases, and destruction or incapacitation of *Aedes* breeding grounds. It was only after Archbishop Placide Louis Chapelle died of yellow fever that the basins of holy water in St. Louis Cathedral were found to be teeming with churchgoing *Aedes* larvae. The priests kept them empty for the remainder of the epidemic. The mayor declared a citywide holiday and asked businesses to close so the citizens could participate in the cleanup campaign. The epidemic reached its peak in mid-August, when in one day it felled a hundred victims. After this peak, the combined effects of the local, state, and federal governments and the lay citizenry began to pay off. It took two more months for the disease to be completely controlled, and by the end of October, the flames of yellow fever were for the last time extinguished in the United States. The final grim toll in New Orleans and Louisiana was almost ten thousand cases and over nine hundred deaths, a deadly farewell to epidemic yellow fever in North America.

Chapter 16

Yellow Fever after Walter Reed

IN 1897, FREDERICK T. GATES RECOMMENDED TO JOHN D. ROCKEfeller Sr. that he endow a medical research institute. Characteristic of Rockefeller's caution, it was several years before an actual institute was established. In 1901, Rockefeller offered grants for medical research to be conducted in existing laboratories. Distinguished, nationally known physicians were asked to serve as expert decision makers on where the money should go. William Welch of Johns Hopkins agreed to chair the group, and he personally oversaw the efforts to get the institute established; in 1902, Dr. Simon Flexner agreed to be its first director. He served until 1935. It was Flexner's brother, Abraham, who wrote in 1910 a startling report on the state of medical education in the United States that produced revolutionary changes in the way physicians were taught and trained. The Rockefeller Institute purchased land in Manhattan along the East River, and construction began in 1903 for its permanent home, which opened in 1904.

Almost ten years later, the Rockefeller Foundation was chartered by the state of New York in 1913 with its mission "to promote the well-being of mankind throughout the world."[1] The Rockefeller Foundation was another effort to use John D. Rockefeller's enormous wealth in positive, beneficial ways, as Rockefeller money had already gone to many different philanthropic efforts through the Rockefeller Institute and the General Education Board, with the overarching goal of improving standards of living and education both in the United States and abroad.

Following his appointment as director-general of the International Health Commission (later called board and then division) of the Rockefeller Foundation, Dr. Wickliffe Rose went abroad in 1914 to initiate contacts with health officials and gather information on possible projects. Yellow fever had never occurred in Asia or the islands of the Pacific; however, in 1910, a Japanese steamer en route from Manzanillo, Mexico, rounded Diamond Head and arrived in Honolulu carrying yellow fever. The nonimmune population of Honolulu was fortunate in that the disease remained confined to one case and did not spread. The following year, the same ship returned to Honolulu carrying another case, and this time, a quarantine guard developed yellow fever. Luckily this was the only secondary case that occurred in Hawaii. Three years later, the opening of the Panama Canal in 1914 completely changed the world of commerce and travel and greatly increased the potential for the spread of disease. The canal opened the waters of the Pacific Ocean and the lands and people of Asia to the Caribbean and all it possessed—including, because of the increased rapidity of travel, the even greater possibility of yellow fever. Public health officials were concerned that the possible introduction of this dreadful disease to the immunologically naive masses of Asia had the potential to be a disaster of catastrophic proportions.

On his return, Rose met with William C. Gorgas, now surgeon general of the U.S. Army and a longtime advocate for the eradication of yellow fever. Following their discussions, Rose decided to make worldwide eradication of yellow fever a goal of the Rockefeller Foundation. Its first step along that daunting path was to form a Yellow Fever Commission with members that included, among others, Gorgas and his friends from Cuba, Henry Rose Carter and Juan Guitéras, and Gorgas's nephew, Theodore C. Lyster.

The Rockefeller Foundation targeted Brazil as one of the countries in South America where they would make significant efforts to improve public health. At the Second Pan-American Scientific Congress held in Washington, D.C., in 1915–1916, the Rockefeller Foundation unveiled its plans to begin work on eradication of yellow fever in Brazil. Gorgas was elected the chairman of the Medical Section of the Congress, which then passed a resolution proposing the eradication of yellow fever in the Americas.

In October 1916, Gorgas, along with the other members of the Rockefeller Foundation Yellow Fever Commission, including Carter and Guitéras, made an initial visit to Ecuador, Peru, Colombia, Venezuela, and Brazil to gather firsthand knowledge of the situation. At this time, the fight against yellow fever was based on two assumptions. First was that *Aedes aegypti* was the only vector for the disease; second was the "key center" theory. The first assumption was, of course, based on the investigative work of Walter Reed and the follow-up work of Gorgas in Havana and Panama, where destruction of *Aedes* had ended yellow fever. The "key center" assumption said that there were endemic centers of yellow fever that served as "seed beds" from which the epidemics arose. Based on his experience in

Cuba and Panama, Gorgas believed that yellow fever would disappear if the "seed beds" were wiped out. No one could seriously argue with either assumption, based on Gorgas's extraordinary results; yellow fever no longer existed in either country. When the Gorgas expedition returned home, their conclusion was that Guayaquil, Ecuador's major seaport on the Pacific, was the only endemic center of yellow fever in existence at that time.

Gorgas was still surgeon general of the U.S. Army and had his hands full in preparing his Medical Department for entry into World War I. When the United States joined the fight in April 1917, he was unable to pay much attention to yellow fever. In addition, the 1918 influenza pandemic, which claimed at least 20 million lives worldwide, diverted interest and health care resources; thus little thought was given to yellow fever.

Gorgas retired as surgeon general of the army in October 1918 and was then able to turn his full attention to the work of the Rockefeller Foundation Yellow Fever Commission. One of its first successes came in a campaign to eradicate yellow fever from Guayaquil. Following Gorgas's successful techniques from Panama, that is, primarily attacking the breeding places of the *Aedes aegypti* mosquito instead of killing the adults by fumigation, yellow fever disappeared from Ecuador in eight short months. During this campaign, Hideyo Noguchi, a member of the Rockefeller Institute, worked independently in Ecuador and reported isolating a new germ as the etiologic agent of yellow fever, a spirochete that he named *Leptospira icteroides*.

Noguchi, born in Japan in 1876, had become famous working for Simon Flexner at the Rockefeller Institute. He was the first to demonstrate with Flexner the spirochete of syphilis in the brains of patients who succumbed to neurosyphilis. Noguchi, ambitious beyond measure and safety, was in a rush to glory and fame. He worked tirelessly, almost always alone, with many different agents of disease. He claimed to be able to accomplish remarkable things that others could not. He was able to grow in a test tube the spirochete that caused syphilis when others failed. He also grew the organisms of rabies, polio, and trachoma. No one was ever able to repeat his work. He was either a genius or a scientific shyster; yellow fever would distinguish the truth where humans could not.

Noguchi made several extraordinary claims about yellow fever: first, that the new agent he had found was the etiologic agent of yellow fever; second, that it was a spirochete, visible with an ordinary microscope, that no one else had ever seen. This was in direct contradiction to James Carroll's finding that the yellow fever germ was an ultramicroscopic agent that passed through the smallest available filters. Noguchi claimed he had transmitted yellow fever caused by this organism to animals and between animals. He also reported that he had produced and successfully tested in animals a vaccine based on this organism. His claims were eerily reminiscent of those made by Guiseppe Sanarelli some twenty years before. Sanarelli's were all proven to be false, but what about Noguchi's? Almost immediately, others working in the field began to raise doubts about the veracity of his work and continued to do so over the next few years as they were unable to reproduce his results. Many thought he had confused his organism *Leptospira icteroides* with *Leptospira icterohemorrhagiae*, the known cause of leptospirosis or Weil's disease. His supporters theorized that the cases he had seen in Ecuador were misdiagnosed by the local physicians as yellow fever when they were, in fact, Weil's disease all along. Thus, he had made an understandable mistake when he was misled to the diagnosis. Noguchi never admitted that he could have made a mistake.

In 1924, Aristides Agramonte, who had lived in Cuba since the completion of the work of the U.S. Army Board, read a paper at the International Conference on Health Problems in Tropical America. Noguchi was in the audience, and Agramonte challenged him to produce a natural case of yellow fever by way of a controlled experiment. Noguchi was unable to do so. Several others failed to substantiate his claims; even more workers, including a young investigator at Harvard, Dr. Max Theiler, concluded that *Leptospira icteroides* and *Leptospira icterohemorrhagiae* were identical. These events were again eerily reminiscent of the past history of yellow fever research, when Walter Reed had proved that Sanarelli's organism, *Bacillus icteroides*, was identical to common hog cholera.

In 1920, the Rockefeller Foundation sent a commission to the coast of West Africa in response to a reported epidemic of what was thought to be yellow fever; Gorgas was named to lead it. On his way to Africa, he stopped in London to be honored by King George V with the Knight Commander of the Most Distinguished Order of St. Michael and St. George. While there, he suffered a stroke and was not able to attend the ceremony. The king came to his bedside at the Queen Alexandra Military Hospital and presented Gorgas his knighthood. Four weeks later, Gorgas, having never left the hospital, died. He was sixty-six years old.

It would be five years before the Rockefeller Foundation returned to Africa and Dr. Henry Beeuwkes, a U.S. Army colonel, established the West African Yellow Fever Commission headquarters and laboratory in Yaba, near Lagos, Nigeria. The other commission staff included Drs. Johannes H. Bauer, N. Paul Hudson, Alexander F. Mahaffy, and Adrian Stokes. Unfortunately, very little progress was made for several years, as Rockefeller scientists were mired in the misguided theories of Noguchi and made no significant discoveries until 1927.

In late June 1927, Dr. Alexander F. Mahaffy examined several people in the Gold Coast (now Ghana) town of Kpeve, made the clinical diagnosis of yellow fever, and drew blood from two yellow fever patients. One of those he drew blood from was a twenty-eight-year-old African man named Asibi. Unknown to them at the time, the name of the young African who was only mildly ill with yellow fever would become famous in public health circles the world over. The name of the young doctor who drew the blood and took it to Accra, where it was injected into two monkeys and two guinea pigs, would fade into history essentially unknown.

One of the monkeys Mahaffy inoculated was a *Macacus rhesus* acquired from India; it was designated as rhesus 253-A. It died four days later of yellow fever. The other monkey, a marmoset, and the guinea pigs remained well. Blood was taken from 253-A and injected into another rhesus, 253-B. Because there were no proper facilities for mosquito experiments in Accra, 253-B was transported to the larger laboratory in Lagos. Several days later when 253-B became ill, *Aedes aegypti* mosquitoes were allowed to feed on it. Monkey 253-B died six days after it received the virus-laden blood from 253-A. Altogether about thirty monkeys were infected with the Asibi yellow fever virus and all but one died. The commission also successfully transmitted the Asibi strain via mosquito bites. The West African Yellow Fever Commission also showed that the agent of yellow fever passed through a Berkefeld filter, confirming the experiments of James Carroll from 1901. In addition, they demonstrated that convalescent serum from the severe cases of yellow fever that they had produced protected susceptible monkeys from the virus.

Their discovery that yellow fever could be transmitted to and therefore studied in laboratory animals was a major breakthrough, but it was not without a price. Tragically, the elusive mistress proved just as deadly in the laboratory as she had in nature. One of the Rockefeller men, Dr. Adrian Stokes, contracted yellow fever while working in the laboratory and died. The forty-year-old Stokes, from London, was the great-grandson of the Irish physician William Stokes, whose name is widely known to those who work in the medical field, as it is attached to a syndrome of fainting triggered by cardiac arrythymia (Stokes-Adams syndrome) and a pattern of abnormal or periodic breathing most often associated with congestive heart failure or neurologic damage (Cheyne-Stokes respirations). Although it is not known for certain how Adrian Stokes contracted yellow fever, it is known he was not exposed to loaded mosquitoes. He did not wear gloves when he worked with the monkeys, and he probably contracted the infection in the laboratory working with monkey blood and tissue infected with the Asibi virus. He was the first of many to become infected in this manner. Stokes, who had been in West Africa just a little over four months, had not been working with *Leptospira*, and there was none in their laboratory. *Leptospira* was clearly not associated with yellow fever.

Hideyo Noguchi arrived in Africa in November 1927, dying to defend himself. He would do exactly that. Working alone in Accra, as had been his routine, Noguchi placed many demands on the West African Yellow Fever Commission for space, equipment, and laboratory animals. He worked with both *Leptospira* and the Asibi virus that had been isolated in Lagos. In an effort to explain why the Rockefeller workers in Lagos had isolated a virus shown to cause yellow fever, he theorized that South American yellow fever was distinct from African yellow fever. Around Christmas, he became ill with what he called yellow fever; no one knew for sure. During his illness, he had a monkey injected with his blood. He claimed the monkey became ill with typical yellow fever, but the illness he described did not fit the normal pattern. When the monkey died almost three weeks later, Noguchi claimed that the autopsy revealed the most typical case of yellow fever he had ever seen. He failed to explain why the monkey had no fever, jaundice, or albumin in its urine.

After his recovery, Noguchi worked furiously, demanding even more monkeys for his private studies. Many of his results were confusing to others experienced with yellow fever. He was sure his research was precedent setting; in a cable home, he wrote, "My work is so revolutionary that it is going to upset all our old ideas of yellow fever."[2] In May 1928, he was preparing to return to New York with his self-proclaimed revolutionary discoveries, but while on a trip to Lagos, he became ill. He returned to Accra, where Alexander Mahaffy thought he had yellow fever. Several days into his illness, Noguchi had black vomit, an ominous prognostic sign. Despite his claim to have had the disease previously, everyone knew that this time he truly had yellow fever. After the black vomit that usually heralded death, Noguchi rallied, but a week later, on May 20, he died of kidney failure. Dr.

William A. Young, the director of the Medical Research Institute at Accra and the only trained scientist that Noguchi had allowed in his laboratory, performed the autopsy. The tragedy of Noguchi's death was compounded ten days later, when Young also died of yellow fever. Young was thirty-nine.

The fact that Young became ill five days after performing Noguchi's autopsy would fit the usual incubation period of yellow fever, and it is presumed that he contracted yellow fever in this way. How many hundreds if not thousands of autopsies had been done on yellow fever victims over the years with no evidence that it could be transmitted by contact? Reed and the U.S. Army Yellow Fever Board had shown that regardless of the severity of the case, the virus is no longer in the blood of a victim after about the third day of illness. It is now known that even though the virus is cleared from the bloodstream, it can in some instances reside in the internal organs, especially the liver, for much longer. It is also known that yellow fever can, at least in rare instances in the laboratory, be aerosolized. The timing is such that it is hard to deny that Young got yellow fever from performing Noguchi's autopsy. How Noguchi became infected was open to much speculation. Had he finally realized that there was no way out of the scientific corner he had painted himself into? Had he committed medical hara-kiri? His supporters who knew him well thought this was extremely unlikely and saw him as a medical martyr. Others, more skeptical, felt that he had succumbed to a laboratory-acquired infection, simply a victim of his own life-long sloppy laboratory habits. Noguchi is still revered by many as a scientific genius; however, *A History of the Rockefeller Institute*, the official published history of the Rockefeller Institute, supplied a measured epitaph: "His habit of working with an almost unmanageably large assortment of culture tubes, not always labeled, was not conducive to precision. More enthusiastic than experienced in pathology, he sometimes mistook the lesions in his experimental animals for those characteristic of human disease."[3]

The deaths in Africa of so many good men shocked the Rockefeller Foundation. The director of the International Health Division, Colonel Frederick F. Russell, formerly the head of the Division of Laboratories and Infectious Disease for the Army Surgeon General's Office, wanted to get control of the situation. In 1928, just a month after Noguchi and Young died, he established the Rockefeller Foundation Yellow Fever Laboratory in New York City. Wilbur A. Sawyer was appointed to be the first director. The Rockefeller Foundation obviously did not want any more of its men to die, or to lose its position at the forefront of yellow fever research.

Several other laboratories were active in yellow fever research, including that of Andrew W. Sellards at Harvard, where the first work with the yellow fever virus in the United States took place. Sellards had acquired the "French" strain of yellow fever at the Institut Pasteur in Dakar, the capital of French Equatorial Africa (now Senegal). The French strain had originated in a Syrian patient, François Mayali, and had been passed through mosquitoes to a monkey in a manner similar to the way the Asibi strain had been processed by the Rockefeller men in Lagos. These two different strains of yellow fever virus, the Asibi strain and the French strain, became the standards used in laboratory research. The Asibi strain had been responsible for the deaths of Adrian Stokes, William Young, and possibly Hideyo Noguchi. Despite its deadly beginnings, the Asibi virus would later be used to save thousands of lives.

During the first year of operation of the New York City laboratory, Sawyer contracted yellow fever. Other workers in yellow fever laboratories around the world were also taken ill. Fortunately, Sawyer survived; some of the others were not as lucky. In June 1929, a Rockefeller Foundation worker in Brazil, Dr. Paul A. Lewis, who was still trying to prove Noguchi's theory about *Leptospira*, became ill and died of yellow fever. Sawyer said that Lewis's death was "the last gasp of the *leptospira* question."[4]

One more Rockefeller scientist would die of yellow fever. Dr. Theodore B. Hayne attended medical school in his native South Carolina and had completed one tour in West Africa with the foundation's Yellow Fever Commission. He returned home in January 1930 to be married on January 27. In late March, he left his pregnant bride and returned to Africa for his second tour. Back in Nigeria, he took charge of the Entomology Laboratory and its dangerous cache of loaded mosquitoes; apparently it was one of his charges that bit him and transmitted his fatal case of yellow fever. He had been receiving injections of serum from donors who had had yellow fever, but not in a great enough volume to provide any protection. Theodore Hayne was just a few days short of his thirty-second birthday when he died in August 1930 in Lagos. He was the eighth and last researcher to die of yellow fever while trying to solve its mysteries.

There were over thirty laboratory workers who contracted yellow fever, but strangely the eight who died were all physicians. U.S. Army Contract Surgeon Jesse Lazear died in Cuba in September 1900. Walter Myers from the Liverpool School of Tropical Medicine died in South America in 1901. Dr. Howard B. Cross, thirty-three, a graduate of Johns Hopkins School of

Medicine, was the first of six Rockefeller Foundation scientists to die from yellow fever, on December 26, 1921, in Tuxtepec, Mexico, where he was on duty for the International Health Division. In Africa, there were three shocking deaths—Adrian Stokes, Hideyo Noguchi, and William Young. No less difficult were the deaths of Paul A. Lewis in 1929 and Theodore Hayne in 1930. Eight loyal and fearless soldiers in the war against an invisible foe had, in the noblest sentiments of the profession, died in hopes of saving others. Yellow fever claims another grim distinction in that no other virus in the history of laboratory research has taken away so many of those working to solve its mysteries.

The idea of a yellow fever vaccine was obviously not new, but the startling deaths of the five Rockefeller men between 1927 and 1930 had upped the ante on developing one. Guiseppe Sanarelli and others had tried passive immunization for the prevention of yellow fever in the late 1800s. Passive immunization consisted of using serum from a person or an animal that had recovered from an exposure to the offending agent, in this case yellow fever, in the hopes that the convalescent serum contained antibodies that would protect the recipient against the disease. Convalescent serum against yellow fever was difficult to come by, as those who had had yellow fever were scattered across several continents and oceans and were difficult to locate, and large volumes of serum were required. Animals (nonhuman primates, horses, goats) were used in a successful attempt to acquire more convalescent serum, but animal serum could not be used repeatedly in humans without severe allergic reactions. When animal serum was combined with a partially attenuated virus (the French strain), it produced active immunity. Initially, there were few significant side effects noted, and it became standard practice in the early 1930s. It was useful for health care workers and researchers; however, it was still cumbersome and could not be used for mass immunization programs. After isolation of the virus in 1927, attempts were made to develop an inactivated vaccine, but those met with limited success.

Max Theiler, working with Sellards at Harvard, showed in 1930 that common albino mice were susceptible to the yellow fever virus if it was inoculated into their brain. This finding opened up a whole new arena for research, as it was obviously much easier to work with laboratory mice than monkeys, not to mention the significant cost savings accrued by using these much smaller and lower-maintenance animals. Theiler also developed a test that was used to demonstrate an individual's immunity. Persons were shown to have had yellow fever if their serum could protect a laboratory mouse from a challenge with the yellow fever virus. When expanded to a large population, this mouse protection test permitted surveys of immunity that were previously unavailable. These population surveys provided information that helped lead to the conclusion that yellow fever had occurred without the presence of *Aedes aegypti*, a very important point in the later full understanding of the epidemiology of yellow fever. Somewhat later in 1930, Theiler was recruited to join the Rockefeller Foundation.

Active immunization with an attenuated version of the French strain and without the addition of convalescent serum was begun in 1932 in Africa. In 1934, reports began to come in that there were some dangerous complications associated with the French strain vaccine. Because of this danger, American and English researchers chose not to use the vaccine produced from the French strain for routine use and looked for an alternative. During the years 1934 to 1937, Theiler and others, including Hugh Smith at the Rockefeller Foundation Yellow Fever Laboratory in New York City, working with the Asibi strain of yellow fever, developed, by multiple passages through mouse embryos and then chick embryos with their central nervous systems removed, a strain that was known as subculture strain 17D. This strain greatly reduced the risk of viscerotropism (damage to the visceral organs, principally the liver) and neurotropism (damage to the brain) that plagued the French-strain vaccine. After successful animal studies, Theiler and Smith, who were already immune, tried the vaccine on themselves in November 1936, looking for potential complications. There were none. Trials were then conducted with other human volunteers; they were all successful.

Wilbur Sawyer had been elevated to the head of the International Health Division with overall charge of the yellow fever program. Sawyer and Fred Soper, the director of the Rockefeller Foundation's efforts in Brazil, agreed that Brazil was the place to conduct the first field trials of the vaccine. Hugh Smith was sent to direct the production of vaccine and the field trials of the vaccine in Brazil. Smith, working with Brazilian Dr. Henrique Penna, started slowly with only six people. By the end of 1937, they had vaccinated thirty-eight thousand; by the end of the next year, they had vaccinated over a million people. It would have been unrealistic to expect that there would be no problems with such a huge program. For some time, it had been common practice to mix vaccines with human serum. At first, the serum was convalescent serum from the disease itself, and it provided some passive immunity. By the time the 17D vaccine was being produced for widespread use, human serum was added to help keep the virus alive.

The yellow fever scientists were all aware of an unusual illness that had been seen in England in some recipients of a different yellow fever vaccine than the one Rockefeller had developed. In 1936, Dr. G. Marshall Findlay, working for the Wellcome Bureau of Scientific Research, told the Rockefeller men about a young doctor who had received the vaccine and had developed an illness associated with jaundice. Serum hepatitis was an unknown entity at the time. During the following two years, Findlay encountered over a hundred cases of hepatitis in about five thousand people who received the vaccine. The jaundice and other evidence of hepatitis could not be yellow fever, as they developed anywhere from five weeks to seven months after the vaccination, much too delayed an illness for yellow fever. In 1938, while presenting at a tropical medicine meeting in London, Findlay said, "We are dealing with another virus introduced into the yellow fever tissue culture with the apparently normal human serum. This virus is similar to, and probably identical with, the virus of epidemic catarrhal jaundice or . . . infective hepatitis."[5] Given the state-of-the-art knowledge and equipment available to them, it was impossible to pin down the actual culprit. Further work in Brazil solidified the belief that it was the human serum added to the vaccine that caused hepatitis in some vaccine recipients. To protect against this, the serum was heated to 133 degrees Fahrenheit before being added to the vaccine; this appeared to work, but not in every situation. Much later it was learned that a temperature of over 170 degrees Fahrenheit was required to inactivate or kill the virus of serum hepatitis. In Brazil, work was renewed on a serum-free vaccine that was put into use in December 1940.

In June 1940, the National Research Council recommended that all U.S. military personnel be vaccinated with the yellow fever vaccine if there was any possibility that they might be assigned in or travel to the tropics. This greatly increased the demand for a vaccine that at the time was only produced by the Rockefeller International Health Division. Despite the concerns about hepatitis and the early success with the serum-free vaccine in Brazil, Sawyer decided to stay with the standard process of vaccine production using human serum; by January 1941, Sawyer and his team were producing fifty thousand doses a week.

Theiler and others were concerned about the possibility of hepatitis from the use of human serum and began work on a serum-free vaccine of their own. However, Sawyer was not convinced it was a problem and felt that the serum-free vaccine had not been field-tested enough to vouch for its potency and stability. There was no time to complete the further testing, as a yellow fever epidemic in the Nuba Mountains in Sudan had sickened fifteen thousand, with at least fifteen hundred deaths, and as the likelihood of another world war approached, the army was pushing to get its troops vaccinated. Theiler warned Sawyer that there was a potential disaster in the making.

The military needed more vaccine and proposed adding another laboratory to increase production. The Rockefeller laboratory volunteered to produce all the vaccine for free after it heard that civilian contractors were in discussions with the government to provide the vaccine for a dollar a dose; the lab was currently producing it for pennies a dose. Increased production meant the need for more human serum, and when a former Rockefeller man working at Johns Hopkins proposed that Hopkins medical students, interns, nurses, and technicians would provide the serum as paid volunteers, everyone was happy. The student doctors and nurses were glad to contribute to the war effort and to get the extra income. Rockefeller scientists could not possibly think of a better-educated, cleaner-living, or healthier group. In reality, health care workers are one of the highest-risk groups of donors for the transmission of serum hepatitis. By April 1942, the Rockefeller laboratory had produced 7 million doses of the yellow fever vaccine, all with human serum.

In early 1942, an increased incidence of hepatitis was being reported from military posts and bases in the West. Over the next few months, similar reports came in from around the world. Sawyer found out about the hepatitis problem in mid-March; he was not inclined to think it was the vaccine. Hepatitis was known to be common in crowded military camps and could have been acquired from the local civilian population. But evidence to the contrary quickly mounted, and on April 1, he called the military and suggested they stop using the vaccine except in situations with high risk of exposure to yellow fever. Two weeks later, its use was halted completely. Theiler had been working on a serum-free 17D vaccine that was quickly put into production; by June 1942, the military began to use it. The yellow fever vaccine containing human serum would never be used again. There were over forty-nine thousand cases of hepatitis in the military, most of which were linked to the yellow fever vaccine. There were eighty-four deaths. The other side of this coin was that during the years of

World War II, not a single U.S. soldier, sailor, or Marine, deployed all over the world, contracted yellow fever. Wilbur Sawyer took full responsibility and sharp criticism for his decisions. After publishing a full report, he retired in 1944. Despite the tragic results for those involved, medical knowledge had been significantly advanced. The existence of serum hepatitis, its differences from infectious hepatitis, the importance of previous clinical history in blood donors, and the potential dangers of human blood and blood products all had major public health impacts in the decades to come.

In sub-Saharan Africa during the 1930s, the French continued to use a vaccine produced from the French strain of the yellow fever virus that Max Theiler had developed but since had himself abandoned. Despite some reports of complications (encephalitis, or inflammation of the brain), French public health officials made the decision that the real threat of yellow fever outweighed the concerns about vaccine complications. In 1939, a new technique was developed to deliver the yellow fever vaccine concomitantly with the smallpox vaccine, using the scarification method already in use for smallpox. In just one year, over a hundred thousand people were immunized by this method without recognized side effects and with a greater than 95 percent success rate in producing protection against yellow fever. The French vaccine did not contain human serum. By 1941, 1.9 million people had been immunized using this technique in francophone Africa. With the rush to get the masses immunized, there was no careful follow-up on complications. Later, a more careful and thorough assessment revealed that encephalitis was a serious complication, especially in children, and that it could have a mortality rate as high as 40 percent.

Over a period of about twenty-five years, the French virus-based vaccine was given to more than 40 million people in French West Africa. Yellow fever was essentially eliminated except for sporadic cases. Because of the complications of encephalitis in young children, the French stopped giving their vaccine to children under ten years of age. An epidemic in Senegal, West Africa, in the mid-1960s caused about 140 deaths, mostly in children under ten who had not received the French vaccine. At that time, they switched over to the 17D vaccine, which has become the world standard and for almost forty years has been the only yellow fever strain used to produce a vaccine.

As the vaccine was being developed and put into practice, others continued to sort out yellow fever's pathology and epidemiology. Dr. Fred L. Soper of the Rockefeller Foundation first arrived in Brazil in 1920 and was assigned to work on the hookworm problem. For the next seven years, except for two years of additional postgraduate study in the United States, he was involved with the organization and administration of the hookworm prevention program in Brazil and Paraguay. In 1927, he was reassigned to work on yellow fever, which was considered Brazil's number one public health problem.

Historically, little importance was placed on the anatomic diagnosis of yellow fever by examination of the internal organs at autopsy, as this was obviously after the fact, and during an epidemic the clinical diagnosis was pretty straightforward. Some members of the U.S. Army Board in 1900 and 1901 did autopsies on yellow fever victims, usually declaring the results consistent with the clinical diagnosis. They were probably familiar with William T. Councilman's 1890 description of microscopic changes in the liver associated with yellow fever, the so-called "Councilman bodies."[6] The yellow fever epidemic in Rio de Janeiro in 1928 that lasted more than a year provided a large amount of pathologic material for study. Brazilian pathologists were able to confirm the work of another Brazilian, Henrique da Rocha Lima, who twenty years earlier had been the first to extensively describe the changes in the visceral organs due to yellow fever, using modern staining methods. By 1930, there was general agreement that yellow fever could be diagnosed by histologic study of the liver alone. A new procedure was devised called viscerotomy, which was the practice of collecting liver tissue from the body of a person who had died after a febrile illness of less than eleven days' duration. After appropriate training, the procedure was performed by nonmedical personnel with an instrument called a viscerotome. The viscerotome was specifically made for this purpose and was patterned after an instrument used to sample coffee beans without damage to the coffee sack. After initial difficulties over customs and religious beliefs (including some gun fights and deaths), viscerotomy became routine in appropriate circumstances, greatly assisting in the elucidation of the epidemiology of yellow fever. In June 1930, Soper became the head of the Cooperative Yellow Fever Service, a joint venture of the Rockefeller Foundation and the Brazilian government.

Using Theiler's mouse protection test, which had been further developed by Wilbur Sawyer and Wray Lloyd, evidence was found that yellow fever had occurred in many areas where it was not expected and not reported. In some situations, the prevalence of yellow fever was higher in rural and jungle areas than it was in the urban areas where the outbreaks had occurred. These findings did not fit the conventional wisdom that yellow fever did not occur without *Aedes aegypti* mosquitoes.

In 1932, Soper and his colleagues investigated an outbreak of yellow fever in a rural area of Brazil where there were no *Aedes aegypti*. However, it took several more similar outbreaks over the next couple of years in rural areas of Brazil, Colombia, and Bolivia to convince Soper he was seeing something completely different from the well-known urban yellow fever.

In 1935, Soper presented his conclusions before the Brazilian National Academy of Medicine. Soper spoke in Portuguese that he had taught himself and for the first time used the term "jungle yellow fever." He gave historical background that suggested the existence of jungle yellow fever as early as 1907. Soper preferred the term "jungle" over the word "sylvan" as more descriptive of the tropical rain forest where these cases occurred; both terms are used today.[7] Urban and jungle yellow fever are the same disease clinically; the terms simply refer to the epidemiology of the disease.

The complete transmission cycle was unknown to Soper at the time, but was later determined to involve tree-top-dwelling mosquitoes (*Haemagogus* species) whose victims were monkeys who shared the same treetops. When nonimmune humans entered the jungle to work or play, they could become victims of *Haemagogus*'s deadly bite. Soper's elucidation of jungle yellow fever put a stop to any hopes the Rockefeller Foundation had for the worldwide eradication of yellow fever. Despite this setback to the vision he had shared with the Rockefeller Foundation, Fred Soper continued to work toward the eradication of yellow fever by elimination of the *Aedes aegypti* mosquito. In 1950, when he became the director of the Pan-American Sanitary Bureau, later the Pan-American Health Organization, he continued to lead efforts to control the yellow fever vector, and by 1972, *Aedes aegypti* had been eliminated from over 70 percent of the land area it had originally inhabited.

It is now known that the enzootic, or animal-to-human, transmission cycle of yellow fever involves nonhuman primates and tree-hole-breeding mosquitoes, primarily *Haemagogus sp.* in South America and *Aedes sp.* (non-*aegypti*) in Africa. This is the true way that yellow fever is maintained in nature. The awful epidemics of urban yellow fever that ravaged the East and Gulf coasts of North America, the Caribbean, and Central and South America, killing literally hundreds of thousands, were for centuries caused by mosquito-to-man-to-mosquito transmission, the only cycle known at the time. As these epidemics were confined to urban areas, they were effectively controlled by destruction of the vector, *Aedes aegypti*. At this point in time, it is generally accepted that jungle yellow fever will never be eradicated because the vastness of the jungles in South America and Africa makes it impossible to eliminate the mosquitoes.

On October 13, 1951, Max Theiler was notified that he had been selected to receive the Nobel Prize in Physiology or Medicine for his "discoveries concerning yellow fever and how to combat it."[8] Theiler would become the only scientist among the many who battled yellow fever to be recognized for his accomplishments with the Nobel Prize. Theiler's achievements in the laboratory were many: early on while at Harvard, he identified the virus that served as the basis of the French neurotropic vaccine; he demonstrated the usefulness of mice as a laboratory vehicle for the study of yellow fever; his mouse protection test was used worldwide to survey yellow fever immunity; and most important, his patient and persistent passage of the Asibi virus through multiple mouse and then chick embryos produced the 17D strain and the resultant highly successful 17D vaccine. Theiler was somewhat embarrassed that other Rockefeller workers, especially Hugh Smith, had not been named co-winners with him. But Theiler was an obvious choice, mostly because of his advances in basic scientific research, but also because he was not tainted by the "Rockefeller disease,"[9] as the epidemic of serum hepatitis associated with the contaminated yellow fever vaccine during World War II came to be known. His boss, the director of the International Health Division, Wilbur Sawyer, had been tainted by the episode. A basic scientist who gave up the laboratory for an administrative leadership role, Sawyer expectantly saw himself as deserving of the prize. After all, he had overseen all aspects of the program. Sawyer saw the awarding of the Nobel Prize to anyone else in the field as a repudiation of his entire career. By the time Theiler made his acceptance speech in Stockholm on December 11, 1951, Wilbur Sawyer had been dead a month. His wife frankly said that the award of the Nobel Prize to Max Theiler killed her husband.

In a somewhat twisted way, some considered Wilbur Sawyer to be the last Rockefeller man to become a victim of yellow fever.

Epilogue: After Cuba

D R. JAMES CARROLL, SECOND IN CHARGE OF THE ARMY YEL-
low Fever Board after Walter Reed, was married with five children
at the time he voluntarily participated in the early yellow fever experiments.
At forty-six years old, he knew, as did the others, that the mortality from
yellow fever rapidly increased with age. He developed a very severe case,
and although it was not diagnosed at the time, he almost certainly suffered
with the complication of myocarditis. His damaged heart continued to
plague him for the remainder of his life.

At the outbreak of the Spanish-American War, Carroll, who was serving as an enlisted man despite his medical degree, was hired as a contract
surgeon. He served in this capacity during his work with the Yellow Fever
Board. After the successes of the board, Generals Wood and Sternberg recommended that Carroll be promoted to major, but this was denied due to
a moratorium on promotions. He applied for and received a regular army
commission as first lieutenant in late 1902 and later served, after Reed's
death, as the curator of the Army Medical Museum. He wrote widely on
yellow fever in national and international journals. He also spoke at many
national meetings and became a jealous guardian of the historical accounts
of the Yellow Fever Board's work. His last publication was the chapter on
yellow fever in William Osler's *Systems of Medicine*.

Carroll was finally promoted by Special Act of Congress from first
lieutenant to major on March 9, 1907. He died in Washington, D.C., on
September 16, 1907, from complications of valvular heart disease that
some thought was brought on by his experimental case of yellow fever. He
was fifty-four. Carroll was buried in Arlington National Cemetery. A
bronze plaque in his memory was placed at the University of Maryland

Medical School in Baltimore, and during World War II, a liberty ship, built by Bethlehem-Fairfield Shipyard in Baltimore, was named in his honor in November 1943.

Aristides Agramonte, who had also served the board as a contract surgeon, remained in his native Cuba for some years. He became a professor of bacteriology and experimental pathology at the University of Havana. Although the role he played on the U.S. Army Yellow Fever Board was smaller than the others, after 1907, he was the sole surviving member and was called upon to represent the group, such as in 1924 when he challenged Hideyo Noguchi at an international meeting. In December 1915, he published in *Scientific Monthly* his memories of the board's work, a paper entitled "The Inside History of a Great Medical Discovery." At the time of his death in 1931, he was professor of tropical medicine at Louisiana State University in New Orleans.

Dr. Carlos Finlay had publicly proposed in 1881 that the female *Aedes* mosquito was "the intermediate agent in the transmission of yellow fever."[1] Finlay, who had been unable to convincingly prove it, had been derisively called by some in his native Cuba "the mosquito man." After the success of the Yellow Fever Board, he became the toast of Havana. He was praised and feted around the country and the world. He received international recognition and appointments to various boards and associations. In 1904, 1906, and 1907, he was nominated for the Nobel Prize but did not win. In honor of his mosquito theory, the Philadelphia College of Physicians made him an honorary Fellow. This was the same college that Benjamin Rush had resigned from in protest following the 1793 Philadelphia epidemic. Finlay died in Havana in 1915 at age eighty-two.

As governor general of Cuba, Leonard Wood had provided financial and command support for the work of the Yellow Fever Board. While serving as governor general, he was a member of the U.S. Volunteers. By the time he completed that assignment in 1902, his good friend Theodore Roosevelt was in the White House, and Wood received a commission as brigadier general in the regular army. He ultimately became chief of staff of the U.S. Army (1910–1914) and was an unsuccessful candidate for the Republican presidential nomination in 1920. He served as governor general of the Philippines from 1921 until 1927. The recurrence of a benign brain tumor caused him increasing debility, and he returned to the United States in 1927. He died in Boston immediately following surgery performed by Dr. Harvey Cushing. Fort Leonard Wood in Missouri and its hospital, the General Leonard Wood U.S. Army Hospital, memorialize his name.

The first Nobel Prize for Physiology or Medicine was awarded in 1901. Sir Ronald Ross won the prize in 1902 for his discovery that malaria is transmitted by mosquitoes. Walter Reed's death made him ineligible, as Alfred Nobel had specified in his will that the awards not be given posthumously. There were several campaigns for the surviving members of the Yellow Fever Board, as well as Carlos Finlay, to receive the prize, but this was not to be. Max Theiler received the prize in 1951 for his work with yellow fever and the production of a successful vaccine.

Both Walter Reed (1945) and William Gorgas (1950) were elected to the New York University Hall of Fame of Great Americans, the only two army physicians so honored in the 102-member Hall. The Hall is an outdoor display built as part of the university's University Heights campus and is now part of the Bronx Community College campus.

In 1927, the Virginia Medical Society restored the small cottage in Gloucester County, Virginia, where Walter Reed was born. Today it is maintained by the Joseph Bryan Branch of the Association for the Preservation of Virginia Antiquities. The house is open to the public in September on the Sunday closest to Walter Reed's birthday (September 13) and during Historic Garden Week every spring.

In 1929, the seventieth U.S. Congress passed Public Law No. 858, "To recognize the high public service rendered by Major Walter Reed and those associated with him in the discovery of the cause and means of transmission of yellow fever." It read:

> Be it enacted by the Senate and House of Representatives of the United States of America in Congress assembled, That in special recognition of the high public service rendered and disabilities contracted in the interest of humanity and science as voluntary

subjects for the experimentations during the yellow-fever investigations in Cuba, the Secretary of War, be, and he is hereby, authorized and directed to publish annually in the Army Register a roll of honor on which shall be carried the following names: Walter Reed, James Carroll, Jesse W. Lazear, Aristides Agramonte, James H. Andrus, John R. Bullard, A. W. Covington, William H. Dean, Wallace W. Forbes, Levi E. Folk, Paul Hamann, James L. Hanberry, Warren G. Jernegan, John R. Kissinger, John J. Moran, William Olsen, Charles G. Sonntag, Clyde L. West, Doctor R. P. Cooke, Thomas M. England, James Hildebrand, and Edward Weatherwalks.

This Act of Congress also entitled these individuals (or their survivors) to a Congressional Gold Medal and a monthly pension. A Special Act of Congress in July 1957 amended Public Law 858—Seventieth Congress, to include the names of Gustaf E. Lambert and Roger P. Ames.

Brigadier General Albert E. Truby had been a lieutenant in the Medical Corps assigned to Cuba during this extraordinary work of the U.S. Army Board. In 1943, following his retirement, he published *Memoir of Walter Reed: The Yellow Fever Episode.* His admiration for the enlisted men was still obvious some forty years later, when he wrote,

> The hospital corps detachment consisted of from forty to seventy men with about seven non-commissioned officers (hospital stewards and acting hospital stewards). This group of men was as loyal and efficient as any I have ever known during my long service in the Medical Department. Their service in various camp hospitals had thoroughly fitted them for the duties at our hospital. Their heroism was shown in their daily work with typhoid fever and more especially when volunteers were needed to test the mosquito theory concerning yellow fever.[2]

In concluding his remarks to the Fourth International Congress on Tropical Medicine and Malaria in 1948, Philip S. Hench, the Mayo Clinic physician who by that time had spent twenty years studying the work of the Yellow Fever Board, said the following:

In these days when man's inhumanity to man is still so pathetically apparent, it is well for us to note the example of these men who banded together for high adventure, not to kill or even die for one country but to die if need be for their fellow men of all countries. These 25 men included 3 Cubans, 16 Americans, 1 Englishman, 1 Irishman, and 4 Spaniards. Some were Catholic, some were Protestant, some were Hebrews. United in a common cause they demonstrated magnificently the human capacity for greatness and courage. It is such as they who reassure us of the inherent decency and dignity of man.[3]

Dr. Hench's comments of over half a century ago still ring true today. These little known but remarkable men demonstrated uncommon courage and commitment as they participated in and made possible the U.S. Army Medical Department's most extraordinary contribution to medicine, world health, and commerce. The measure of this contribution was quickly made evident by the successful completion of the Panama Canal, and today can be gauged by the fact that to the vast majority of all physicians throughout the world, yellow fever is an unknown disease.

Afterword: Yellow Fever Today

THE YELLOW FEVER VIRUS IS A MEMBER OF THE FLAVIVIRIDAE family, which is within the group of viruses that are called arboviruses because they are transmitted by arthropod vectors. Most of the viruses of this family that do cause disease are transmitted to humans by mosquitoes or ticks. There are three subgroups of mosquito-borne viruses: yellow fever, dengue and dengue hemorrhagic fever, and Japanese encephalitis (including West Nile virus). Dengue is asymptomatic in 80 percent of children, and when it does cause illness, it cannot be distinguished from other common childhood infections. In adults, the disease is more severe, causing chills, fever, frontal headache, severe musculoskeletal pain, and rash. Dengue fever has also been known as breakbone fever. The Japanese encephalitis viruses, including West Nile, attack the brain and central nervous system.

Yellow fever is a single-strained RNA virus of 10,862 nucleotides; the yellow fever virion is an enveloped particle with a diameter of about 50 nanometers, many times smaller than the bacteria that Reed and his associates were able to see through their microscopes. Today yellow fever occurs only in South America and Africa. The New Orleans epidemic in 1905 was the last appearance of yellow fever in North America, but it continued to occur elsewhere in the Western Hemisphere. Rio de Janeiro had an epidemic in 1928 after a twenty-year hiatus. The last urban yellow fever in the Americas occurred in 1954. Jungle yellow fever invaded Central America in the 1950s and 1960s; since then, there have been repeated small outbreaks of jungle yellow fever scattered throughout South America, usually less than three hundred cases each. It is still occurring today; in December 2003 and January 2004, the Colombian Ministry of Social Protection reported twenty-seven confirmed cases of yellow fever with at least eight deaths that occurred in a tourist area along its Caribbean coast.

Yellow fever in Africa has been much more common and widespread. There were serious epidemics in every decade of the twentieth century. Between 1958 and 1966, there were a number of epidemics in Central and East Africa that claimed thousands of lives. Dr. Thomas Monath, currently one of the world's leading experts on yellow fever, said that the 1960s "was ushered in by the largest epidemic of yellow fever ever recorded, affecting 10% of the 1,000,000 residents of southwestern Ethiopia, and causing about 30,000 deaths."[1] Epidemics occurred in Ghana (formerly Gold Coast) in the 1970s that killed hundreds, and in Nigeria in the 1980s that killed thousands, including five thousand in 1987. Smaller and less murderous epidemics occurred in the early 1990s. In January 2003, the World Health Organization reported that new cases of yellow fever had occurred in several West African locations and in the southern Sudan, with at least sixty deaths.

To this day, yellow fever has not occurred in Asia. The dengue fever virus, which shares the same flaviviridae family as yellow fever, is hyperendemic in most Asian countries, making some scientists speculate that the populace is protected from yellow fever by its immunity to dengue fever. In addition, there is speculation that the *Aedes aegypti* mosquitoes that are abundant in Asia may not be as well suited for transmitting yellow fever as their sister *Aedes aegypti* found in South America and Africa. Regardless of the reasons, Asia has been spared this deadly plague.

The United States government's Centers for Disease Control and Prevention estimates that worldwide, several hundred cases of yellow fever occur each year. However, some experts think that due to underreporting and lack of recognition of the disease, the actual incidence of yellow fever is hundreds to thousands of times higher. The clinical spectrum of signs and symptoms with acute yellow fever has not changed over the centuries, and neither has the fatality rate of severe yellow fever, approximately 20 percent. Definitive diagnosis is made by culturing the virus from blood or tissue specimens or by identification of yellow fever virus antigen or viral particles in body tissues using highly sophisticated immunologic studies. Treatment for yellow fever consists of providing general supportive care, and it varies, depending on which organ systems are involved. No effective specific antiviral therapy against yellow fever has been developed.

Some public health officials are concerned about the possibility of yellow fever reemerging. The urban yellow fever vector *Aedes aegypti* has reinvaded a number of countries where it had been eradicated. Human populations and transportation systems have grown into some enzootic areas due to efforts to colonize these forested areas. In addition, the ready availability and speed of international air travel contribute to the possibility of the introduction of yellow fever to unprepared populations. The 1982 occurrence of epidemic *Aedes aegypti*–borne dengue fever in an urban center in Brazil brought to light this potential danger. Despite the availability of 17D vaccine and its proven safety and efficacy, large populations remain unvaccinated. This situation has been demonstrated repeatedly in Africa with its periodic epidemics. Latin America has fared much better because of its more systematic use of vaccine.

Between 1996 and 2002, there were five cases of yellow fever among travelers to South America and Africa from the United States and Europe, including the case presented in the introduction of this book. All were unvaccinated and tragically all died. Prevention is obviously the best approach and is easily accomplished with the 17D vaccine. All yellow fever vaccines currently in use are live attenuated vaccines derived from the 17D strain. Yellow fever vaccine is still given in a dose of 0.5 milliliter, subcutaneously, usually in the upper arm. Persons who receive the yellow fever vaccines should get it at least ten days prior to any potential exposure. Despite the fact that vaccine immunity may be lifelong, international health regulations require revaccination every ten years. Administration of the yellow fever vaccine simultaneous with other vaccines is generally acceptable. Current pricing for the vaccine supplied to the World Health Organization is about twenty cents a dose; however, the price could be significantly higher for individual patients depending on where they receive their vaccine.

Reactions to the 17D yellow fever vaccine are typically mild. Some persons receiving the vaccine have reported mild headaches, muscle aches, low-grade fevers, or other minor symptoms for five to ten days. Only about 1 percent of those who receive the vaccine curtail regular activities. Immediate hypersensitivity reactions, characterized by rash, urticaria, or asthma, are uncommon and typically occur among individuals with histories of allergies to egg or other substances.

Historically, the most common serious adverse event associated with yellow fever vaccine, encephalitis (inflammation of the brain), has occurred in children. This complication, formerly known as postvaccinal encephalitis, is now known as vaccine-associated neurotropic disease. Since 1945, with literally millions of doses given, fewer than two dozen cases of encephalitis temporally associated with or confirmed to be caused by the 17D vaccine have been reported; of these, over half have occurred among children younger than nine months, thus it is recommended that children younger than nine months of age not be vaccinated.

Recently, a new serious adverse reaction syndrome has been described among recipients of different 17D yellow fever vaccines. Previously known as febrile multiple organ system failure, this syndrome is now known as vaccine-associated viscerotropic disease. In July 2001, the first seven case reports of this syndrome appeared. These cases occurred between 1996 and 2001, with each patient having severe multiple organ system failure; six of the seven patients died. Subsequently, additional suspected cases have been identified. These cases demonstrate that the 17D vaccine virus has the potential to cause serious illness and even death in certain persons. Evidence exists that individuals are most at risk for yellow fever vaccine-associated viscerotropic disease after their first vaccination, as all cases reported thus far have occurred in persons after their first vaccination.

With over one and a half million doses of the yellow fever vaccine distributed between 1990 and 1998, four cases of yellow fever vaccine-associated viscerotropic disease were reported. This equates to an estimated reported incidence of 1 in 400,000 doses distributed.

However, the recent receipt of yellow fever vaccination and the similarity of the clinical symptoms among all four U.S. cases indicate that the yellow fever vaccine is a probable cause of the disease in these cases. Whether and in what way underlying factors in the vaccine recipient (genetic or acquired) or preexisting clinical conditions might have contributed to the course or outcome of yellow fever vaccine-associated viscerotropic disease is unknown.

Because of the recent reports of yellow fever deaths among unvaccinated travelers to areas endemic for yellow fever and of these reports of vaccine–associated viscerotropic disease, physicians should be careful to administer the yellow fever vaccine only to persons truly at risk for exposure to yellow fever. Additional information is available at www.cdc.gov.

Acknowledgments

Over time, many people have given us the encouragement to indulge our curiosity and allowed us time for research and thus the opportunity to tell the story of yellow fever and its conquerors. Their support led to our opportunity to write this book. Many of those people are named below; others are unnamed but not unthanked. We fully realize that while the book, and all that is right and wrong it it, may be ours, our thoughts and words were guided over the years by many people.

At Walter Reed Army Medical Center: Generals Ronald Blanck, Michael Kussman, Leslie Burger, Harold Timboe, and Kevin Kiley, and Carolyn Stoneburner. At the Walter Reed Army Institute of Research: Colonel Patrick W. Kelley. At the Office of the Surgeon General, U.S. Army: Dr. John Greenwood. At the Uniformed Services University of the Health Sciences: Drs. Robert Joy, Dale Smith, Earl Fauver, and Val Hemming. At the Department of Veterans Affairs: Dr. Clark Sawin. Archivists and librarians at the National Archives and Records Administration, the Walter Reed Army Medical Center, the Walter Reed Army Institute of Research, the Department of Veterans Affairs Central Office, the Department of Veterans Affairs Record Management Center, the University of Virginia's Claude Moore Health Sciences Library, the National Museum of Health and Medicine, the National Library of Medicine, the New York Academy of Medicine, and the interlibrary loan and Twinbrook Community Library staff of the Montgomery County Public Library.

Finally, Stephen S. Power, our editor at John Wiley & Sons, who took a chance on us and gave us the opportunity to tell this great story to a larger audience than we ever thought we would reach.

Notes

ABBREVIATIONS

NARA: National Archives and Records Administration

PH-WRC: Philip S. Hench Walter Reed Yellow Fever Collection, Claude Moore Health Sciences Library, University of Virginia Health Center

TJP-LOC: Thomas Jefferson Papers, Library of Congress, accessed at http://memory.loc.gov/ammem/mtjhtml/mtjhome.html

INTRODUCTION: THE FORGOTTEN SCOURGE

1. Centers for Disease Control and Prevention, "Fatal Yellow Fever in a Traveler Returning from Amazonas, Brazil, 2002," p. 324.

2. Corpus Christi *Caller-Times*, March 27, 2002.

3. PH-WRC, letter from Walter Reed to Emilie Reed, December 31, 1900.

CHAPTER 1. YELLOW FEVER COMES TO AMERICA

1. T. P. Monath, *Tropical Infectious Diseases*, p. 1259.

2. M. D. C. Creighton, "The Origin of Yellow Fever," p. 339.

3. Ibid., p. 338.

4. Cogolludo, *Historia de Yucathan*, quoted in H. R. Carter, et al., *Yellow Fever: An Epidemiological and Historical Study of Its Place of Origin*, p. 147.

5. H. R. Carter, et al., *Yellow Fever: An Epidemiological and Historical Study of Its Place of Origin*, p. 148.

6. Cogolludo, *Historia de Yucathan*, quoted in H. R. Carter, et al., *Yellow Fever: An Epidemiological and Historical Study of Its Place of Origin*, p. 148.

7. Ibid., p. 149.

8. Ibid.

9. C. L. R. James, *The Black Jacobins: Toussaint L'Ouverture and the San Domingo Revolution*, p. 330.

10. Ibid., p. 331.

11. TJP-LOC, letter from Thomas Jefferson to Benjamin Rush, September 23, 1800.

12. King James Bible, 1 Leviticus 14:46.

13. Anonymous, "Quarantine and Hygiene," p. 447.

14. Ibid., p. 449.

15. D. F. Stickle, "Death and Class in Baltimore: The Yellow Fever Epidemic of 1800," p. 293.

CHAPTER 2. THE CAPITAL UNDER SIEGE

1. E. Kornfeld, "Crisis in the Capital: The Cultural Significance of Philadelphia's Great Yellow Fever Epidemic," p. 191.

2. M. Carey, *Short Account of the Malignant Fever, Lately Prevalent in Philadelphia: With a Statement of the Proceedings That Took Place on the Subject in Different Parts of the United States.*

3. Ibid.

4. E. Kornfeld, "Crisis in the Capital: The Cultural Significance of Philadelphia's Great Yellow Fever Epidemic," p. 194.

5. W. A. Currie, *Sketch of the Rise and Progress of the Yellow Fever.*

6. B. Rush, *An Account of the Bilious Remitting Yellow Fever as It Appeared in the City of Philadelphia in the Year 1793*, p. 14.

7. Ibid.

8. J. H. Powell, *Bring Out Your Dead: The Great Plague of Yellow Fever in Philadelphia in 1793*, p. 7.

9. M. Carey, *Short Account of the Malignant Fever, Lately Prevalent in Philadelphia: With a Statement of the Proceedings That Took Place on the Subject in Different Parts of the United States.*

10. L. H. Butterfield (ed.), *Letters of Benjamin Rush: Vol. II, 1793–1813*, letter from B. Rush to Julia Rush, August 21, 1793, p. 637.

11. Ibid., letter from B. Rush to Julia Rush, August 22, 1793, p. 639.

12. Ibid., letter from B. Rush to Julia Rush, August 25, 1793, p. 641.

13. M. Carey, *Short Account of the Malignant Fever, Lately Prevalent in Philadelphia: With a Statement of the Proceedings That Took Place on the Subject in Different Parts of the United States.*

14. L. H. Butterfield (ed.), *Letters of Benjamin Rush: Vol. II, 1793–1813*, letter from B. Rush to Julia Rush, August 26, 1793, p. 642.

15. Ibid., letter from B. Rush to Julia Rush, August 27, 1793, p. 643.

16. J. H. Powell, *Bring Out Your Dead: The Great Plague of Yellow Fever in Philadelphia in 1793*, p. 54.

17. Ibid., p. 55.

18. Ibid.

19. M. Carey, *Short Account of the Malignant Fever, Lately Prevalent in Philadelphia: With a Statement of the Proceedings That Took Place on the Subject in Different Parts of the United States.*

20. L. H. Butterfield (ed.), *Letters of Benjamin Rush: Vol. II, 1793–1813*, letter from B. Rush to Julia Rush, September 18, 1793, p. 669.

21. J. L. Gardner (ed.), *John Adams: A Biography in His Own Words*, p. 343.

22. L. H. Butterfield (ed.), *Letters of Benjamin Rush: Vol. II, 1793–1813*, letter from B. Rush to Julia Rush, August 29, 1793, p. 644.

23. Ibid.

24. Ibid.

25. Ibid., letter from B. Rush to Julia Rush, September 1, 1793, p. 646.

26. TJP-LOC, letter from Thomas Jefferson to James Madison, September 8, 1793, accessed at www.memory.loc.gov/ammem/mtjhtml/mtjhome.html.

CHAPTER 3. NOTHING BUT A YELLOW FEVER

1. M. Workman, "Medical Practice in Philadelphia at the Time of the Yellow Fever Epidemic, 1793," p. 34.

2. Ibid.

3. L. H. Butterfield (ed.), *Letters of Benjamin Rush: Vol. II, 1793–1813*, letter from B. Rush to Nicholas Belleville, September 3, 1793, p. 648.

4. Ibid., letter from B. Rush to Julia Rush, September 8, 1793, p. 655.

5. R. H. Shryock, "The Medical Reputation of Benjamin Rush: Contrasts Over Two Centuries," p. 508.

6. Ibid.

7. L. H. Butterfield (ed.), *Letters of Benjamin Rush: Vol. II, 1793–1813*, letter from B. Rush to Nicholas Belleville, September 6, 1793, p. 653.

8. E. Kornfeld, "Crisis in the Capital: The Cultural Significance of Philadelphia's Great Yellow Fever Epidemic," p. 203.

9. Ibid., p. 196.

10. L. H. Butterfield (ed.), *Letters of Benjamin Rush: Vol. II, 1793–1813*, letter from B. Rush to Julia Rush, September 13, 1793, p. 663.

11. Ibid., letter from B. Rush to Julia Rush, September 21, 1793, p. 673.

12. J. H. Powell, *Bring Out Your Dead: The Great Plague of Yellow Fever in Philadelphia in 1793*, p. 79.

13. Ibid., p. 226.

14. J. T. Flexnar, *Washington: The Indispensable Man*, p. 303.

15. A. Jones and R. Allen, "A Narrative of the Proceeding of the Black People during the late Awful Calamity in Philadelphia in the Year 1793," accessed at www.geocities.com/bobarnebeck/allen.html.

16. M. Carey, *Short Account of the Malignant Fever, Lately Prevalent in Philadelphia: With a Statement of the Proceedings That Took Place on the Subject in Different Parts of the United States*.

17. L. H. Butterfield (ed.), *Letters of Benjamin Rush: Vol. II, 1793–1813*, letter from B. Rush to Julia Rush, September 18, 1793, p. 669.

18. J. H. Powell, *Bring Out Your Dead: The Great Plague of Yellow Fever in Philadelphia in 1793*, p. 155.

19. Ibid., p. 161.

20. Ibid., p. 172.

21. Ibid., p. 167.

22. Ibid., p. 197.

23. M. Carey, *Short Account of the Malignant Fever, Lately Prevalent in Philadelphia: With a Statement of the Proceedings That Took Place on the Subject in Different Parts of the United States*.

24. J. H. Powell, *Bring Out Your Dead: The Great Plague of Yellow Fever in Philadelphia in 1793*, p. 204.

25. Ibid., p. 208.

26. B. Rush, *An Account of the Bilious Remitting Yellow Fever as It Appeared in the City of Philadelphia in the Year 1793*, p. 14.

27. L. H. Butterfield (ed.), *Letters of Benjamin Rush: Vol. II, 1793–1813*, letter from B. Rush to Julia Rush, October 14, 1793, p. 715.

28. Ibid., letter from B. Rush to Julia Rush, October 17, 1793, p. 716.

29. Ibid., letter from B. Rush to Julia Rush, November 7, 1793, p. 740.

30. G. W. Corner (ed.), *The Autobiography of Benjamin Rush: His Travels Through Life*, p. 98.

31. Ibid., p. 95.

32. Ibid., p. 97.

33. S. Peller, "Walter Reed, C. Finlay, and Their Predecessors Around 1800," p. 202.

34. Ibid., p. 204.

CHAPTER 4. YELLOW FEVER MOVES SOUTH

1. J. A. Carrigan, *The Saffron Scourge: A History of Yellow Fever in Louisiana*, p. 235.

2. Ibid., p. 237.

3. Ibid., p. 239.

4. T. L. Savitt and J. H. Young (eds.), *Disease and Distinctiveness in the American South*, p. 61.

5. Ibid.

6. History of Mississippi: Yellow Fever Epidemics, p. 3, accessed at www.usgennet.org/usa/ms/state/yellowfever.html.

7. Ibid.

8. M. Humphries, *Yellow Fever and the South*, p. 21.

9. Ibid., p. 23.

10. J. C. Nott, "Yellow Fever Contrasted with Bilious Fever—Reasons for Believing It a Disease Sui Generis—Its Mode of Propagation—Remote Cause—Probable Insect or Animalcular Origin, &c.," p. 527.

11. Ibid., p. 590.

12. M. Humphries, *Yellow Fever and the South*, p. 24.

13. D. R. Goldfield, "Disease and Urban Image: Yellow Fever in Norfolk 1855," p. 36.

14. Ibid., p. 34.

15. Ibid., p. 40.

16. Sanitary Commission, Report of a Committee of the Associate Members of the Sanitary Commission, on the Subject of the Nature and Treatment of Yellow Fever, p. 5.

17. Ibid., p. 8.

18. Ibid., p. 10.

19. Ibid., p. 23.

20. B. Butler, "Some Experiences with Yellow Fever and Its Prevention," p. 530.

21. Ibid., p. 528.

22. Ibid., p. 529.

23. J. A. Carrigan, *The Saffron Scourge: A History of Yellow Fever in Louisiana*, p. 89.

CHAPTER 5. THE NATION THREATENED

1. J. A. Carrigan, *The Saffron Scourge: A History of Yellow Fever in Louisiana*, p. 97.

2. J. H. Ellis, *Yellow Fever and Public Health in the South*, p. 39.

3. K. J. Bloom, *The Mississippi Valley's Great Yellow Fever Epidemic of 1878*, p. 87.

4. S. R. Bruesch, "Yellow Fever in Tennessee in 1878. Part I," p. 890.

5. Ibid.

6. K. J. Bloom, *The Mississippi Valley's Great Yellow Fever Epidemic of 1878*, p. 90.

7. Ibid., p. 100.

8. M. S. Legan, "Mississippi and the Yellow Fever Epidemics of 1878–1879," p. 205.

9. P. Robbins, "Alas, Memphis!" p. 43.

10. J. H. Ellis, *Yellow Fever and Public Health in the South*, p. 43.

11. K. J. Bloom, *The Mississippi Valley's Great Yellow Fever Epidemic of 1878*, p. 128.

12. F. M. Wright, "Annie Cook: 'The Mary Magdalene of Memphis,'" p. 52.

13. S. R. Bruesch, "Yellow Fever in Tennessee in 1878. Part II," p. 102.

14. Ibid., p. 103.

15. Ibid.

16. J. H. Ellis, *Yellow Fever and Public Health in the South*, p. 61.

17. Ibid., p. 60.

18. Ibid., p. 66.

19. Ibid., p. 67.

20. Ibid.

21. Proceeding of the Board of Experts Authorized by Congress to Investigate the Yellow Fever Epidemic of 1878. January 29, 1879.

22. Ibid.

23. Ibid.

24. Ibid.

25. Ibid.

CHAPTER 6. YELLOW FEVER'S ODD COUPLE

1. J. W. Boshell (ed.), *Yellow Fever: A Symposium in Commemoration of Carlos Juan Finlay*, p. 5.

2. J. L. Sánchez, *Carlos J. Finlay: His Life and Work*, p. 190.

3. G. M. Sternberg, "Report on the Etiology and Prevention of Yellow Fever," p. 47.

4. PH-WRC, Report, extracts from an account of Dr. Louis-Daniel Beauperthuy: A Pioneer in Yellow Fever Research by Aristides Agramonte, and Mosquito or Man by Sir Rupert Boyce, June 11, 1908.

5. C. J. Finlay, "The Mosquito Hypothetically Considered as the Agent of Transmission of Yellow Fever," p. 612.

6. S. Peller, "Walter Reed, C. Finlay, and Their Predecessors Around 1800," p. 198.

7. Ibid., p. 197.

8. C. E. Finlay, *Carlos Finlay and Yellow Fever*, p. 25.

9. Ibid., p. 38.

10. P. P. Mortimer, "The Bacteria Craze of the 1880s," p. 584.

11. M. L. Sternberg, *George Miller Sternberg: A Biography*, p. 104.

12. Ibid., p. 111.

13. G. M. Sternberg, "Report on the Etiology and Prevention of Yellow Fever," p. 221.

14. Ibid., p. 223.

CHAPTER 7. WALTER REED

1. J. A. Graves, *The History of the Bedford Light Artillery*, p. 39.

2. PH-WRC, letter from Walter Reed to Emilie Lawrence, July 18, 1874.

3. Ibid.

4. Ibid., letter from Walter Reed to Emilie Lawrence, August 12, 1874.

5. Ibid., Examination Paper: Hygiene by Walter Reed, February 8, 1875.

6. Ibid., letter from Walter Reed to Emilie Lawrence, March 24, 1875.

7. Ibid., letter from Walter Reed to Emilie Lawrence, July 29, 1875.

8. Ibid., Letter from Walter Reed to Emilie Lawrence, August 30, 1875.

9. T. M. Fink, "Before Yellow Fever and Cuba, Walter Reed in Arizona," p. 194.

10. Ibid., p. 195.

11. W. B. Bean, *Walter Reed: A Biography*, p. 44.

12. M. Sandoz, *Old Jules*, p. 52.

13. W. Reed, "Geronimo and His Warriors in Captivity," pp. 231–235.

14. PH-WRC, Essay by William Welch Concerning Walter Reed's Work at Johns Hopkins University, undated.

15. W. B. Bean, *Walter Reed: A Biography*, p. 72.

16. G. Sanarelli, "A Lecture on Yellow Fever with a Description of Bacillus Icteroides," pp. 7–11.

17. G. Sanarelli, "Some Observations and Controversial Remarks on the Specific Cause of Yellow Fever," pp. 193–199.

18. Ibid.

19. Anonymous, "The Microbe of Yellow Fever," p. 672.

20. Ibid.

21. E. Wasdin and H. D. Geddings, Report to the Secretary of Treasury, July 10, 1899, Transmittal Letter.

22. E. Wasdin and H. D. Geddings, "The Etiology of Yellow Fever," pp. 299–302.

23. W. C. Gorgas, *Sanitation in Panama*, pp. 7–8.

CHAPTER 8. SPANISH BULLETS AND YELLOW FEVER

1. G. J. A. O'Toole, *The Spanish War: An American Epic—1898*, p. 82.

2. TJP-LOC, letter from Thomas Jefferson to James Monroe, October 24, 1823.

3. PH-WRC, letter from Walter Reed to Jefferson Kean, April 23, 1898.

4. Ibid.

5. M. C. Gillett, *The Army Medical Department, 1865–1917*, p. 149.

6. C. J. Post, *The Little War of Private Post: The Spanish-American War Seen Up Close*, pp. 260–261.

7. R. A. Alger, *The Spanish-American War*, p. 255.

8. Ibid., p. 257.

9. C. J. Post, *The Little War of Private Post: The Spanish-American War Seen Up Close*, p. 304.

10. T. R. Roosevelt, *The Rough Riders*, p. 204.

11. R. A. Alger, *The Spanish-American War*, p. 264.

12. D. F. Trask, *The War with Spain in 1898*, p. 330.

13. R. A. Alger, *The Spanish-American War*, p. 256.

14. T. R. Roosevelt, *The Rough Riders*, p. 280.

15. R. A. Alger, *The Spanish-American War*, p. 266.

16. Ibid., p. 270.

17. C. J. Post, *The Little War of Private Post: The Spanish-American War Seen Up Close*, p. 312.

18. M. C. Gillett, *The Army Medical Department, 1865–1917*, p. 232.

19. Ibid., p. 234.

20. Senate Document No. 822, Yellow Fever—A Compilation of Various Publications, p. 244.

21. PH-WRC, letter from Leonard Wood to Francis Greene, July 12, 1899.

22. Anonymous, "The Microbe of Yellow Fever," p. 672.

23. A. Agramonte, "Report of Bacteriological Investigations upon Yellow Fever," pp. 203–212, 249–256.

24. A. E. Truby, *Memoir of Walter Reed: The Yellow Fever Episode*, p. 73.

25. Senate Document No. 822, Yellow Fever—A Compilation of Various Publications, p. 235.

26. M. C. Gorgas and B. J. Hendrick, *William Crawford Gorgas: His Life and Work*, p. 85.

27. W. C. Gorgas, *Sanitation in Panama*, p. 6.

28. NARA Record Group 112, Memorandum from the Surgeon General to the Adjutant General, May 23, 1900.

29. NARA Record Group 112, Special Order No. 122, Department of the Army, Washington, D.C., May 24, 1900.

30. NARA Record Group 112, Memorandum George Miller Sternberg to Walter Reed, May 29, 1900.

31. Ibid.

32. Ibid.

33. PH-WRC, letter from Henry M. Hurd to Howard Kelly, February 11, 1905.

CHAPTER 9. THE OPPORTUNITY OF A LIFETIME

1. PH-WRC, letter from Jesse Lazear to Mabel Lazear, July 15, 1900.

2. PH-WRC, letter from Walter Reed to Emilie Lawrence Reed, June 25, 1900.

3. PH-WRC, letter from Walter Reed to Emilie Lawrence Reed, June 25, 1900.

4. A. Agramonte, "One Contribution of Army Medical Officers to Science," p. 558.

5. Ibid., p. 558.

6. PH-WRC, letter from Walter Reed to Emilie Lawrence Reed, July 20, 1900.

7. PH-WRC, letter from Walter Reed to Emilie Lawrence Reed, July 13, 1900.

8. PH-WRC, letter from Leonard Wood to Walter Reed, January 27, 1899.

9. PH-WRC, letter from Walter Reed to Emilie Lawrence Reed, July 2, 1900.

10. PH-WRC, letter from Walter Reed to Emilie Lawrence Reed, July 7, 1900.

11. PH-WRC, letter from Walter Reed to Emilie Lawrence Reed, July 8, 1900.

12. W. Osler, *The Practice and Principles of Medicine*, p. 125.

13. PH-WRC, letter from Alexander Stark to Guy Godfrey, July 24, 1900.

14. PH-WRC, letter from Alexander Stark to Robert Cooke, July 24, 1900.

15. Senate Document No. 822, Yellow Fever—A Compilation of Various Publications, p. 137.

16. T. E. Woodward, "Epidemiologic Classics of Carter, Maxey, Trudeau, and Smith," p. 236.

17. Henry Rose Carter Collection, National Library of Medicine.

18. PH-WRC, letter from Walter Reed to George Miller Sternberg, July 24, 1900.

19. PH-WRC, letter from James C. Carroll to Howard A. Kelly, June 23, 1906.

20. PH-WRC, letter from Walter Reed to George M. Sternberg, July 24, 1900.

21. PH-WRC, letter from James Carroll to the Editor, June 26, 1903.

22. PH-WRC, letter from Philip Hench to Mary Standlee, August 4, 1951.

23. A. E. Truby, *Memoir of Walter Reed: The Yellow Fever Episode*, p. 104.

CHAPTER 10. "A SOLDIER'S CHANCES"

1. *New York Times*, September 23, 1900.

2. PH-WRC, letter from James C. Carroll to the Editor, June 26, 1903.

3. A. Agramonte, "The Inside History of a Great Medical Discovery," pp. 210–211.

4. W. Reed, J. C. Carroll, A. Agramonte, and J. P. Lazear, "The Etiology of Yellow Fever: A Preliminary Note," p. 795.

5. PH-WRC, letter from Jesse Lazear to Mabel Lazear, September 8, 1900.

6. PH-WRC, letter from Jesse Lazear to Charlotte Sweitzer, September 10, 1900.

7. PH-WRC, letter from Walter Reed to James Carroll, September 24, 1900.

8. Ibid.

9. PH-WRC, letter from Walter Reed to Jefferson Randolph Kean, September 25, 1900.

10. PH-WRC, letter from Jefferson Randolph Kean to Mabel Lazear, September 25, 1900.

11. A. E. Truby, *Memoir of Walter Reed: The Yellow Fever Episode*, p. 112.

12. W. Reed, J. C. Carroll, A. Agramonte, and J. W. Lazear, "The Etiology of Yellow Fever: A Preliminary Note," p. 796.

13. A. E. Truby, *Memoir of Walter Reed: The Yellow Fever Episode*, p. 126.

14. G. M. Sternberg, "Report on the Etiology and Prevention of Yellow Fever," p. 1040.

15. PH-WRC, documents from New York Academy of Medicine laboratory notebook.

16. Yellow Fever Board, Laboratory Notebook. Collection of the New York Academy of Medicine.

CHAPTER 11. PUTTING IT ALL TOGETHER

1. A. E. Truby, *Memoir of Walter Reed: The Yellow Fever Episode*, p. 115.

2. Ibid., p. 122.

3. H. E. Durham and W. Myers, "Preliminary Report of the Yellow Fever Expedition to Para, Brazil," p. 656.

4. H. Hagedorn, *Leonard Wood: A Biography*, vol. 1, pp. 325–326.

5. W. B. Bean, *Walter Reed: A Biography*, p. 139.

6. PH-WRC, Chief Surgeon's Office, Headquarters Department of Western Cuba, Quemados, October 13, 1900.

7. PH-WRC, Headquarters Department of Western Cuba, Quemados, October 15, 1900, Circular No. 8.

8. W. Reed, J. C. Carroll, A. Agramonte, and J. W. Lazear, "The Etiology of Yellow Fever: A Preliminary Note." p. 796.

9. *Indianapolis Journal*, October 24, 1900.

10. *Indianapolis Sentinel*, May 24, 1900.

11. *Washington Post*, November 2, 1900.

12. PH-WRC, letter from Walter Reed to Emilie Lawrence Reed, November 5, 1900.

CHAPTER 12. AFFIRMATION

1. A. Agramonte, "One Contribution of Army Medical Officers to Science," pp. 562–563.

2. A. Agramonte, "The Inside History of a Great Medical Discovery," p. 234.

3. V. Vaughan and W. Osler, "Discussion of G. M. Sternberg, The *Bacillus icteroides* (Sanarelli) and the *Bacillus X* (Sternberg)," pp. 70–71.

4. A. E. Truby, *Memoir of Walter Reed: The Yellow Fever Episode*, p. 152.

5. J. R. Kean, Walter Reed: Dedication of His Birthplace," p. 301.

6. S. Lederer, *Subjected to Science*, p. 21.

7. W. B. Bean, "Walter Reed and Yellow Fever," p. 662.

8. Senate Document No. 822, Yellow Fever—A Compilation of Various Publications, p. 98.

9. H. A. Kelly, *Walter Reed and Yellow Fever*, p. 139.

10. PH-WRC, letter from Henry Hurd to Howard Kelly, February 11, 1905.

11. Senate Document No. 822, Yellow Fever—A Compilation of Various Publications, p. 98.

12. E. Wasdin, "The Etiology of Yellow Fever," pp. 950–952.

13. Ibid.

14. Ibid.

15. A. Agramonte, "The Inside History of a Great Medical Discovery," p. 235.

16. Ibid., p. 235.

17. A. E. Truby, *Memoir of Walter Reed: The Yellow Fever Episode*, p. 153.

18. W. Reed, J. C. Carroll, and A. Agramonte, "The Etiology of Yellow Fever—An Additional Note," p. 438.

19. W. B. Bean, *Walter Reed: A Biography*, p. 151.

20. PH-WRC, P. S. Hench, Summary of Research, August 20, 1940.

21. PH-WRC, J. R. Kissinger, Experiences with the Yellow Fever Commission in Cuba 1900.

22. W. B. Bean, *Walter Reed: A Biography*, p. 151.

23. PH-WRC, letter from Walter Reed to Emilie Lawrence Reed, December 9, 1900.

24. PH-WRC, J. R. Kissinger, Experiences with the Yellow Fever Commission in Cuba 1900.

25. A. Agramonte, "The Inside History of a Great Medical Discovery," p. 235.

26. W. C. Gorgas, *Sanitation in Panama*, pp. 30–31.

27. A. Agramonte, "The Inside History of a Great Medical Discovery," pp. 231–232.

28. PH-WRC, letter from Walter Reed to Emilie Lawrence Reed, December 23, 1900.

29. W. B. Bean, *Walter Reed: A Biography*, p. 157.

30. PH-WRC, J. J. Moran, The Story of John Moran.

31. PH-WRC, letter from Walter Reed to Emilie Lawrence Reed, December 31, 1900.

CHAPTER 13. PRESENTATION

1. PC-WRC, letter from John H. Andrus to John J. Moran, August 30, 1947.

2. Ibid.

3. M. L. Sternberg, *George Miller Sternberg: A Biography*, p. 227.

4. Senate Document No. 822, Yellow Fever—A Compilation of Various Publications, pp. 101–102.

5. W. Reed, J. C. Carroll, and A. Agramonte, "The Etiology of Yellow Fever—An Additional Note," pp. 439–440.

6. PC-WRC, letter from Walter Reed to Emilie Lawrence Reed, February 5, 1901.

7. Anonymous, "The Etiology of Yellow Fever," p. 461.

8. Senate Document No. 822, Yellow Fever—A Compilation of Various Publications, p. 236.

9. M. D. Gorgas and B. J. Hendrick, *William Crawford Gorgas: His Life and Work*, p. 122.

10. A. E. Truby, *Memoir of Walter Reed: The Yellow Fever Episode*, p. 185.

11. Senate Document No. 822, Yellow Fever—A Compilation of Various Publications, p. 236.

12. J. Guitéras, "Experimental Yellow Fever at the Inoculation Station of the Sanitary Department of Havana with a View to Producing Immunization," p. 809.

13. Ibid., p. 817.

14. W. Reed, J. C. Carroll, and A. Agramonte, "The Etiology of Yellow Fever—An Additional Note," p. 438.

15. Ibid., p. 438.

CHAPTER 14. RECOGNITION

1. Henry Rose Carter papers, National Library of Medicine, letter from Walter Reed to Henry Rose Carter, February 26, 1901.

2. PH-WRC, letter from Jefferson Randolph Kean to Walter Reed, November 9, 1901.

3. Ibid.

4. PH-WRC, letter from Walter Reed to Emilie Lawrence Reed, December 31, 1900.

5. W. B. Bean, *Walter Reed: A Biography*, p. 177.

6. H. A. Kelly, *Walter Reed and Yellow Fever*, p. 242.

7. W. B. Bean, *Walter Reed: A Biography*, p. 181.

8. PH-WRC, letter from Emilie Lawrence Reed to Laura Blincoe Reed, January 7, 1903.

9. PH-WRC, Minutes of the meeting of the General Committee of the Walter Reed Memorial Association held at Bar Harbor, Maine, August 15, 1903.

10. B. Furman, *A Profile of the United States Public Health Service 1798–1948*, p. 244.

CHAPTER 15. HISTORIC APPLICATION

1. W. C. Gorgas, *Sanitation in Panama*, p. 153.

2. M. D. Gorgas and B. J. Hendrick, *William Crawford Gorgas: His Life and Work*, p. 201.

3. Ibid., p. 141.

CHAPTER 16. YELLOW FEVER AFTER WALTER REED

1. www.rockfound.org

2. G. Eckstein, *Noguchi*, p. 414.

3. G. W. Corner, *A History of the Rockefeller Institute 1901–1953*, p. 188.

4. G. Williams, *The Plague Killers: Untold Stories of Three Great Campaigns Against Disease*, p. 254.

5. Ibid., p. 299.

6. W. T. Councilman, "Description of Pathological Histology of Yellow Fever," pp. 151–159.

7. F. L. Soper, "Jungle Yellow Fever. A New Epidemiological Entity in South America," pp. 1–39.

8. G. Williams, *The Plague Killers: Untold Stories of Three Great Campaigns Against Disease*, pp. 322.

9. Ibid., p. 312.

EPILOGUE

1. C. J. Finlay, Presented before the Royal Academy of Medical, Physical, and Natural Sciences in Havana, August 14, 1881, and published in *Anales dela Ciencir Medicas, Fisicas y Naturales de la Habana*, vol. 17, p. 147.

2. A. E. Truby, *Memoir of Walter Reed: The Yellow Fever Episode*, p. 49.

3. Proceedings from the Fourth International Congress on Tropical Medicine and Malaria, Volume One, Washington, D.C., May 10–18, 1948, Department of State. p. 54.

AFTERWORD: YELLOW FEVER TODAY

1. T. P. Monath, "Yellow Fever: Victor, Victoria? Conqueror, Conquest? Epidemics and Research in the Last Forty Years and Prospects for the Future," p. 11.

Bibliography

COLLECTIONS, OFFICIAL REPORTS, AND OTHER PRIMARY SOURCES

American Public Health Association. Proceeding, 29th Annual Meeting, September 1901.

Annual Report of the Supervising Surgeon-General of the Marine Hospital Service of the United States for the Fiscal Year 1898, Article on "Yellow Fever: Its Nature, Treatment, and Prophylaxis, and Quarantine Regulations Relating Thereto." Washington, D.C., 1899.

Bergstrand, H. Presentation Speech, the Nobel Prize in Physiology or Medicine, 1951.

Cabell, J. L. The National Board of Health and the International Sanitary Conference of Washington. Philadelphia: Collins, 1881.

Chief Sanitary Officer, Havana, Report to the Governor General of Cuba, July 12, 1902.

Chief Surgeon, Department of Cuba, Report to the Adjutant General: "Yellow Fever, Especially from the Viewpoint of the Sanitarian." February 8, 1901.

George Miller Sternberg Papers. National Library of Medicine, Bethesda, Maryland.

Gorgas, William C. Report of Major W. C. Gorgas, Medical Corps, United States Army, July 12, 1902.

Holt, D. Handbill: "Dr. Holt's Prescription for the Treatment of Yellow Fever." New Orleans, October 1, 1843.

Letters of the Civil War. www.lettersoftheCivil War.com/11-28-62-neworleans.html. Accessed October 20, 2003.

New York Times, various issues, 1898–1901.

Philip S. Hench, Walter Reed, Yellow Fever Collection, Claude Moore Health Science Center, University of Virginia, Charlottesville, Virginia.

National Archives and Record Administration, Record Group 112.

Proceedings of the Board of Experts Authorized by Congress to Investigate the Yellow Fever Epidemic of 1878. Washington, D.C., 1878.

Reed, W., V. C. Vaughan, and E. O. Shakespeare. Report on the Origin and Spread of Typhoid Fever in US Military Camps During the Spanish War of 1898. Washington, D.C.: Government Printing Office, 1904.

Sanitary Commission. Report of a Committee of the Associate Members of the Sanitary Commission, on the Subject of the Nature and Treatment of Yellow Fever. New York: Wm. C. Bryant & Co., 1862.

Senate Document No. 822, Yellow Fever—A Compilation of Various Publications, 61st Congress. Washington, D.C.: Government Printing Office, 1911.

Special Order No. 122. Department of the Army, Washington, D.C., May 24, 1900.

Sternberg, George M. Report on the Etiology and Prevention of Yellow Fever. Washington, D.C.: Government Printing Office, 1890.

Surgeon General, U.S. Army. Memorandum to the Adjutant General of the Army. Washington, D.C., May 23, 1900.

Surgeon General, U.S. Army. Memorandum to Major Walter Reed. Washington, D.C., May 29, 1900.
Theiler, M. Nobel Lecture: "The Development of Vaccines Against Yellow Fever," December 11, 1951.
Woodworth, J. M. Conclusions of the Board of Experts Authorized by Congress to Investigate the Yellow Fever Epidemic of 1878. Washington, D.C., January 29, 1879.
Yellow Fever Board, Laboratory Notebook. Collection of the New York Academy of Medicine, 1900.

ARTICLES

Agramonte, A. "Dr. Carlos Finlay—A Biographical Sketch." *Transactions of the American Society of Tropical Medicine*, vol. 10, 1916: 27–31.
——. "The Inside History of a Great Medical Discovery." *Scientific Monthly*, vol. 1, 1916: 209–237.
——. "Letter of the Editor." *Journal of the American Medical Association*, vol. 40, 1903: 1661a.
——. "One Contribution of Army Medical Officers to Science." *The Military Surgeon*, vol. 67, November 1930: 557.
——. "Report of Bacteriological Investigations upon Yellow Fever." *Medical News*, vol. 76, 1900: 203–212, 249–256.
Amster, L. J. "Carlos J. Finlay: The Mosquito Man." *Hospital Practice*, vol. 15, May 1987: 223–246.
Anonymous. "The Deadly Camp Fevers." *Journal of the American Medical Association*, vol. 30, 1898: 1359.
——. "Deaths, Edward O. Shakespeare." *Journal of the American Medical Association*, vol. 34, 1900: 1504–1505.
——. "Deaths, Henry Rose Carter." *Journal of the American Medical Association*, vol. 85, 1925: 993.
——. "Deaths, William Crawford Gorgas." *Journal of the American Medical Association*, vol. 75, 1920: 123.
——. "History and the Incidents of the Plague in New Orleans." *Harper's New Monthly Magazine*, vol. 7, no. 42, November 1853: 797–806.
——. "How to Arrest Yellow Fever." *Manufacturer and Builder*, vol. 10, no. 11, November 1878: 253–254.
——. "The Late Stephen Girard." *New England Magazine*, vol. 2, no. 2, February 1832: 149–154.
——. "Medical Essays of Miner and Tully." *North American Review*, vol. 17, no. 41, October 1823: 323–340.
——. "The Microbe of Yellow Fever." *Journal of the American Medical Association*, vol. 33, 1899: 672.
——. "Notice of Deceased Member, Theobold Smith." *Journal of Pathology and Bacteriology*, vol. 40, 1935: 621–635.
——. "The Prevention and Cure of Yellow Fever." *Medical Record*, vol. 54, 1898: 125.
——. "Quarantine and Hygiene." *North American Review*, vol. 91, no. 189, October 1860: 438–491.
——. "Reed and Carroll's Reply to Sanarelli." *Journal of the American Medical Association*, vol. 33, 1899: 735.
——. "Sanarelli's Autobiography." *Journal of the American Medical Association*, vol. 33, 1899: 677.
——. "Sanarelli's Bacillus Not the Cause of Yellow Fever." *Medical News*, vol. 75, 1899: 119.
——. "Sanarelli and the Pathogenic Role of Bacillus Icteroides." *Medical News*, vol. 75, 1899: 209–210.
——. "Yellow Fever." *Harper's New Monthly Magazine*, vol. 13, no. 78, November 1856: 784–793.
——. "Yellow Fever." *Harper's New Monthly Magazine*, vol. 15 no. 85, June 1857: 61–70.
——. "The Yellow Fever." *Medical Record*, vol. 54, 1898: 128.
——. "Yellow Fever Etiology." *Journal of the American Medical Association*, vol. 35, 1900: 1039–1040.
——. "Yellow Fever and Mosquitoes." *British Medical Journal*, vol. 2, 1900: 1391b.
Barrie, H. J. "Diary Notes on a Trip to West Africa in Relation to a Yellow Fever Expedition Under the Auspices of the Rockefeller Foundation, 1926, by Oskar Klotz." *Canadian Bulletin of Medical History*, vol. 14, no. 1, 1997: 133–163.
Bauer, J. H., and N. P. Hudson. "The Incubation Period of Yellow Fever in the Mosquito." *Journal of Experimental Medicine*, vol. 48, 1928: 147–153.
Bean, W. B. "The Fielding H. Garrison Lecture: Walter Reed and the Ordeal of Human Experiments." *Bulletin of the History of Medicine*, vol. 51, no. 1, Spring 1977: 75–92.

———. "Josiah Clark Nott, a Southern Physician." *Bulletin of the New York Academy of Medicine*, vol. 50, no. 4, 1974: 529–535.

———. "Walter Reed: He Gave to Man Control of the Dreadful Scourge Yellow Fever." *Archives of Internal Medicine*, vol. 89, 1952: 171–187.

———. "Walter Reed and Yellow Fever." *Journal of the American Medical Association*, vol. 250, 1983: 659–662.

Bendiner, E. "Max Theiler: Yellow Jack and the Jackpot." *Hospital Practice*, vol. 23, no. 6, June 1988: 211–212, 214–215, 219–222 passim.

Berry, G. P., and S. F. Kitchen. "Yellow Fever Accidentally Contracted in the Laboratory." *American Journal of Tropical Medicine*, 1931, 11: 365–434.

Blake, J. B. "Yellow Fever in Eighteenth-Century North America." *Bulletin of the New York Academy of Medicine*, vol. 44, no. 6, June 1968: 673–686.

Bloch, H. "Yellow Fever in the City of New York. Notes on Epidemic of 1798." *New York State Journal of Medicine*, vol. 73, no. 20, October 1973: 2503–2505.

———. "Yellow Fever Epidemic in Philadelphia, 1793. Physicians in Dispute." *New York State Journal of Medicine*, vol. 73, no. 21, November 1973: 2606–2609.

Borden, W. C. "History of Doctor Walter Reed's Illness from Appendicitis." *Washington Medical Annuals*, vol. 1, 1902: 425–426.

———. "Walter Reed General Hospital of the U.S. Army." *The Military Surgeon*, vol. 20, 1907: 20–35.

Bowen, T. E. "William Crawford Gorgas, Physician to the World." *Military Medicine*, vol. 148, 1983: 917–920.

Bowers, J. Z., and King, E. E. "The Conquest of Yellow Fever: The Rockefeller Foundation." *Journal of the Medical Society of New Jersey*, vol. 78, no. 7, July 1981: 539–541.

Brès, P. L. J. "A Century of Progress in Combating Yellow Fever." *Bulletin of the World Health Organization*, vol. 64, 1986: 775–786.

Brouwer, N. "Defending New York City's Eastern Gateways: A Brief History of Fort Totten on Willetts Point." www.hoflink.com/~bayside/brouwer.html. Accessed on February 21, 2004.

Bruesch, S. R. "Yellow Fever in Tennessee in 1878. Part I." *Journal of the Tennessee Medical Association*, vol. 71, no. 12, December 1978: 887–896.

———. "Yellow Fever in Tennessee in 1878. Part II." *Journal of the Tennessee Medical Association*, vol. 72, no. 2, February 1979: 91–104.

———. "Yellow Fever in Tennessee in 1878. Part III." *Journal of the Tennessee Medical Association*, vol. 72, no. 3, March 1979: 193–205.

Bryan, C. S. "Eulogy Written in a Country Churchyard." *Journal of the South Carolina Medical Association*, vol. 84, no. 2, February 1988: 94–95.

Butler, B. "Some Experiences with Yellow Fever and Its Prevention." *North American Review*, vol. 147, no. 384, November 1888: 525–542.

Bynum, W. F. "Mosquitoes Bite More Than Once." *Science*, vol. 295, no. 5552, 2002: 47–49.

Carmichael, E. B. "Henry Rose Carter, Jr.—Epidemiologist—Sanitarian." *Alabama Journal of Medicine and Science*, vol. 6, no. 3, 1969: 348–353.

———. "Jesse William Lazear." *Alabama Journal of Medical Science*, vol. 9, no. 1, 1972: 102–114.

Carrigan, J. A. "Mass Communication and Public Health: The 1905 Campaign Against Yellow Fever in New Orleans." *Louisiana History*, vol. 29, no. 1, 1988: 5–20.

———. "Privilege, Prejudice, and the Stranger's Disease in Nineteenth-Century New Orleans." *Journal of Southern History*, vol. 36, 1970: 568–578.

Carroll, J. C. "A Brief Review of the Aetiology of Yellow Fever." *New York Medical Journal and Philadelphia Medical Journal*, vol. 79, 1904: 214–245, 307–310.

———. "Fatal Yellow Fever in a Traveler Returning from Venezuela, 1999." *Morbidity and Mortality Weekly Report*, vol. 49, no. 14, April 14, 2000.

———. "The Transmission of Yellow Fever." *Journal of the American Medical Association*, vol. 20, 1903: 1429–1433.

———. "Treatment of Yellow Fever." *Journal of the American Medical Association*, vol. 34, 1902: 117–124.

———. "Yellow Fever: A Popular Lecture." *Bulletin of the University of Texas*, June 15, 1905: 3–32.

Carter, H. R. "A Note on the Interval Between Infecting and Secondary Cases of Yellow Fever from the Records of Yellow Fever at Orwood and Taylor, Mississippi, in 1898." *New Orleans Medical and Surgical Journal*, vol. 52, 1900: 617–636.

Centers for Disease Control and Prevention. "Fatal Yellow Fever in a Traveler Returning from Amazonas, Brazil, 2002." *Morbidity and Mortality Weekly Report*, vol. 51, no. 15, April 19, 2002.

Chappell, G. S. "Surgeon at Fort Sidney: Captain Walter Reed's Experiences at a Nebraska Military Post, 1883–1884." *Nebraska History*, vol. 54, 1973: 419–443.

Chernin, E. "Josiah Clark Nott, Insects, and Yellow Fever." *Bulletin of the New York Academy of Medicine*, vol. 59, no. 9, November 1983: 790–802.

Choppin, S. "History of the Importation of Yellow Fever into the United States, 1693–1878." *Public Health Papers, American Public Health Association*, vol. 4, 1877–1878.

Christie, A. "Medical Conquest of the Big Ditch." *Southern Medical Journal*, vol. 71, no. 6. 1978: 717–723.

Cirillo, V. J. "Fever and Reform: The Typhoid Epidemic in the Spanish-American War." *Journal of the History of Medicine*, vol. 55, 2000: 363–397.

———. "'The Patriotic Odor': Sanitation and Typhoid Fever in the National Encampments During the Spanish-American War." *Army History*, 2000, vol. 49: 17–23.

Coan, T. M. "Some Peculiarities of Yellow Jack." *Harper's New Monthly Magazine*, vol. 58, no. 343, December 1878: 126–131.

Cockerell, T. D. A. "The Epic of Yellow Fever." *Scientific Monthly*, vol. 54, 1942: 43–48.

Corbett, B. "The Haitian Revolution of 1791–1803: An Historical Essay in Four Parts." webster.edu/~corbetre/haiti/history/revolution/. Accessed May 13, 2003.

Coker, W. S., and J. R. McNeill. "Dr. Tomas Romay's Unpublished Manuscript on Yellow Fever, June 27, 1804." *Journal of the Florida Medical Association*, vol. 71, no. 7, July 1984: 456–462.

Cosmas, G. A. "Securing the Fruits of Victory: The U.S. Army Occupies Cuba 1898–1899." *Military Affairs*, vol. 38, 1974: 85–91.

Councilman, W. T. "Description of Pathological Histology of Yellow Fever," in Sternberg, G. M., Report on Etiology and Prevention of Yellow Fever. U.S. Marine Hospital Service Public Health Bulletin No. 2: 151–159, 1890.

Craig, S. C. "Dr. George M. Sternberg on the Kansas Plains, 1866–1870." *Kansas History*, vol. 21, no. 3, Autumn 1998: 188–206.

Creighton, M. D. C. "The Origin of Yellow Fever." *North American Review*, vol. 139, no. 35, October 1884: 335–348.

Curtin, P. D. "Disease Exchange Across the Tropical Atlantic." *History of Philosophy and Life Science*, vol. 15, no. 3, 1993: 329–356.

Davis, J. H. "Two Martyrs of the Yellow Fever Epidemic of 1878." *West Tennessee History Society Papers*, vol. 26, 1972: 20–39.

Del Regato, J. A. "Carlos Finlay and the Carrier of Death." *Jefferson Medical College Alumni*, Bulletin 20, Summer 1971: 2–17.

———. "Carlos Juan Finlay (1833–1915)." *Journal of Public Health Policy.*, vol. 22, no. 1, 2001: 98–104.

———. "Jesse William Lazear: The Successful Experimental Transmission of Yellow Fever by the Mosquito." *Medical Heritage*, vol. 2, no. 6, November–December 1986: 443–452.

———. "Jesse W. Lazear." *Physicians and Surgeons Quarterly*, vol. 16, 1971: 11–17, 21.

Diaz, H. F. "A Possible Connection Between the 1878 Yellow Fever Epidemic in the Southern United States and the 1877–1878 El Nino Episode." *Bulletin of the American Meteorological Society*, vol. 80, no. 1, 1999: 21.

Dolman, C. E. "Theobold Smith 1859–1934." *New York State Medical Journal*, vol. 69, 1969: 2801–2816.

Doty, A. H. "The Scientific Prevention of Yellow Fever." *North American Review*, vol. 167, no. 505, December 1898: 681–689.

Downs, W. G. "History of Epidemiological Aspects of Yellow Fever." *Yale Journal of Biological Medicine*, vol. 55, no. 3-4, May–August 1982: 179–185.

———. "The Known and the Unknown in Yellow Fever Ecology and Epidemiology." *Ecology of Disease*, vol. 1, no. 2-3, 1982: 103–110.

———. "The Story of Yellow Fever Since Walter Reed." *Bulletin of the New York Academy of Medicine*, vol. 44, 1968: 721–727.

Duffy, J. "Yellow Fever in the Continental United States During the Nineteenth Century." *Bulletin of the New York Academy of Medicine*, vol. 44, no. 6, June 1968: 687–701.

Dunham, H. E, and W. Myers. "Preliminary Report of the Yellow Fever Expedition to Para, Brazil." *British Medical Journal*, vol. 2, 1900: 656–657.

Eckert, J. "In the Days of the Epidemic: The 1793 Yellow Fever Outbreak in Philadelphia as Seen by Physicians." *Transactions and Studies of the College of Physicians of Philadelphia*, vol. 15, no 5, December 1993: 31–38.

Etheridge, E. W. "Yellow Fever, Polio, and the New Public Health." *Revised American History*, vol. 21, no. 2, June 1993: 297–302.

Fink, T. M. "Before Yellow Fever and Cuba, Walter Reed in Arizona." *Journal of Arizona History*, vol. 42, 2001: 181–200.

Finlay, C. J. "Method of Stamping Out Yellow Fever Suggested Since 1899." *Medicine*, March 1903: 175–178.

———. "The Mosquito Hypothetically Considered as the Agent of Transmission of Yellow Fever." Reprinted in *Medical Classics* 2, 1938: 569–612. Originally published as "El Mosquito hipoteti-camente considerado como agente de transmission de la fiebre amarilla." *Anales de la Ciencir Medicas, Fisicas y Naturales de la Habana*, vol. 18, 1881–1882: 147–169.

———. "Two Different Ways Yellow Fever May Be Transmitted." *Journal of the American Medical Association*, November 23, 1901: 1387–1389.

Flaumenhaft, E., and C. Flaumenhaft. "Evolution of America's Pioneer Bacteriologist: George M. Sternberg's Formative Years." *Military Medicine*, vol. 158, no. 7, 1993: 448–457.

Foster, K. R., M. F. Jenkins, and A. C. Toogood. "The Philadelphia Yellow Fever Epidemic of 1793." *Scientific American*, vol. 279, 1998: 88–93.

Ganter, M. N. "Yellow Jack: The American Plague." *Early American Homes*, June 1996: 41–44.

Geggus, D. "Yellow Fever in the 1790s: The British Army in Occupied Saint Domingue." *Medical History*, vol. 23, no. 1, January 1979: 38–58.

Goldfield, D. R. "Disease and Urban Image: Yellow Fever in Norfolk 1855." *Virginia Cavalcade*, vol. 23, Autumn 1973: 34–41.

Goodyear, J. D. "The Sugar Connection: A New Perspective on the History of Yellow Fever." *Bulletin of the History of Medicine*, vol. 52, no. 1, Spring 1978: 5–21.

Greenleaf, C. "An Object Lesson in Military Sanitation." *Boston Medical and Surgical Journal*, vol. 141, 1899: 485–487.

Gribbin, W. "Divine Providence or Miasma? The Yellow Fever Epidemic of 1822." *New York History*, vol. 53, no. 3, 1972: 283–298.

Guitéras, J. "Experimental Yellow Fever at the Inoculation Station of the Sanitary Department of Havana with a View to Producing Immunization." *American Medicine*, vol. 2, 1901: 809–817.

Haines, R., et al. "Mortality and Voyage Length in the Middle Passage Revisited." *Explorations in Economic History*, vol. 38, 2001: 503–533.

Hardy, J. L., G. Apperson, and S. M. Asman. "Selection of a Strain of *Culex tarsalis* Highly Resistant to Infection Following Ingestion of Western Equine Encephalomyelitis Virus." *American Journal of Tropical Medicine and Hygiene*, vol. 27, 1978: 313.

Harvey, A. M. "Johns Hopkins and Yellow Fever: A Story of Tragedy and Triumph." *Johns Hopkins Medical Journal*, vol. 149, no. 1, 1981: 25–39.

Havard, V. "Sanitation and Yellow Fever in Havana." *Sanitarian*, vol. 47, 1901: 13–21, 121–128.

Haydock, M. D. "'This Means War!'" *American History*, February 1998.

Hench, P. S. "Conquerors of Yellow Fever." *Hygenia*, October 1, 1941.

Hendricks, M. "Do Unto Yourself." *Johns Hopkins Magazine*, vol. 48, no. 2, April 1996: 14–19.

Holmes, C. "Benjamin Rush and the Yellow Fever." *Bulletin of the History of Medicine*, vol. 40, no. 3, May–June 1966: 246–263.

Ireland, M. W. "The Conquest of Yellow Fever." *The Military Surgeon*, vol. 64, 1929: 244–251.

Jenkins J. S. "Life and Society in Old Cuba." *The Century: A Popular Quarterly*, vol. 56, no. 5, September 1898: 742–753.

Joy, R. J. T. "Book Review, Walter Reed—A Biography." *New England Journal of Medicine*, vol. 307, 1982: 322–323.

Kean, J. R. "Editorial—William Crawford Gorgas." *The Military Surgeon*, vol. 56, 1925: 366–370.

———. "Hospitals and Charities in Cuba." *Journal of the Association of Military Surgeons of the United States*, vol. 12, 1903: 140–149.

———. "Walter Reed: Dedication of His Birthplace." *The Military Surgeon*, vol. 62, 1928: 293–304.

Kiple, K. L., and V. H. Kiple. "Black Yellow Fever Immunities, Innate and Acquired, as Revealed in the American South." *Social Science and History*, vol. 1, no. 4, 1977: 419–436.

Koide, S. S. "Hideyo Noguchi's Last Stand: The Yellow Fever Commission in Accra, Africa (1927–1928)." *Journal of Medical Biography*, vol. 8, no. 2, May 2000: 97–101.

Kornfeld, E. "Crisis in the Capital: The Cultural Significance of Philadelphia's Great Yellow Fever Epidemic." *Pennsylvania History*, vol. 51, no. 3, 1984: 189–205.

Lazear, J. W. "Pathology of Malarial Fevers, Structure of the Parasites and Changes in Tissue." *Journal of the American Medical Association*, vol. 35, 1900: 917–920.

Legan, M. S. "Mississippi and the Yellow Fever Epidemics of 1878–1879." *Journal of Mississippi History*, vol. 33, 1971: 199–217.

Leland, T. M. "Josiah Clark Nott, M.D. 1804–1873." *Journal of the South Carolina Medical Association*, vol. 82, no. 2, February 1986: 100–101.

Leonard, J. "Carlos Finlay's Life and the Death of Yellow Jack." *Bulletin of the Pan-American Health Organization*, vol. 23, no. 4, 1989: 438–452.

———. "William Gorgas, Soldier of Public Health." *Bulletin of the Pan-American Health Organization*, vol. 25, no. 2, 1991: 166–185.

Lewis, P. B., and D. W. Lewis. "Deathstorm: The Yellow Fever Epidemic of 1855." *Virginia Medical Quarterly*, vol. 122, no. 1, Winter 1995: 38–41.

Litsios, S. "William Crawford Gorgas (1854–1920)." *Perspectives in Biological Medicine*, vol. 44, no. 3, 2001: 368–378.

Loesh, Z. "Dr. Walter Reed: Gloucester County's Modern Medical Hero from the Last Century." *The Chesopiean: A Journal of North Amercan Archeology*, vol. 36, no. 2, 1998: 15–24.

Lowy, I. "Epidemiology, Immunology, and Yellow Fever: The Rockefeller Foundation in Brazil, 1923–1939." *Journal of the History of Biology*, vol. 30, no. 3, Fall 1997: 397–417.

Lull, G. F. "A Brief History of the Army Medical School, 1893–1933." *The Military Surgeon*, vol. 74, no. 2, February 1934.

Middleton, W. S. "The Yellow Fever Epidemic of 1793 in Philadelphia." *Annals of Medical History*, vol. 10, 1928: 434–450.

Miles, N. A. "The War with Spain II." *North American Review*, vol. 168, no. 511, June 1899: 749–761.

———. "The War with Spain III." *North American Review*, vol. 168, no. 512, July 1899: 125–138.

Milton, H. A. "Tennessee-Material and Spiritual Value of the Yellow Fever Fund." *American Missionary*, vol. 33, no. 5, May 1879: 149–150.

Monath, T. P. "Yellow Fever: A Medically Neglected Disease. Report on a Seminar." *Reviews of Infectious Disease*, vol. 9, no. 1, 1987: 165–175.

———. "Yellow Fever: Victor, Victoria? Conqueror, Conquest? Epidemics and Research in the Last Forty Years and Prospects for the Future." *American Journal of Tropical Medicine*, vol. 45, no. 1, 1991: 1–43.

Mortimer, P. P. "The Bacteria Craze of the 1880s." *Lancet*, vol. 353, 1999: 581–585.

National Center for Infectious Diseases. "Notice: Yellow Fever Outbreak, Colombia, 2003." *Centers for Disease Control and Prevention*, January 23, 2004.

———. "Yellow Fever: West and Central Africa, 2003." *Centers for Disease Control and Prevention*, May 20, 2004 .

New York Landmarks Commission. "Fort Totten Historic District, Queens." www.ci.nyc.ny.us/html/lpc/html/designation/summaries/forttotten_print.html. Accessed February 21, 2004.

Norman, C. "The Unsung Hero of Yellow Fever?" *Science*, vol. 223, 1984: 1370–1372.

Nott, J. C. "Sketch of the Epidemic of Yellow Fever of 1847 in Mobile." *Charleston Medical Journal and Review*, January 1848: vol. 3, no. 1.

———. "Yellow Fever Contrasted with Bilious Fever—Reasons for Believing It a Disease Sui Generis—Its Mode of Propagation—Remote Cause—Probable Insect or Animalcular Origin, &c." *New Orleans Medical and Surgical Journal*, vol. 4, 1848: 563–601.

Patterson, K. D. "Dr. William Gorgas and His War with the Mosquito." *Canadian Medical Association Journal*, vol. 141, 1989: 596–599.

———. "Yellow Fever Epidemics and Mortality in the United States, 1693–1905." *Social Science and Medicine*, vol. 34, no. 8, April 1992: 855–865.

Peller, S. "Walter Reed, C. Finlay, and Their Predecessors Around 1800." *Bulletin of the History of Medicine*, vol. 33, no. 3, May–June 1959: 195–211.

Peterson, R. K. D. "Insects, Disease, and Military History: The Napoleonic Campaigns and Historical Perception." *American Entomologist*, vol. 41, 1995: 147–160.

Raynor-Smallman, M., and A. D. Cliff. "The Spatial Dynamics of Epidemic Diseases in War and Peace: Cuba and the Insurrection Against Spain, 1895–1898." *Transactions of the Institute of British Geography*, vol. 24, 1999: 331–352.

Reed, W. "Geronimo and His Warriors in Captivity." *The Illustrated American*, vol. 3, 1890: 231–235.

Reed, W., and J. C. Carroll. "A Comparative Study—*Bacillus X, Bacillus icteroides*, and Hog Cholera." *Journal of Experimental Medicine*, 1900: 215–271.

———. "Bacillus Icteroides and Bacillus Cholerae Suis—A Preliminary Note." *Medical News*, vol. 74, 1899: 513–514.

———. "The Etiology of Yellow Fever—A Supplemental Note." *American Medicine*, vol. 3, 1902: 301–305.

———. "The Specific Cause of Yellow Fever. A Reply to Dr. G. Sanarelli." *Medical News*, vol. 75, 1899: 321–329.

Reed, W., J. C. Carroll, and A. Agramonte. "The Etiology of Yellow Fever—An Additional Note." *Journal of the American Medical Association*, vol. 36, 1901: 431–440.

———. "Experimental Yellow Fever." *American Medicine*, vol. 2, 1901: 15–23.

Reed W., J. C. Carroll, A. Agramonte, and J. Lazear. "The Etiology of Yellow Fever: A Preliminary Note." *Philadelphia Medical Journal*, vol. 6, 1900: 790–796.

Reese, D. M. "Contagion and Fever of the Last Season." *North American Review*, vol. 10, no. 27, April 1820: 394–418.

Richter, E. D. "Henry R. Carter—An Overlooked Skeptical Epidemiologist." *New England Journal of Medicine*, vol. 277, no. 14, 1967: 734–738.

Robbins, P. "Alas, Memphis!" *American History Illustrated*, vol. 16, no. 9, 1982: 38–46.

Sakula, A. "Louis-Daniel Beauperthuy: Pioneer in Yellow Fever and Leprosy Research." *Journal of the Royal College of Physicians*, vol. 20, no. 2, April 1986: 146–150.

Sanarelli, G. "Etiologic et pathogénic de la fiévre jaune." *Annales de l'Institut Pasteur*, 1897, vol. 11: 433–514.

———. "A Lecture on Yellow Fever with a Description of Bacillus Icteroides." *British Medical Journal*, July 3, 1897: 7–11.

———. "Some Observations and Controversial Remarks on the Specific Cause of Yellow Fever." *Medical News*, vol. 75, 1899: 193–199.

Smart, C. "The Germ of Yellow Fever." *Philadelphia Medical Journal*, vol. 6, 1900: 754b.

Sehdev, P. S. "The Origin of Quarantine." *Clinical Infectious Disease*, vol. 35, no. 9, November 2002: 1071–1072.

Shryock, R. H. "The Medical Reputation of Benjamin Rush: Contrasts Over Two Centuries." *Bulletin of the History of Medicine*, vol. 45, no. 6, November–December 1971: 507–552.

Simstein, N. L. "Leonard Wood as the Modern Renaissance Man." *Surgery, Gynecology and Obstetrics*, vol. 173, 1972: 64–70.

Slosek, J. "*Aedes aegypti* Mosquitoes in the Americas: A Review of Their Interactions with the Human Population." *Social Science and Medicine*, vol. 23, no. 3, 1986: 249–257.

Snape, W. J., and E. L. Wolfe. "The Studies of Yellow Fever by Noah Webster and John Conrad Otto at Red Bank, New Jersey." *Bulletin of the Gloucester County Historical Society*, vol. 19, no. 4, June 1984: 25–32.

Soper, F. L. "Jungle Yellow Fever. A New Epidemiological Entity in South America." *Revista Higiene Saúde Pública* vol. 10, 1936: 1–39.

Sternberg, G. M. "The Address of the President." *Journal of the American Medical Association*, vol. 30, 1898: 1373–1380.

———. "*Bacillus icteroides* and *Bacillus X*." *Journal of the American Medical Association*, vol. 30, 1898: 233–234.

———. "The *Bacillus icteroides* as the Cause of Yellow Fever, A Reply to Sanarelli." *Medical News*, vol. 75, 1899: 225–228, 767–768.

———. "Dr. Finlay's Mosquito Inoculation." *American Journal of the Medical Sciences*, vol. 102, 1891: 627–628.

———. "A National Health Bureau." *North American Review*, vol. 158, no. 450, May 1894: 529–534.

———. "Sanitary Lessons of the War." *Journal of the American Medical Association*, vol. 21, 1899: 1287–1294.

———. "The Sanitary Regeneration of Havana, by the Surgeon General of the Army." *The Century: A Popular Quarterly*, vol. 56, no. 4, August 1898: 578–583.

Stickle, D. F. "Death and Class in Baltimore: The Yellow Fever Epidemic of 1800." *Maryland History Magazine*, vol. 74, no. 3 1979: 282–299.

Stokes, A., J. H. Bauer, and N. P. Hudson. "Experimental Transmission of Yellow Fever to Laboratory Animals." *American Journal of Tropical Medicine*, vol. 8, 1928: 103–164.

Sullivan, R. B. "Sanguine Practices: A Historical and Historiographic Reconsideration of Heroic Therapy in the Age of Rush." *Bulletin of the History of Medicine*, vol. 68, no. 2, Summer 1994: 211–234.

Theiler, M., and H. H. Smith. "The Effect of Prolonged Cultivation In Vitro upon the Pathogenicity of Yellow Fever Virus." *Journal of Experimental Medicine*, vol. 65, 1937: 767–786.

———. "The Use of Yellow Fever Virus Modified by In Vitro Cultivation for Human Immunization." *Journal of Experimental Medicine*, vol. 65, 1937: 787–800.

Tiggertt, H. B., and Tiggertt, W. D. "Clara Louise Maass: A Nurse Volunteer for Yellow Fever Inoculations." *Military Medicine*, vol. 148, 1983: 252–253.

Tone, J. L. "How the Mosquito (Man) Liberated Cuba." *History and Technology*, vol. 14, no 4, 2002: 277–308.

Vaughan, V., and W. Osler. "Discussion of G. M. Sternberg, The *Bacillus icteroides* (Sanarelli) and the *Bacillus X* (Sternberg)." *Transactions of the Association American Physicians*, vol. 13, 1898: 70–71.

Victory, J. "CDC Confirms Man Died of Yellow Fever: Oil Executive Is Third American in 78 Years to Be Killed by Mosquito-Borne Illness." *Corpus Christi (Texas) Caller Times*, March 27, 2002.

Walls, E. "Observations on the New Orleans Yellow Fever Epidemic, 1878." *Louisiana History*, vol. 23, Winter 1982: 60–67.

Warner, M. "Hunting the Yellow Fever Germ: The Principle and Practice of Etiological Proof in Late Nineteenth-Century America." *Bulletin of the History of Medicine*, vol. 59, no. 3, Fall 1985: 361–382.

Wasdin, E. "The Etiology of Yellow Fever." *Philadelphia Medical Journal*, vol. 6, 1900: 950–952.

———. "Yellow Fever: Its Nature and Cause." *Journal of the American Medical Association*, vol. 35, 1900: 867–875.

Wasdin, E., and H. D. Geddings. "The Etiology of Yellow Fever." *New York Medical Journal*, vol. 70, 1899: 299–302.

Weisberger, B. A. "Epidemic." *American Heritage*, vol. 35, no. 6, 1984: 57–64.

White, C. S. "The Last Illness of Major Walter Reed." *Medical Annals of the District of Columbia*, vol. 24, 1955: 396–398.

Wilkinson, R. L. "Yellow Fever: Ecology, Epidemiology, and Role in the Collapse of the Classic Lowland Maya Civilization." *Medical Anthropology*, vol. 16, no. 3, July 1995: 269–294.

Winter, F. "The Romantic Side of the Conquest of Yellow Fever." *The Military Surgeon*, vol. 61, 1927: 439–440.

Woodward, T. E. "Epidemiologic Classics of Carter, Maxcy, Trudeau and Smith." *Journal of Infectious Disease*, vol. 165, 1992: 235–244.

Workman, M. "Medical Practice in Philadelphia at the Time of the Yellow Fever Epidemic, 1793." *Pennsylvania Folklife*, vol. 27, no. 4, 1978: 33–39.

Wright, F. M. "Annie Cook: 'The Mary Magdalene of Memphis.'" *West Tennessee Historical Society Papers*, vol. 43, 1989: 44–54.

———. "The 1878 Yellow Fever Epidemic in Memphis." *Journal of the Mississippi State Medical Association*, vol. 42, no. 1, 2001: 9–13.

Writer, J. V. "'Did the Mosquito Do It?'" *American History*, February 1997: 45–51.

BOOKS

Alger, R. A. *The Spanish-American War*. Freeport, New York: Books for Libraries Press, 1971 (reprint of 1901 edition).

Altman, L. K. *Who Goes First? The Story of Self-Experimentation in Medicine*. Berkeley: University of California Press, 1986.

Anonymous. *The Army Medical Service Graduate School: Sixtieth Anniversary, 1893–1953*. Washington, D.C., 1953.

Arnebeck, B. *Destroying Angel: Benjamin Rush, Yellow Fever and the Birth of Modern Medicine*, accessed at www.geocities.com/bobarnebeck/fever1793.html, 1999.

Bean, W. B. *Walter Reed: A Biography*. Charlottesville: University of Virginia Press, 1982.

Bloom, K. J. *The Mississippi Valley's Great Yellow Fever Epidemic of 1878*. Baton Rouge: Louisiana State University Press, 1992.

Boshell, J. W. (ed.). *Yellow Fever: A Symposium in Commemoration of Carlos Juan Finlay*. Philadelphia: Jefferson Medical College, 1955.

Brands, H. W. *The Reckless Decade: America in the 1890s*. New York: St. Martin's Press, 1995.

Bray, R. S. *Armies of Pestilence: The Impact of Disease on History*. Barnes and Noble Books, New York, 1996.

Brock, T. D. *Robert Koch: A Life in Medicine*. Washington, D.C.: ASM Press, 1999.

Bryan, C. S. *A Most Satisfactory Man: The Story of Theodore Brevard Hayne, Last Martyr of Yellow Fever*. Spartanburg, S.C.: The Reprint Company, 1996.

Burnside, M. *Spirits of the Passage: The Transatlantic Slave Trade in the Seventeenth Century*. New York: Simon and Schuster, 1997.

Butterfield, L. H. (ed.). *Letters of Benjamin Rush: Vol. II, 1793–1813*. Princeton, N.J.: Princeton University Press, 1951.

Carey, M. *Short Account of the Malignant Fever, Lately Prevalent in Philadelphia: With a Statement of the Proceedings That Took Place on the Subject in Different Parts of the United States*. Philadelphia: Printed by the author, 1793.

Carrigan, J. A. *The Saffron Scourge: A History of Yellow Fever in Louisiana*. Lafayette: University of Louisiana Press, 1994.

Carter, H. R., and L. A. Carter, and W. H. Frost (eds.). *Yellow Fever: An Epidemiological and Historical Study of Its Place of Origin*. Baltimore: Williams and Wilkins, 1931.

Chin, J. (ed.). *Control of Communicable Diseases Manual*, 17th edition. Washington, D.C.: American Public Health Association, 2000.

Cook, G. C. (ed.). *Manson's Tropical Diseases*. London, W. B. Saunders, 2003.

Corner, G. W. (ed.). *The Autobiography of Benjamin Rush: His Travels Through Life*. Philadelphia: American Philosophical Society, 1948.

———. *A History of the Rockefeller Institute 1901–1953: Origins and Growth*. New York: Rockefeller Institute Press, 1964.

Cosmas, G. A. *An Army for Empire: The United States Army in the Spanish-American War*. Columbia: University of Missouri Press, 1971,

Currie, W. A. *Sketch of the Rise and Progress of the Yellow Fever*. Philadelphia: Publisher unknown, 1800.

DeKriuf, P. *The Microbe Hunters*. San Diego: Harcourt Brace and Co., 1965.

Delaporte, F. *History of Yellow Fever: An Essay on the Birth of Tropical Medicine.* Cambridge, Mass.: M.I.T. Press, 1991.

Diamond, J. *Guns, Germs and Steel.* New York: W.W. Norton, 1999.

Eckstein, G. *Noguchi.* New York: Harper and Brothers, 1931.

Ellis, J. H. *Yellow Fever and Public Health in the South.* Lexington: University of Kentucky Press, 1992.

Ferguson, J. *A Traveler's History of the Caribbean.* New York: Interlink Books, 1999.

Finlay, C. E. *Carlos Finlay and Yellow Fever.* New York: Oxford University Press, 1940.

Flexnar, J. T. *Washington: The Indispensable Man.* Boston: Little, Brown and Co., 1984.

Fosdick, R. B. *The Story of the Rockefeller Foundation.* New York: Harper and Brothers, 1962.

Franklin, J., and J. Sutherland. *Guinea Pig Doctors.* New York: William Morrow, 1984.

Furman, B. *A Profile of the Unites States Public Health Service 1798–1948.* U.S. Department of Health, Education and Welfare. DHEW Publication No. (NIH) 73–369, U.S. Government Printing Office, 1973.

Gardner, J. L. (ed.). *John Adams: A Biography in His Own Words.* New York: Harper and Row, 1978.

Gibson, J. M. *Soldier in White: The Life of General George Miller Sternberg.* Durham, N.C.: Duke University Press, 1958.

Gillett, M. C. *The Army Medical Department, 1865–1917.* Washington, D.C.: Center for Military History, 1995.

Goddard, J. *Physician's Guide to Arthropods of Medical Importance.* Boca Raton, Fla.: CRC Press, 2003.

Gorgas, M. D., and B. J. Hendrick. *William Crawford Gorgas: His Life and Work.* Garden City, N.Y.: Doubleday and Page and Company, 1924.

Gorgas, W. C. *Sanitation in Panama.* New York: D. Appleton and Company, 1915.

Graves, J. A. *The History of the Bedford Light Artillery.* Bedford City, Va.: Press of the Bedford Democrat, 1903.

Hagedorn, H. *Leonard Wood: A Biography.* New York: Harper and Brothers, 1931.

Harrison, G. *Mosquitoes, Malaria and Man: A History of the Hostilities since 1880.* New York: E.P. Dutton, 1978.

Hearn, C. G. *When the Devil Came Down to Dixie: Ben Butler in New Orleans.* Baton Rouge: Louisiana State University Press, 1997.

Hill, R. N. *The Doctors Who Conquered Yellow Fever.* New York: Random House, 1957.

Honigsbaum, M. *The Fever Trail: In Search of the Cure for Malaria.* New York: Farrar, Straus and Giroux, 2001.

Howard, L. O. *Mosquitoes: How They Live; How They Carry Disease; How They Are Classified; How They May Be Destroyed.* New York: McClure, Phillips, 1901.

Howard, L. O. *A History of Applied Entomology.* Washington, D.C.: The Smithsonian Institute, 1930.

Humphries, M. *Yellow Fever and the South.* New Brunswick, N.J.: Rutgers University Press, 1992.

James, C. L. R. *The Black Jacobins: Toussaint L'Ouverture and the San Domingo Revolution.* New York: Vintage Press, 1989.

Kelly, H. A. *Walter Reed and Yellow Fever.* New York: McClure, Phillips and Company, 1908.

Klein, H. S. *African Slavery in Latin America and the Caribbean.* New York: Oxford University Press, 1986.

Koprowski, H., and M. B. A. Oldstone. *Microbe Hunters: Then and Now.* Bloomington, Ill.: Medi-Ed Press, 1996.

La Roche, R. *Yellow Fever, Considered in Its Historical, Pathological, Etiological, and Therapeutical Relations.* Philadelphia: Blanchard and Lea, 1855.

Lederer, S. E. *Subjected to Science: Human Experimentation in America Before the Second World War.* Baltimore: Johns Hopkins University Press, 1995.

McCullough, D. *John Adams.* New York: Simon and Schuster, 2001.

———. *Mornings on Horseback: The Story of An Extraordinary Family, a Vanished Way of Life and the Unique Child Who Became Theodore Roosevelt.* New York: Simon and Schuster, 1981.

———. *The Path Between the Seas: The Creation of the Panama Canal 1870–1914.* New York: Simon and Schuster, 1977.

McNeill, W. H. *Plagues and Peoples.* New York: Anchor Press, 1976.

Millis, W. *The Martial Spirit.* Boston: Houghton Mifflin, 1931.

Monath, T. P. "Yellow Fever." In *The Arboviruses: Epidemiology and Ecology*, Volume V, edited by T. P. Monath. Boca Raton, Fla.: CRC Press, 1988.

———. "Yellow Fever." In *Tropical Infectious Diseases: Principles, Pathogens, and Practice*, edited by R. L. Guerrant, D. H. Walker, and P. F. Walker. Philadelphia: Churchill Livingstone, 1999.

———. "Yellow Fever." In *Vaccines*, edited by S. A. Plotkin and W. A. Orenstein. Philadelphia: W.B. Saunders, 1999.

Morris, E. *The Rise of Theodore Roosevelt.* New York: Coward, McCann and Geoghegan, 1979.

Musicant, I. *Empire by Default: The Spanish-American War and the Dawn of the American Century.* New York: Henry Holt and Company, 1998.

Nuland, S. B. *Doctors: The Biography of Medicine.* New York: Alfred Knopf, 1988.

O'Toole, G. J. A. *The Spanish War: An American Epic—1898.* New York: W. W. Norton, 1984.

Oldstone, M. B. A. *Viruses, Plagues and History.* New York: Oxford University Press, 1998.

Osler, W. (ed.). *Modern Medicine: Its Theory and Practice.* Philadelphia: Lea Brothers, 1907.

Osler, W. *The Practice and Principles of Medicine*, New York: D. Appleton and Company, 1892.

Pérez, L. A. (ed.). *Impressions of Cuba in the Nineteenth Century: The Travel Diary of Joseph J. Dimock.* Wilmington, Del.: Scholarly Resources, 1998.

Post, C. J. *The Little War of Private Post: The Spanish-American War Seen Up Close.* Boston: Little, Brown and Co., 1960.

Porter, R. (ed.). *The Cambridge Illustrated History of Medicine.* London: Cambridge University Press, 1996.

Powell, J. H. *Bring Out Your Dead: The Great Plague of Yellow Fever in Philadelphia in 1793.* Philadelphia: University of Pennsylvania Press, 1949.

Rogozinski, J. *A Brief History of the Caribbean.* New York: Facts on File, 1999.

Roosevelt, T. R. *The Rough Riders.* New York: Scribners, 1902.

Rosenkrantz, B. (ed.). *Yellow Fever Studies: An Original Anthology (Public Health in America Series).* New York: Arno Press, 1977.

Rush, B. *An Account of the Bilious Remitting Yellow Fever as It Appeared in the City of Philadelphia in the Year 1793.* Edinburgh: John Moir, 1796.

Sánchez, J. L. *Carlos J. Finlay: His Life and Work.* Havana: Editorial José Martí, 1999.

Sandoz, M. *Old Jules.* Boston: Little, Brown and Co., 1935.

Sarnecky, M. T. *A History of the U.S. Army Nurse Corps.* Philadelphia: University of Pennsylvania Press, 1999.

Savitt, T. L., and J. H. Young (eds.). *Disease and Distinctiveness in the American South.* Knoxville: University of Tennessee Press, 1988.

Sears, J. H. *The Career of Leonard Wood.* New York: D. Appleton and Company, 1919.

Simmons, J. G. *Doctors and Discoveries: Lives That Created Medicine.* Boston: Houghton Mifflin, 2002.

Smith, P. *America Enters the World: A People's History of the Progressive Era and World War I.* New York: McGraw-Hill, 1985.

———. *The Rise of Industrial America: A People's History of the Post-Reconstruction Era.* New York: McGraw-Hill, 1984.

Spielman, A., and M. D'Antonio, *Mosquito: A Natural History of Our Most Persistent and Deadly Foe.* New York: Hyperion, 2001.

Starr, P. *The Transformation of American Medicine.* New York: Basic Books, 1982.

Sternberg, G. M. *Infection and Immunity, with Special Reference to the Prevention of Infectious Diseases.* New York: G.P. Putnam's Sons, 1903.

———. *A Manual of Microbiology.* New York: Wood, 1892.

Sternberg, M. L. *George Miller Sternberg: A Biography.* Chicago: American Medical Association, 1920.

Strode, G. K. *Yellow Fever.* New York: McGraw-Hill, 1951.

Sullivan, M. *Our Times: The Turn of the Century.* New York: Scribners, 1926.

Thomas, H. *The Slave Trade: The Story of the Atlantic Slave Trade, 1440–1870.* New York: Simon and Schuster, 1997.

Thomas, H. *Cuba: Or the Pursuit of Freedom.* New York: Da Capo Press, 1998.

Trask, D. F. *The War with Spain in 1898.* New York: Macmillan, 1981.

Truby, A. E. *Memoir of Walter Reed: The Yellow Fever Episode.* New York: Paul B. Hoeber, Inc., 1943.

Tucker, J. B. *Scourge: The Once and Future Threat of Smallpox.* New York: Grove Press, 2001.

Vaughan, V. C. *A Doctor's Memories.* Indianapolis: Bobbs-Merrill, 1926.

Watts, S. *Epidemics and History: Disease, Power and Imperialism.* New Haven, Conn.: Yale University Press, 1999.

Williams, G. *The Plague Killers: Untold Stories of Three Great Campaigns Against Disease.* New York: Charles Scribner's Sons, 1969.

Wood, L. N. *Walter Reed: Doctor in Uniform.* New York: Julian Messner, 1943.

Zinsser, H. *Rats, Lice and History.* London: Routledge, 1934.

WEB SITES

www.cdc.gov/mmwr

www.cdc.gov/travel/diseases/yellowfever

www.nlm.nih.gov/hmd/medtour/nmhm.html

www.healthsystem.virginia.edu

Index

Page numbers in italics refer to illustrations